TEACHER'S EDITION
SCIENCE
DAYBOOK

In Collaboration with **NSTA**

D1129406

GReaT S♯uRCe®
EDUCATION GROUP
A Division of Houghton Mifflin Company

Acknowledgments

Reviewers

Deb Barnes
6th Grade Science – Team 4
Fort Riley Middle School USD #475
Fort Riley, Kansas

Marilyn Cook
Teacher
Port Aransas ISD
Port Aransas, Texas

Charles Harmon
Science Teacher
Belvedere Middle School
Los Angeles Unified School District
Los Angeles, California

Marilyn R. LeRud
Retired Elementary Teacher
Tucson Unified School District
Tucson, Arizona

Maxine Rosenberg
Science Curriculum Consultant
Newton, Massachusetts

Dwight Sieggreen
Science Teacher
Hillside Middle School
Northville, Michigan

Nadine A. Solomon
Elementary Science Specialist
Arlington Public Schools
Arlington, Massachusetts

Richard Sturgeon
Teacher Earth/Space and Biology
Glastonbury High School
Glastonbury, Connecticut

Nancy Thornblad
Curriculum Facilitator
Millard Public Schools
Omaha, Nebraska

Thomas Vaughn
Lead Science Teacher
Arlington Public Schools
Arlington, Massachusetts

Karen Lang
Teacher
Monticello Central Schools
Monticello, New York

Credits

Writing: Sarah Martin, Marianne Knowles
Editorial: Carl Proujan; Great Source: Claire Boivin, Kathy Kellman, Susan Rogalski
Design: Brown Publishing Network
Production Management: Great Source: Evelyn Curley
Cover Design: Brown Publishing Network

Cover

(c): ©Buddy Mays/CORBIS; (bml): © Ruth Cole/Animals, Animals/Earth Scenes; (bmr): ©Bill Lea/Dembinsky Photo Associates; (br): Fran Jarvis; (bl): ©Don Farrall/ PhotoDisc/Getty Images; (bkgrnd): ©Chris Collins/CORBIS

National Science Teachers Association:

Dave Anderson, Tyson Brown, Carol Duval, Carole Hayward, Caryn Long, Pat Warren

Photos

Page 20: ©M.J. O'Riain & J. Jarvis/Visuals Unlimited; 23: ©Wildlife Conservation Society, headquartered at the Bronx Zoo; 25: ©Adam Jones/Visuals Unlimited; 27: ©W. Perry Conway/CORBIS; 30(l): ©Joseph Van Os/Image Bank/Getty Images; 30(c): ©Ken Lucas/Taxi/Getty Images; 30(r): ©Carolina Biological/Visuals Unlimited; 32: Courtesy of Dr. Gavin Hunt; 41(t): ©Oliver J.Troisfontaines/SuperStock; 41(l): ©Barry Koffler/feathersite.com; 41(r): ©Barry Koffler/feathersite.com; 44: ©Sullivan and Rogers/Bruce Coleman, Inc.; 46: ©E.R. Derringer/Bruce Coleman, Inc.; 52: ©Arnold Genthe/Arnold Genthe Collection/Library of Congress; 53: ©Arnold Genthe/Arnold Genthe Collection/Library of Congress; 54: R. Decker/United States Geological Survey; 58: ©Hans Strand/Getty Images; 59: ©Ann and Peter Bosted; 64: ©Gerald French/ CORBIS; 65: ©Bettmann/CORBIS; 66: ©David Frazier/Photo Researchers, Inc.; 69: ©American Museum of Natural History/ neg. 5401; 76: ©DonFarrall/ PhotoDisc/Getty Images; 77: ©Jim Reed/CORBIS; 82: ©Reynir Eyjolfsson; 84: ©Mike Brinson/ Image Bank/Getty Images; 85(l, c, r): ©Reynir Eyjolfsson; 90 (tr): ©Michael & Patricia Fogden/CORBIS; 90 (c): ©Buddy Mays/CORBIS; 90 (bl): ©David A. North-cott/CORBIS; 90(br): ©Kevin Schafer/CORBIS; 91: ©Michael & Patricia Fodgen/CORBIS; 95: William L. Clements Library/The University of Michigan; 102: Bob Goldberg/ Feature Photo Service; 106: Courtesy of Pasco Scientific; 108: CORBIS; 109: Univer-sity of Kentucky Library; 114: Courtesty of Mohammed Bah Abba; 119: ©Nick Koudis/ Photodisc/Getty Images; 128: ©John Swedberg/Bruce Coleman, Inc.; 131 (l): ©Nigel Bean/naturepl.com (Nature Place); 131(r): ©Mark Edwards/Peter Arnold, Inc.; 133: Courtesy of Dr. Joseph Kiesecker/Penn State University; 134: ©Sheldon Allen Blake/Animals Animals, Earth Scenes; 135: ©Annette Coolridge/Photo Edit, Inc.; 136: ©Randy M. Ury/CORBIS; 137: ©Bill Lea/Dembinsky Photo Associates; 143: ©Hulton–Deutsch/ CORBIS; 144: ©Sheila Terry/Photo Researchers, Inc.; 147: ©Royalty-free/CORBIS; 150: ©Richard Shell/Animals Animals/Earth Scenes; 155: Photo courtesy of Sylvia Campbell/NIWRA; 158: Photo courtesy of Sylvia Campbell/ NIWRA; 159: THE INCREDIBLE HULK: TM & ©2005 Marvel Characters, Inc. Used with permission; 160: Courtesy of Universal Studios Licensing LLLP

Illustration

Pages 6, 21: Gene Barretta; 13, 35, 43, 48, 51, 63, 81, 113, 139: Amy Vangsgard; 14, 15: Lane Smith; 17, 18, 37: Grace Lin; 19, 103: Jessica Flick; 22: Barroux; 26, 34: Tammy Smith; 28: Linda Bleck; 29, 61, 83 (all), 93, 97 (t), 99, 100, 111, 123, 151, 152: Mike Wesley; 31, 75, 89, 101, 107, 119, 127: ©Linda Bronson; 38, 39: Louis Darling; 55, 56, 129 (t): Sophie Kitteridge; 67 (all): Fran Jarvis; 71, 73 (t), 114, 115, 116, 153: Viviana Garofoli; 73 (b): Teen Liu; 79 (l, r): Doug Ross; 97 (b): © Dean Stanton; 105, 112, 121 (br, cr), 124: Roberto Sabas; 120, 142: Shennen Bersani; 122: Armstrong Sperry; 129 (b), 161: Pamela Thomson; 132 (l, r): Ann Barrow; 138, 140: Kristen Balouch; 149: John O'Brien; 164: Jason Peltz.

Scientists write letters, argue incessantly, make mistakes, suffer from jealousy, exhibit both vanity and generosity — all the while striving in diverse ways to enlarge human understanding. Among the most important skills they possess is the ability to communicate ideas, defend them against critics, and modify their own positions in the face of contravening evidence. Every literate person — every scientifically literate person — must do this.

The National Science Teachers Association (NSTA) is pleased to participate in the publication of these Science Daybooks because they bring together science, reading, and writing. Most important: The primary sources in the Daybooks — first-hand accounts that scientists and researchers use to communicate their ideas — firmly place science in the context of human endeavor.

What NSTA Did

From the outset, NSTA staff and members collaborated with Great Source and developers to ensure that the Daybooks were created from a teacher's perspective and were based on the National Science Education Standards. We helped link important topic areas with primary sources. We suggested activity ideas at the pilot stage and reviewed those submitted by authors during development. We supported the lessons with brief activities taken from articles in NSTA's journals, *Science* and *Children* and *Science Scope*. NSTA also provides the sciLINKS extensions that appear throughout the book, directing readers to Web sites that offer further information, additional lessons, and activities.

What is NSTA?

NSTA is the largest organization in the world committed to promoting excellence and innovation in science teaching and learning for all. To address subjects of critical interest to science educators, the NSTA Press publishes projects of significant relevance and value to teachers of science — books on best teaching practices, books that explain and tie in with the National Science Education Standards, books that apply the latest science education research, and classroom activity books. NSTA also considers novel treatments of core science content and is especially eager to publish works that link science to other key curriculum areas such as mathematics and language arts. Hence this project.

Let Us Hear From You

We hope teachers and students benefit from this innovative approach to learning science. Tell us what you think of this joint effort by e-mailing daybooks@nsta.org. For more information about NSTA, please visit our Web site at www.nsta.org.

Sources

The readings in this Science Daybook come from the following sources.

14 From *James and the Giant Peach* by Roald Dahl, Copyright 1961 by Roald Dahl. Text copyright renewed 1989 by Roald Dahl. Alfred A. Knopf, an imprint of Random House Children's Books, a division of Random House, Inc.

20 Reprinted by permission of Carus Publishing Company from *Muse* magazine, February 2003, Vol. 7, No. 2, © 2003 by Carus Publishing Company.

26 *A Moment of Science* radio series, WFIU-FM, Indiana University.

32 *Science News for Kids,* March 26, 2003. (www.sciencenewsforkids.org)

34 From *Pets and Wildlife* column, Gary Bogue, Contra Costa Times, April 16, 2003.

38 From *The Enormous Egg* by Oliver Butterworth. Copyright © 1956 by Oliver Butterworth; Copyright © renewed 1984 by Oliver Butterworth. By permission of Little, Brown and Company, (Inc.).

44, 46 Reprinted by permission of Carus Publishing Company from *ASK* magazine, July/Aug 2003, Vol. 2, No. 4, © 2003 by Catherine Ripley.

52 From *Dragonwings* by Laurence Yep. Copyright © 1975 by Laurence Yep. Used by permission of Harper Collins Publishers.

58 Copyright *Richmond Times-Dispatch,* August 14, 2003. Used with permission.

64 Excerpt from *Sing Down the Moon* by Scott O'Dell. Copyright © 1970 by Scott O'Dell, renewed 1998 by Elizabeth Hall. Reprinted by permission of Houghton Mifflin Company. All rights reserved.

70, 72 From *Tracking Dinosaurs in the Gobi* by Margery Facklam. Copyright © 1997 by Margery Facklam. Twenty-First Century Books, a division of Henry Holt and Company, Inc. Reprinted by permission of Margery Facklam. All rights reserved.

76 From *Nature's Fury: Eyewitness Reports of Natural Disasters* by Carole Garbuny Vogel. Copyright © 2000 Carole Garbuny Vogel. Reprinted by permission of Scholastic, Inc.

82, 84 *Talk of the Nation: Science Friday,* May 9, 2003, second hour. National Public Radio.

90 *Science News for Kids,* Sept 10, 2003. (www.sciencenewsforkids.org)

96 Reprinted by permission of Carus Publishing Company from *ASK* magazine, January/February 2003, Vol. 2, No.1, text © 2002 by Carus Publishing Company, illustrations © 2002 by Dean Stanton.

102 *Science News for Kids,* Aug 27, 2003. (www.sciencenewsforkids.org)

108 Reprinted by permission of Carus Publishing Company from *Muse* magazine, May/June 2003, Vol. 7, No. 5, © 2003 by David Lindley.

114 *A Moment of Science* radio series, WFIU-FM, Indiana University.

120 Excerpt from *Island of the Blue Dolphins* by Scott O'Dell. Copyright © 1960, renewed 1988 by Scott O'Dell. Reprinted by permission of Houghton Mifflin Company. All rights reserved.

122 From *Call It Courage* by Armstrong Sperry. Copyright 1940 by Macmillan Publishing Company. Copyright renewed by Armstrong Sperry. Reprinted by permission of the Armstrong Sperry estate.

128 *Science News for Kids,* August 13, 2003. (www.sciencenewsforkids.org)

134 *National Geographic World,* March 2002, National Geographic Society.

140 "Silly Pilly" from *Laugh-Eteria,* copyright © 1999 by Douglas Florian, reprinted by permission of Harcourt, Inc.

142 From *Accidents May Happen* by Charlotte Foltz Jones. Illustrations by John O'Brien, copyright © 1996 by Charlotte Foltz Jones. Used by permission of Random House Children's Books, a division of Random House, Inc.

148 From *Accidents May Happen* by Charlotte Foltz Jones. Illustrations by John O'Brien, copyright © 1996 by Charlotte Foltz Jones. Used by permission of Random House Children's Books, a division of Random House, Inc.

154 Reuters News Service. *Planet Ark,* August 19, 2002.

160 *National Geographic Kids,* July/August 2003, National Geographic Society.

Contents

UNIT 2: Earth Science

UNIT 3: Physical Science

How to Use the Science Daybook

The Great Source *Science Daybooks* are flexible resources that you can incorporate into your science curriculum in a variety of ways:

- **Supplement your existing science program.** Content for the *Science Daybooks* aligns with most current textbooks as well as state and national science standards.

- **Weave into a thematic unit.** *Science Daybooks* emphasize the use of original source materials for reading and thinking about science, making *Science Daybooks* well suited for multidisciplinary units.

- **Prepare students for high-stakes assessments.** *Science Daybooks* provide important practice in evaluating and demonstrating comprehension of reading materials, like those found on assessments.

- **Extend science after school or during the summer.** *Science Daybook* readings and activities include concepts in the school curriculum, yet are different from materials students are using in class.

However you use the *Science Daybook,* the *Science Daybook Teacher's Guide* provides you with a wealth of tools and information.

Unit Interleaf

Each six-chapter unit begins with four full pages of teacher support. (Units 4 and 5 have three chapters and two pages of unit support each.)

Concepts and Skills

This chart of science concepts, science skills, and reading and writing skills helps you to determine where each chapter best fits in your curriculum.

NSTA Activities

Every unit interleaf includes an activity adapted from a National Science Teachers Association (NSTA) journal for use with a chapter in this *Science Daybook* unit.

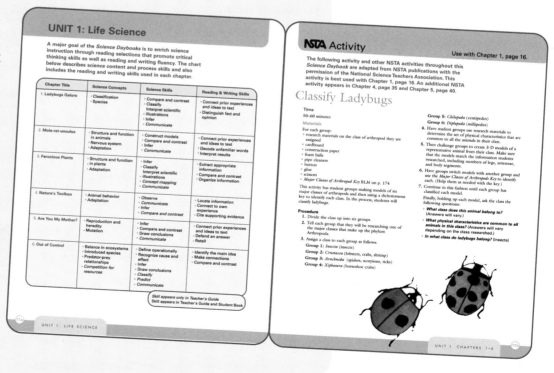

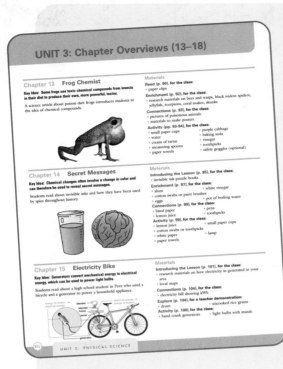

Chapter Overviews show at a glance what to expect in each chapter.

- The **Key Idea** and chapter summary describe what students will learn.

- A **Materials** list helps you plan ahead for hands-on activities and demonstrations.

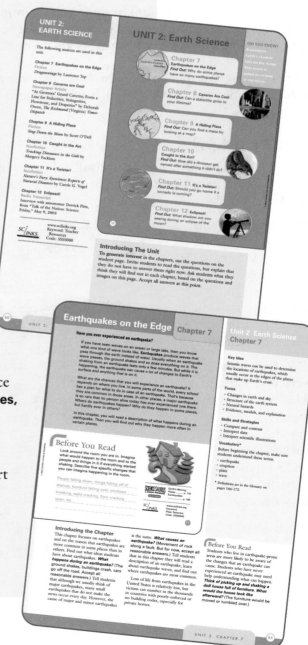

Unit Support

- Each unit begins with a list of the **Sources** for the reading selections in each chapter.

- **Introducing the Unit** suggests how to generate interest using questions on the student page.

Chapter Support

The *Science Daybook* is grounded by solid support on every Teacher's Guide page.

Resources to help you plan are included for every chapter, including:

- the **Key Idea**, a correlation to the National Science Education Standards (**Focus**), **Skills and Strategies**, and **Vocabulary** to review before beginning the chapter.

- a quick chapter description, suggestions for introducing the chapter to your class, and support for **Before You Read**.

- **More Resources** from Great Source and NSTA that you can use to teach the chapter.

- Matching headings for each section—**Before You Read, Read, Look Back, Explore, Activity, Science Journal, Project,** and **Put It All Together** that make it easy to locate teacher support for each part of the student chapter.

- **Check Understanding**, a quick question that you can use to make sure all students are "on board" before moving further.

- For wrapping up each chapter, a reminder to review the **"Find Out" Question**, as well as an **Assessment** for determining how well students have mastered the Key Idea.

- **Science Background** to help you delve deeper into the chapter topic, so you can better answer students' questions and avoid misconceptions.

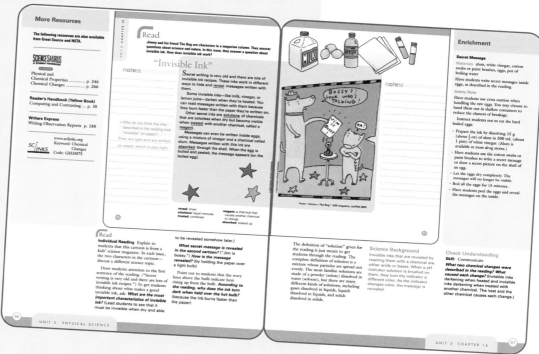

Going Beyond the Chapter

Every chapter in this Teacher's Guide includes additional suggestions for taking your class beyond the typical science lessons.

- **Enrichment** for additional hands-on activities, research projects, and group activities

- **Connections** to other curriculum areas

- **Differentiating Instruction** to help you to reach all your students through activities that address a range of learning styles and needs

- Short **Write to Learn** exercises to help students master concepts by writing about them

- Point-of-Use reference to the **NSTA Activity** that appears on the unit interleaf; Some chapters include complete, additional NSTA Activities at point of use.

Note: Each excerpt has been chosen with attention to age-appropriate content. Before making the entire original work available to your class, however, we recommend you review the contents to judge its suitability for your students.

Unit End

Each unit in the *Science Daybook Teacher's Guide* ends with a suggested Unit Wrap-Up activity that encourages students to make connections among chapters in the unit. Sample answers to "What Did We Learn?" questions are also provided.

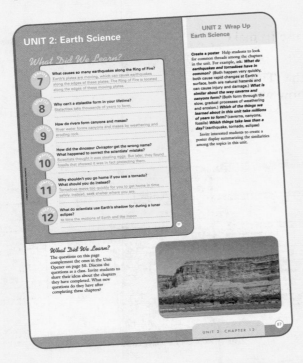

Support continues at the back of the Teacher's Guide...

- The Teacher **Assessment Rubric,** page 173, is a helpful evaluation tool. Use it to assess student work on Science Journal and Projects, and on *Science Daybook Teacher's Guide* features such as Connection, Enrichment, Differentiating Instruction, and Write to Learn.

- **Copymasters,** pages 174–178, are provided as needed to support the NSTA activities and some of the *Science Daybook* Activities. Permission is granted to reproduce these Copymasters for use in your class.

- An **Index,** pages 180–182, helps you to locate specific topics and pages in the *Science Daybook Teacher's Guide.*

Correlation with National Science Education Standards, Grades K–4

Chapter	1	2	3	4	5	6	7	8	9	10	11	12	13	14	15	16	17	18	19	20	21	22	23	24
Unifying Concepts and Processes																								
Systems, order, and organization	■					■						■								■				
Evidence, models, and explanation		■						■	■	■	■	■	■		■	■	■	■	■	■	■	■	■	■
Change, constancy, and measurement					■	■	■	■			■	■	■	■	■	■	■	■		■				
Form and function		■	■	■			■																■	
Science as Inquiry																								
Abilities necessary to do scientific inquiry								■			■		■	■	■		■	■		■				
Understandings about scientific inquiry		■		■				■		■	■		■	■	■	■	■	■			■	■		
Physical Science																								
Properties of objects and materials													■	■			■	■				■	■	
Position and motion of objects															■	■								
Light, heat, electricity, and magnetism															■	■	■	■					■	
Life Science																								
Characteristics of organisms	■	■	■	■	■							■								■			■	
Life cycles of organisms																				■				
Organisms and environments		■	■	■		■						■							■	■	■			
Earth and Space Science																								
Properties of earth materials							■	■																
Objects in the sky											■													
Changes in earth and sky							■	■			■	■												
Science and Technology																								
Abilities of technological design																■	■					■	■	■
Understandings about science and technology																■	■					■	■	■
Distinctions between man-made and natural objects																						■	■	
Science in Personal and Social Perspectives																								
Personal health							■				■							■		■	■		■	
Characteristics and changes in populations	■					■														■				
Types of resources																			■		■			
Changes in environments						■														■	■			
Science and technology in local challenges						■														■				
History and Nature of Science																								
Science as a human endeavor		■								■			■	■					■	■	■	■	■	■

Correlation with National Science Education Standards, Grades 5–8

Chapter	1	2	3	4	5	6	7	8	9	10	11	12	13	14	15	16	17	18	19	20	21	22	23	24
Unifying Concepts and Processes																								
Systems, order, and organization	■					■						■								■				
Evidence, models, and explanation		■						■	■	■	■	■	■	■		■	■	■	■	■	■	■	■	■
Change, constancy, and measurement						■	■	■	■	■		■	■	■	■	■	■	■						
Form and function		■	■	■			■																■	
Science as Inquiry																								
Abilities necessary to do scientific inquiry								■			■		■	■	■		■	■				■		
Understandings about scientific inquiry		■		■				■		■	■		■	■	■	■	■	■	■		■	■		
Physical Science																								
Properties and changes of properties in matter													■	■		■	■	■				■	■	
Motions and forces															■	■								
Transfer of energy															■	■	■							
Life Science																								
Structure and function in living systems	■	■	■	■																■			■	
Reproduction and heredity					■															■				
Regulation and behavior		■		■																■			■	
Populations and ecosystems			■			■													■	■				
Diversity and adaptations of organisms	■	■		■	■							■										■	■	
Earth and Space Science																								
Structure of the earth system							■	■																
Earth's history								■		■														
Earth in the solar system												■												
Science and Technology																								
Abilities of technological design																■	■					■	■	■
Understandings about science and technology																■	■					■	■	■
Science in Personal and Social Perspectives																								
Personal health							■				■						■			■	■		■	
Populations, resources, and environments						■													■	■				
Natural hazards						■	■				■									■				
Science and technology in society						■																■	■	■
History and Nature of Science																								
Science as a human endeavor		■		■							■		■							■	■	■	■	
Nature of science		■		■							■		■				■			■	■			
History of science																■						■	■	

What Is a Science Daybook?

A *Science Daybook* is a workbook that brings together science, reading, and writing. This *Science Daybook* is your very own and, as you use it, you may mark it up with pens and pencils and markers. The more you make it your own, the more valuable the *Daybook* will be to you.

About the Daybook Readings

Each chapter in this book is based on one or two readings. The readings come from a wide variety of sources, including science books, magazines, newspapers, radio shows, web sites, literature, and poetry. Yes, poetry! That's because science is everywhere, not just in science books. (The sources in this book are listed on page 2b.)

What's in a Daybook Chapter?

Each *Science Daybook* chapter is six pages long. Every chapter begins with the same parts: an introduction, Before You Read, and Read. What comes after Read depends on the chapter. Before You Read is described below. The following pages describe all the other kinds of sections you'll find in a chapter.

Before You Read

Each chapter begins with a quick Before You Read feature. As you might expect, this feature gets you to think about the topic of the reading, before you start reading it.

Read

Every chapter in the *Science Daybook* is built around one or two readings. You are encouraged to read the *Daybook* actively. What does it mean to be an active reader? It means that as you read, you are actively marking up the text—writing notes, drawing diagrams, jotting down questions. The more involved you are with the readings in this book, the better you will understand them.

notes:

Jot down your ideas, questions, and drawings in the Notes columns. At the bottom of each column are a few directions or questions. These help you to find the science in the reading.

Vocabulary

Words underlined in the reading are defined at the bottom of the page.

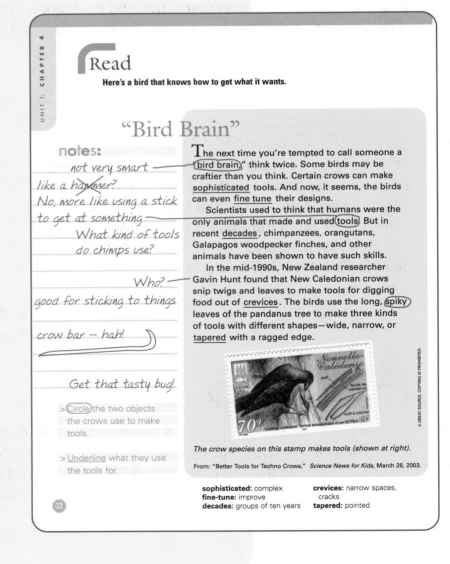

Read

Here's a bird that knows how to get what it wants.

"Bird Brain"

notes:

not very smart

like a hammer?

No, more like using a stick to get at something

What kind of tools do chimps use?

Who?

good for sticking to things

crow bar -- hah!

Get that tasty bug!

> Circle the two objects the crows use to make tools.

> Underline what they use the tools for.

The next time you're tempted to call someone a "bird brain," think twice. Some birds may be craftier than you think. Certain crows can make sophisticated tools. And now, it seems, the birds can even fine tune their designs.

Scientists used to think that humans were the only animals that made and used tools. But in recent decades, chimpanzees, orangutans, Galapagos woodpecker finches, and other animals have been shown to have such skills.

In the mid-1990s, New Zealand researcher Gavin Hunt found that New Caledonian crows snip twigs and leaves to make tools for digging food out of crevices. The birds use the long, spiky leaves of the pandanus tree to make three kinds of tools with different shapes—wide, narrow, or tapered with a ragged edge.

The crow species on this stamp makes tools (shown at right).

From: "Better Tools for Techno Crows," *Science News for Kids*, March 26, 2003.

sophisticated: complex
fine-tune: improve
decades: groups of ten years

crevices: narrow spaces, cracks
tapered: pointed

After the Read section, you will find other kinds of features and activities. These features help you to understand the science related to the reading.

Look Back

Most chapters have a Look Back feature following each reading. Look Back questions help you to notice something important from the reading.

Explore

In Explore, you might answer questions, interpret a diagram, analyze data, or explore a science topic from the reading in some other way.

Glossary Look up unfamiliar words in the glossary on pages 166–172. The glossary gives a simple definition for each word and gives you a chapter page where you can learn more about it.

---

erosion: the movement of weathered rock by water, wind, or ice **(62, 66)**

Activity

Some chapters invite you to do a hands-on activity. Always read the whole activity and get all your materials before you begin. Be sure to follow any special directions from your teacher, along with the ones on the page.

Look Back

What problem did the sea otter face? What solution did it find? What tool was part of its solution?

Problem	Solution
	Tool

Explore

MEETING NEEDS

Look at the picture of the sea otter floating in the ocean. Sea otters are able to float on their backs very comfortably for a long time.

How does the otter use floating on its back to help it get food?

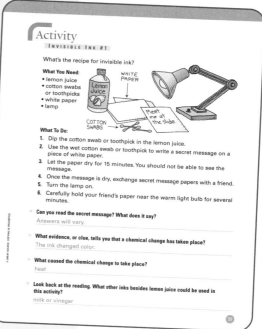

Activity

INVISIBLE INK #1

What's the recipe for invisible ink?

What You Need:
• lemon juice
• cotton swabs or toothpicks
• white paper
• lamp

What To Do:
1. Dip the cotton swab or toothpick in the lemon juice.
2. Use the wet cotton swab or toothpick to write a secret message on a piece of white paper.
3. Let the paper dry for 15 minutes. You should not be able to see the message.
4. Once the message is dry, exchange secret message papers with a friend.
5. Turn the lamp on.
6. Carefully hold your friend's paper near the warm light bulb for several minutes.

Can you read the secret message? What does it say?
Answers will vary.

What evidence, or clue, tells you that a chemical change has taken place?
The ink changed color.

What caused the chemical change to take place?
heat

Look back at the reading. What other inks besides lemon juice could be used in this activity?
milk or vinegar

Science Journal

In this feature, you may be asked to keep a record of science observations, write an essay about topics discussed in the chapter, or write a letter about your experiences with a science topic.

Project

In a Project, you might be asked to research a science topic further, make a display, or make observations of your local area, and report on what you find out.

Put It All Together

Chapters that have two readings often end with this feature. The two readings are related, and Put It All Together helps you make the connection between them.

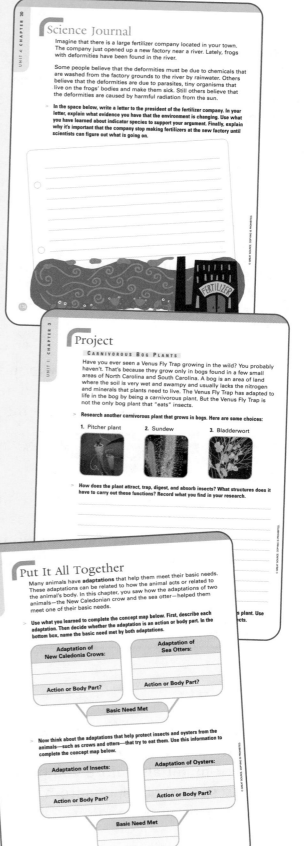

More Resources

ScienceSaurus is a reference book written for students like you. It's filled with information about all kinds of science subjects. It also has instructions about doing science activities, writing up science reports, doing library and internet research, and preparing for tests. Whether you want to know about animals, rocks, machines, weather, or many other subjects, turn to *ScienceSaurus*.

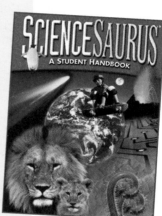

Every chapter in the *Science Daybook* has references to pages in *ScienceSaurus.* The references appear on the second page of the chapter, next to Read. Look on these pages in *ScienceSaurus* for information related to the Daybook chapter.

www.scilinks.org   web address for *Sci*LINKS
Keyword: Behavior   science subject for this link
Code: GSLD12   code to type in at the *Sci*LINKS web site

What is a *Sci*LINK? A *Sci*LINK is a "science link" between a subject you are studying and web sites where you can learn more about the subject.

Most chapters in this *Science Daybook* have at least one *Sci* LINK. The *Sci* LINKS appear on the second page of the chapter, next to Read.

How to use *Sci*LINKS
1. Go to the Sci LINKS web site at www.*Sci*LINKS.org.
2. After you register, sign in by entering your user name and password.
3. Type in the code for the keyword you want to know more about.
4. You will see a list of different web sites that discuss that keyword subject. Click on one of the addresses to get to the site.
5. Go back to the *Sci*LINKS web site and try a different web site.

UNIT 1: Life Science

A major goal of the *Science Daybooks* is to enrich science instruction through reading selections that promote critical thinking skills as well as reading and writing fluency. The chart below describes science content and process skills and also includes the reading and writing skills used in each chapter.

Chapter Title	Science Concepts	Science Skills	Reading & Writing Skills
1. Ladybugs Galore	• Classification • Species	• Compare and contrast • Classify • Interpret scientific illustrations • Infer • *Communicate*	• Connect prior experiences and ideas to text • Distinguish fact and opinion
2. Mole-rat-unculus	• Structure and function in animals • Nervous system • Adaptation	• Construct models • Compare and contrast • Infer • *Communicate*	• Connect prior experiences and ideas to text • Decode unfamiliar words • Interpret results
3. Ferocious Plants	• Structure and function in plants • Adaptation	• Infer • Classify • Interpret scientific illustrations • *Concept mapping* • *Communicate*	• Extract appropriate information • Compare and contrast • Organize information
4. Nature's Toolbox	• Animal behavior • Adaptation	• Observe • *Communicate* • Infer • *Compare and contrast*	• Locate information • Connect to own experience • Cite supporting evidence
5. Are You My Mother?	• Reproduction and heredity • Mutation	• Infer • Compare and contrast • Draw conclusions • *Communicate*	• Connect prior experiences and ideas to text • Defend an answer • Retell
6. Out of Control	• Balance in ecosystems • Introduced species • Predator-prey relationships • *Competition for resources*	• Define operationally • Recognize cause and effect • Infer • Draw conclusions • *Classify* • *Predict* • *Communicate*	• Identify the main idea • Make connections • Compare and contrast

*Skill appears only in Teacher's Guide
Skill appears in Teacher's Guide and Student Book

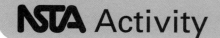
The following activity and other NSTA activities throughout this *Science Daybook* are adapted from NSTA publications with the permission of the National Science Teachers Association. This activity is best used with Chapter 1, page 16. An additional NSTA activity appears in Chapter 4, page 35 and Chapter 5, page 40.

Classify Ladybugs

Time

50–60 minutes

Materials

For each group:
- research materials on the class of arthropod they are assigned
- cardboard
- construction paper
- foam balls
- pipe cleaners
- button
- glue
- scissors
- *Major Classes of Arthropod Key* BLM on p. 174

This activity has student groups making models of six major classes of arthropods and then using a dichotomous key to identify each class. In the process, students will classify ladybugs.

Procedure

1. Divide the class up into six groups.
2. Tell each group that they will be researching one of the major classes that make up the phylum Arthropoda.
3. Assign a class to each group as follows:

    Group 1: *Insecta* (insects)

    Group 2: *Crustacea* (lobsters, crabs, shrimp)

    Group 3: *Arachnida* (spiders, scorpions, ticks)

    Group 4: *Xiphosura* (horseshoe crabs)

Group 5: *Chilopoda* (centipedes)

Group 6: *Diplopoda* (millipedes)

4. Have student groups use research materials to determine the set of physical characteristics that are common to all the animals in their class.
5. Then challenge groups to create 3-D models of a representative animal from their class. Make sure that the models match the information students researched, including numbers of legs, antennae, and body segments.
6. Have groups switch models with another group and use the *Major Classes of Arthropods Key* to identify each. (Help them as needed with the key.)
7. Continue in this fashion until each group has classified each model.

    Finally, holding up each model, ask the class the following questions:

    - ***What class does this animal belong to?*** (Answers will vary.)
    - ***What physical characteristics are common to all animals in this class?*** (Answers will vary depending on the class researched.)
    - ***In what class do ladybugs belong?*** (Insecta)

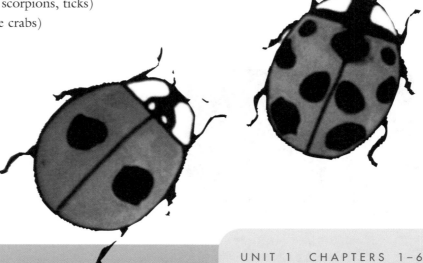

Chapter 1 Ladybugs Galore

Key Idea: Organisms can be classified into groups according to their traits.

A passage from Roald Dahl's classic children's book *James and the Giant Peach* introduces students to the idea of animal classification.

Materials

Introducing the Lesson (p. 13), for teacher demonstration:
• pictures of ladybugs

Connections (p. 15), for the class:
• books by Roald Dahl

NSTA Activity (p. 16), for the class:
• see page 11B

Enrichment (p. 16), for the class:
• research materials on arthropod classification

Differentiating Instruction (p. 17), for the class:
• index cards
• masking tape

Chapter 2 Mole-rat-unculus

Key Idea: The structure of an animal's body part or system is related to the function that it serves.

A magazine article describes how the naked mole-rat is specially adapted to its underground environment.

Materials

Introducing the Lesson (p. 19), for teacher demonstration:
• assorted small objects of varying textures
• cloth or paper bag

Enrichment (p. 22), for the class:
• research materials on bats

Differentiating Instruction (p. 23), for the class:
• gym mats or student desks

Chapter 3 Ferocious Plants

Key Idea: Adaptations to their environment help plants meet their needs.

A transcript from a science radio show introduces students to the Venus Fly Trap, an organism that consumes insects in order to meet its special dietary needs.

Materials

Before You Read (p. 25), for the class:
• cactus plant

Enrichment (p. 28), for the class:
• research materials on sea sponges

Explore (p. 29), for the class:
• Venus Fly Trap plant

Project (p. 30), for the class:
• research materials on carnivorous bog plants
• materials to create posters

Chapter 4   Nature's Toolbox

Key Idea: Behavioral adaptations—including the use of tools—help animals meet their basic needs.

Two articles offer examples of animals in nature that use objects to get at food sources.

Materials

Enrichment (p. 33), for the class:
• stiff, narrow leaves or grasses
• rice (optional)

NSTA Activity (p. 35), for each student pair or group:
• 2-3 pill bugs
• plastic container (salad bar containers work well)
• paper towel
• water

Chapter 5   Are You My Mother?

Key Idea: The traits of offspring are similar to those of their parents.

A passage from *The Enormous Egg* by Oliver Butterworth describes an impossible scene—a dinosaur emerging from a chicken egg.

Materials

Before You Read (p. 37), for the class:
• pictures of the life cycle of an insect that undergoes complete metamorphosis (butterfly, darkling beetle)

Enrichment (p. 39), for the class:
• research materials on dinosaurs

NSTA Activity (p. 40), for each student:
• paper
• pencil

Connections (p. 41), for each student pair or group:
• calculators

Chapter 6   Out of Control

Key Idea: The introduction of a new species into an ecosystem may effect the ecological balance that exists there.

Articles from a science magazine explain how two species introduced to new areas to solve ecological problems ended up creating a whole new set of problems.

Materials

Introducing the Lesson (p. 43), for the class:
• list of plants and animals native to your area (may be available from a local wildlife center)

Connections (p. 45), for the class:
• research materials on the Civilian Conservation Corps (CCC)

Enrichment (p.46), for the class:
• research materials on animals introduced into Australia, materials to create posters

Differentiating Instruction (p. 47), for the class:
• materials for exhibits

Connections (p. 47), for the class:
• *Rikki-Tikki-Tavi* by Rudyard Kipling

The following sources are used in this unit.

Chapter 1 Ladybugs Galore
Fiction
James and the Giant Peach by Roald Dahl

Chapter 2 Mole-rat-unculus
Magazine Article
"Night of the Living Unculus" from *Muse* magazine, February 2003

Chapter 3 Ferocious Plants
Radio Transcript
"What the Heck is a Venus Fly Trap?" from the radio show "A Moment of Science," WFIU and Indiana University

Chapter 4 Nature's Toolbox
Magazine Article
"Better Tools for Techno Crows" from *Science News for Kids*, March 26, 2003

Newspaper Article
Pets and Wildlife column of the Contra Costa Times, April 16, 2003

Chapter 5 Are You My Mother?
Fiction
The Enormous Egg by Oliver Butterworth

Chapter 6 Out of Control
Magazine Article
"Big Mistakes!" from *ASK* magazine, July/Aug 2003.

www.scilinks.org
Keyword: New Teacher
  Resources
Code: GSSD02

UNIT 1: Life Science

Chapter 1 Ladybugs Galore
Find Out: How do scientists tell one kind of ladybug from another?

Chapter 2 Mole-rat-unculus
Find Out: Which parts of a mole-rat's body are most sensitive to touch?

Chapter 3 Fierce Plants
Find Out: Why do some plants eat insects?

Chapter 4 Nature's Toolbox
Find Out: Which animals use tools to help them get food?

Chapter 5
Are You My Mother?
Find Out: Can a chicken lay an egg that doesn't contain a chick?

Chapter 6 Out of Control
Find Out: What if the solution to one environmental problem creates another?

12

Introducing the Unit
To generate interest in the chapters, use the questions on the student page. Invite students to read the questions, but explain that they do not have to answer them right now. Ask students what they think they will find out in each chapter, based on the questions and images on this page. Accept all answers at this point.

Ladybugs Galore

Chapter 1

Are all ladybugs alike?

Here's a challenge: how long would it take you to name every kind of living thing on Earth? Do you think it would take all day? Actually, it could take you months! That's because there are millions of kinds of living things on Earth.

It could take you quite a while just to name the kinds of ladybugs. Ladybugs are a type of insect. You may think all ladybugs are alike, but did you know that there are 450 different kinds of ladybugs in North America? In fact, there are 4500 kinds of ladybugs worldwide. That's a lot of ladybugs!

In this chapter, you'll learn how scientists tell one kind of ladybug from another.

Before You Read

You've probably seen a ladybug walking up the stalk of a garden plant or trapped inside a screen door. Close your eyes and try to remember what it looked like. Draw the ladybug in the space below.

Species .... p. 128
Animals ...... p. 141
Animals With an
Exoskeleton p. 148

www.scilinks.org
Keyword:
Classification
Code: GS5D005

13

Key Idea

Organisms can be classified into groups according to their traits.

Focus

- Systems, order, and organization
- Characteristics of organisms
- Diversity and adaptations of organisms

Skills and Strategies

- Compare and contrast
- Classify
- Interpret scientific illustrations
- Infer
- *Communicate (TG)*

Vocabulary*

Before beginning the chapter, make sure students understand these terms.

- insects
- mammals

* Definitions are in the Glossary on pages 166–172

Introducing the Chapter

Materials pictures of ladybugs

This chapter examines how organisms are classified according to their characteristics. To get students thinking about scientific classification, ask: **What traits do all ladybugs have in common?** (Students may say that ladybugs are small, spotted, have legs, wings, antennae, eyes, and have a smooth body.) Bees make up another group of animals. **What traits do all bees have in common?** (Students may say that bees have stripes, wings, legs, and have a fuzzy body.) **What are some traits of ladybugs that bees don't have?** (Students should use the information above to express their answers.) Show students pictures of ladybugs and bees to help them in their discussion.

Science Background

Scientists have identified approximately 1.4 million different species of organisms on Earth. Almost 1 million of those are insects. Scientists estimate that there are 4–6 million more species of insects that have not been found and identified yet.

Before You Read

Help students, as needed, to describe what a ladybug looks like. If students are having trouble, ask: **What are some of the traits of ladybugs.** (red, black spots, round body, six legs, wings). After students have finished their drawings, ask: **How many spots does your ladybug have?** (Answers will vary.)

More Resources

The following resources are also available from Great Source and NSTA.

SCIENCESAURUS
A STUDENT HANDBOOK
BLUE BOOK

Reader's Handbook (Yellow Book)

SCILINKS.
THE WORLD'S A CLICK AWAY

www.scilinks.org
Keyword: Classification
Code: GS5D05

Read

Seven-year-old James Henry Trotter is on a fantastical journey with a group of animal friends—a grasshopper, a spider, a centipede, a glow-worm, an earthworm, and a ladybug. Sailing through the skies aboard the Giant Peach, James has a chance to ask the ladybug about her spots.

"A Fine Thing To Be"

notes:

> Do all ladybugs have the same number of spots?

No

> Underline what a ladybug's spots tell you about her.

"I think you're wonderful," James told her. "Can I ask you one special question?"

"Please do."

"Well, is it really true that I can tell how old a Ladybug is by counting her spots?"

"Oh no, that's just a children's story," the Ladybug said. "We never change our spots. Some of us, of course, are born with more spots than others, but we never change them. <u>The number of spots that a Ladybug has is simply a way of showing which branch of the family she belongs to.</u> I, for example, as you can see for yourself, am a Nine-Spotted Ladybug. I am very lucky. It is a fine thing to be."

 14

Read

Independent Reading Have students share their answer to the second margin question on page 14. *What do you think the author means by "branch of the family"?* (Students may guess that the phrase implies a relationship among organisms.)

Explain that the three kinds of ladybugs described in the story are related as are members of a larger family. For example, cousins are related to one another but are parts of different branches of a family. They are similar in some ways to one another, but different in other ways. Students will explore this family on the next page.

Write the words "Fact" and "Opinion" on the board. With the help of volunteers, establish the difference between the two. (Fact is truth and has nothing to do with feelings on a subject. Opinion is someone's personal view of a subject.)

Guide students in distinguishing between fact and opinion in the

"It is, indeed," said James, gazing at the beautiful scarlet shell with the nine black spots on it.

"On the other hand," the Ladybug went on, "some of my less fortunate relatives have no more than two spots altogether on their shells! Can you imagine that? They are called Two-Spotted Ladybugs, and very common and ill-mannered they are, I regret to say. And then, of course, you have the Five-Spotted Ladybugs as well. They are much nicer than the Two-Spotted ones, although I myself find them a trifle too saucy for my taste."

"But they are all of them loved?" said James.

"Yes," the Ladybug answered quietly. "They are all of them loved."

From: *James and the Giant Peach* by Roald Dahl.

scarlet: red
trifle: little
saucy: disrespectful

notes:

_____

_____

_____

_____

_____

_____

_____

_____

> List three kinds of ladybugs described in the reading.
Two-Spotted, Five-Spotted, and Nine-Spotted

_____

_____

 15

Materials books by Roald Dahl

Language Arts Have students write out the expressions used to describe the personality traits of the two-spotted (very common and ill-mannered) and five-spotted (a trifle saucy) ladybugs. Explain that the author of the story was an Englishman named Roald Dahl (1916-1990). While these expressions may not be familiar to students, they are commonly used in England.

Have students write paragraphs incorporating the phrases in a different context. For example, students might incorporate the phrase in a sports story a news story, or a short biographical sketch.

reading. ***What part of what the Ladybug says is fact? What part is opinion?*** (The number of spots on each species is fact. The personality traits of each species is opinion.)

Science Background

The three species of ladybug described in the reading are all native to North America, although the story of *James and the Giant Peach* begins in England. The most common ladybug native to Europe is the seven-spotted ladybug, *Coccinella septempunctata*.

Check Understanding

Skill: Communicate

Could a five-spotted ladybug become a nine-spotted ladybug? Why or why not? (No, it could not, because ladybugs have the same number of spots throughout their lives.)

NSTA Activity

Classify Ladybugs

See page 11B for an NSTA activity on classification. Tie this activity in with the Explore section on p. 16. The activity will show students how physical traits are used to classify objects.

Enrichment

Arthropods

Materials research materials on arthropod classification

Remind students that James was on an adventure with some animal friends, including a grasshopper, a spider, and a centipede. Have students do some research to find out how the grasshopper, spider, and centipede are classified. (All are arthropods. The grasshopper is an insect. The spider is an arachnid.)

Then have students draw a Venn diagram to show what body traits the three animals have in common and which are unique to each. (All are arthropods, so all have jointed limbs, segmented bodies, exoskeletons, and compound eyes. Spiders have two main body parts. Grasshoppers have three main body parts. Centipedes have many segments. Spiders have eight legs and grasshoppers have six legs. Centipedes have more than 20 legs. Insects and centipedes have one pair of antennae. Arachnids have no antennae.)

Look Back

A **trait** is a characteristic or feature, such as having brown hair or having two eyes.

> **What trait was used to tell one kind of ladybug from the other?**

the number of spots on each ladybug

Explore

CLASSIFY LADYBUGS

Scientists divide living things into groups based on their traits. These groups form a **classification system**. A classification system makes it easier to see how all living things are related to one another. For example, mammals, insects, and birds all belong to a group that includes all animals. Scientists divide the insect group into even smaller groups. Look at the diagram below. It shows some of the different groups of living things within the animal group.

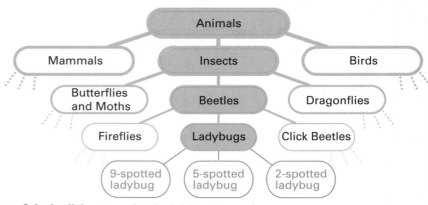

> **Color in all the groups that the ladybugs belong to.**

> **What is the largest group that the ladybugs belong to?** Animals

> **Now add to the diagram ovals for the three kinds of ladybugs described in the reading. Which group should they branch off from? Label your new ovals.**

16

Look Back

Have students describe as many of a ladybug's traits as they can using the drawings on page 17. (They are sort of round, they are curved on top, they are red with black spots, they have two antennae, they have six legs.) Remind students that traits can be observed and are facts.

Explore

Classify Ladybugs Help students as needed to understand the diagram. Point out that only three of the many groups within the animal kingdom are shown in the diagram. Likewise, only three of the many groups within the insect class and beetle order are shown. The short, dashed lines indicate that other groups are missing from the diagram.

To help students answer the question "What is the largest group that the ladybugs belong to?" point to each oval on the diagram and ask: *Are*

the ladybugs a kind of _____? (Students should conclude that a ladybug is a kind of beetle, a kind of insect and a kind of animal.)

You might choose to have students recreate the diagram shown on page 16 on a classroom or school bulletin board using cut-out paper ovals and push pins. Have them illustrate examples of animals from each group by cutting out pictures from magazines and pinning them next to each oval. Point out how the groups have more in common the lower you go.

Explore

COMPARE LADYBUGS

The smallest group that a living thing can belong to is called a species. A **species** is one kind of living thing. For example, the gray wolf is one kind of species. The two-spotted ladybug is another. Only two living things of the same species can mate with each other and produce more members of that species. Look at the pictures of three species of ladybugs, below. How are the ladybugs alike? How are they different?

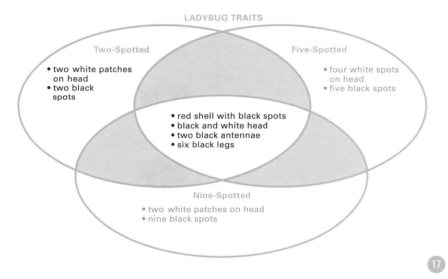

Two-Spotted Ladybug   Five-Spotted Ladybug   Nine-Spotted Ladybug

> **Complete the Venn diagram below to show which traits are unique to each species of ladybug and which traits are shared by all three species.**

LADYBUG TRAITS

Two-Spotted
- two white patches on head
- two black spots

Five-Spotted
- four white spots on head
- five black spots

- red shell with black spots
- black and white head
- two black antennae
- six black legs

Nine-Spotted
- two white patches on head
- nine black spots

Materials index cards, masking tape

Visual/Spatial Invite students to use index cards to construct a physical model of the Venn diagram on page 17. Begin by having students write down each ladybug's individual traits on a separate index card. Have them start with general observations. ("It is red." "It has black spots." "It has a black head with white spots." "It has six legs.") Then have them move on to more specific observations. ("It has two black spots on its red shell." "It has two white patches on its head.")

When all the traits have been written on separate index cards, write the following four category heads on the board: "Two-spotted," "Five-spotted," "Nine-spotted," and "All ladybugs." Finally, invite students to tape each index card under the correct head. Then ask: *What traits are common to all ladybugs?* (red shell, black spots, two black antennae, six black legs) *Which traits vary from one species of ladybug to another?* (number of spots, number of white patches on head)

Explore

Compare Ladybugs Students may think that all ladybugs look pretty much alike, and that they can all mate with each other to produce more ladybugs. Emphasize that animals that look a lot alike to us may still be different species, and in general different species cannot mate to produce young.

Encourage students to think about how the three ladybug species are alike and different before they start filling out their Venn diagrams.

If students have never drawn a Venn diagram before, walk them through the process. Explain that traits unique to each ladybug should be written in the parts of the ovals that are not overlapping. Traits that all the ladybugs share in common should be written in the overlapped section of the Venn diagram. You may want to draw a Venn diagram on the board and complete it as a class exercise.

Once students have completed their charts, have them focus on the overlapped section. Point out that this

collection of traits are what make ladybugs different from other kinds of beetles.

Assessment

Skill: Communicating

Use the following question to assess each student's progress.

What trait would you use to classify ladybugs? (number of spots it has)

Could a five-spotted ladybug and a nine-spotted ladybug mate and produce a seven-spotted ladybug? Why or why not? (No they couldn't do this, because they are different species and generally different species cannot mate to produce young.)

Review "Find Out" Question

Review the question from the Unit Opener on page 12. Ask: *How do scientists tell one kind of ladybug from another?* (Scientists look for different traits to tell one kind of ladybug from another.) Have students use what they learned in the chapter to suggest an answer to the question. Use their responses as the basis for a class discussion.

Explore

WHAT'S IN A NAME?

Each species has a special scientific name. These names may look strange or unfamiliar to you because they use words from languages that people used long ago—such as Latin and Ancient Greek.

For example, the name that scientists use for the ladybug family is "Coccinellidae." Look at the first part of the name: "Cocc-." Replace the "c"s with "k"s. You get "Kokk-." The Greek word *kokkos* means "berry." So the family name for ladybug comes from the Greek word for "berry."

> **Why do you think they used the word "berry" to name the ladybug family?**
> Students should realize that ladybugs are both brightly colored
> and round.

Knowing some Latin and Greek word parts can help you understand scientific names. Look at the chart below of Latin word parts for numbers.

> **Use the information in the chart to match each ladybug to its correct scientific name. (Hint: How many spots does each ladybug have?)**

Number	Word Part
1	un-
2	du-, di-, bi
3	tre-
4	quat-
5	quin-
6	sex-
7	sept-
8	oct-
9	nov-
10	dec-

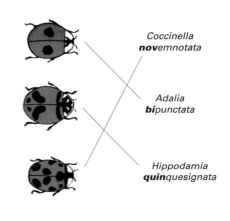

*Coccinella **nov**emnotata*

*Adalia **bi**punctata*

*Hippodamia **quin**quesignata*

Explore

What's in a Name? Explain that each species has a two-part scientific name. The first part tells what genus the organism belongs to. The second part tells what species it belongs to. For example, humans are called *Homo sapiens*. *Homo* is the genus humans belong to, *sapiens* is the species.

Most scientific names tell you a little bit about the organism. For example, homo means "man" and sapiens is from the Latin "to know" or "to be wise." Humans have thinking skills and "wisdom" possessed by no other animals.

Help students see that the five-spotted ladybug has one large spot across the top of its shell that may look a bit like two spots.

How many spots do you think the European ladybug Coccinella septempunctata has? (seven)

Mole-rat-unculus

Chapter 2

If you were a naked mole-rat, how would you find your way around the pitch-black tunnels of your home?

Do you know what a naked mole-rat looks like? Well, you can probably guess that it doesn't have a lot of hair! The naked mole-rat is a small, nearly hairless mammal that lives underground in tunnels. Its whole life is spent in the dark. Unfortunately, it hasn't learned how to use a flashlight, so it has to move around and do all the things it does in total darkness.

In this chapter, you'll read about some scientists who studied the naked mole-rat. They wanted to find out how the naked mole-rat is able to get around so well in the pitch dark.

Before You Read

Smell is one of the senses—touch, taste, smell, sight, and hearing. Imagine that you are standing alone in a house you've never been in before.

> **What senses would you use to get information about your surroundings? What sense would you probably not use?**

Students might suggest sight, hearing, touch, and maybe smell. Taste would probably not be used.

> **Now imagine that all the lights have been turned off and your ears have been plugged. Which senses would be most useful now?**

touch and maybe smell

 SCIENCESAURUS
A STUDENT HANDBOOK
BLUE BOOK

Sensing the Environment p. 90
Sense Organs .... p. 125

 SCiLINKS
THE WORLD'S A CLICK AWAY

www.scilinks.org
Keyword: Adaptations of Animals
Code: GS5D010

(19)

Key Idea

The structure of an animal's body part or system is related to the function that it serves.

Focus

- Form and function
- Characteristics of organisms
- Organisms and environments
- Structure and function in living systems
- Diversity and adaptations of organisms

Skills and Strategies

- Construct models
- Compare and contrast
- Infer
- *Communicate (TG)*

Vocabulary*

Before beginning the chapter, make sure students understand these terms.

- cell
- environment
- mammal
- nerve cells

* Definitions are in the Glossary on pages 166–172.

Introducing the Chapter

Materials assorted small objects of varying textures, cloth or paper bag
This chapter introduces students to the naked mole-rat—an animal that uses touch more than sight to gather information about its environment. To get students thinking about what sort of information they can get from touching an object without seeing it, conduct the following exercise:

Place a number of small objects of varying textures (a paper clip, a rubber eraser, a sea shell, a leaf, a marble, hairpin, shoelace) inside a cloth or paper bag. Have student volunteers place their hand in the bag and try to name each item and share the information gathered by touching the objects. List each volunteer's ideas on the board and then compare the lists. There may be some variety. Which of the five senses do people usually use to identify objects? (sight)

Before You Read

After students have answered the two questions, ask: *How is being in a house with the lights turned off like being a naked mole-rat in a tunnel underground?* (In both cases, sight cannot be used easily to gather information. Touch and other senses become more important.)

More Resources

The following resources are also available from Great Source and NSTA.

www.scilinks.org
Keyword: Adaptations
of Animals
Code: GS5D010

SC LINKS.
THE WORLD'S A CLICK AWAY

Read

Meet the naked mole-rat. It may not be pretty, but it's pretty cool. Find out why this animal is more likely to touch teeth with another naked mole-rat than shake hands.

"Night of the Living Unculus"

notes:

> Which of the senses would be most important to an animal living in a place with no light and little sound?

touch

> How does the size of the body part in the "touch map" relate to the number of nerve cells in the actual body part?

The more nerve cells the actual body part has, the bigger the body part is in the "touch map."

You've probably never asked yourself what it feels like to be a naked mole-rat. Scientists have found out anyway. And they're just bursting to tell you, so here goes.

The naked mole-rat is a <u>bizarre</u> East African beast that spends most of its life <u>scurrying</u> through burrows underground. In order to be a champion tunnel runner, it is nearly hairless and has small eyes and ears. It has been called a hot-dog with teeth, but frankly, we think that's being kind. It's way too ugly to be food.

This past April scientists reported that they had mapped the part of the mole-rat's brain that responds to touch. They put tiny <u>electrodes</u> into the mole-rat's brain, touched a part of its body, and recorded which nerve cells fired. After they had completed the experiment, they drew a naked mole-rat ["touch map"]. The more nerve cells

bizarre: weird
scurrying: running

electrodes: tiny devices that are used to record electrical signals

20

Science Background

The naked mole-rat is found in Kenya, Ethiopia, and Somalia. Scientists have different ideas about why the naked mole-rat does not have fur. Some suggest that fur harbors parasites, and that the absence of fur is a positive adaptation that reduces the chances of parasite infestation.

Read

Paired Reading Explain that nerve cells are cells that send electrical signals between the body and the brain. They are part of the nervous system. Nerve cells are found all over the naked mole-ratís body. But there are more of them in some places than in others.

To help students understand how the experiment described was set up, draw the outline of a mole-rat on the board. Label the brain and indicate where the electrodes were placed (in

the brain). Draw a small dot on the mole-rat's body and explain that this dot represents the place where scientists touched the mole-rat. Explain that if the electrodes in the brain recorded the firing of a nerve cell when this spot was touched, the scientists knew there was a nerve cell on that part of the body. Circle the dot and identify it as a place where a nerve cell is found. Explain that in this way, scientists were able to map out the places of the mole-rat's body that had the most nerve cells.

The Moleratunculus

[the body part had], the bigger they drew the part. The scientific name for this kind of touch map in people is *homunculus*, which is Latin for "little man." So the scientists called their map a moleratunculus. Guess which part of the mole-ratunculus is the biggest?

Fully a third of the mole-rat's "<u>touch cortex</u>" is devoted to those fantastic front choppers, which it uses for <u>eating, digging, dragging things around, and socializing with other mole-rats</u>. In fact, the teeth seem to have taken over an area of the brain devoted to vision in [animals] that are similar but do not spend their lives in the dark.

From: "Night of the Living Unculus," *Muse* magazine, February 2003.

touch cortex: part of the brain that receives information about touch

notes:

_____

_____

_____

_____

_____

_____

_____

_____

_____

_____

_____

 <u>Underline</u> what the naked mole-rat uses its teeth for.

(21)

Connections

Math Tell the students that the mass of a mole-rat's brain is about 2.5% of the mass of its body. then pose the following problem: **You are caring for a mole-rat. You find that the mass of a mole-rat's body is 42 g. What would be your estimate of the mass of its brain?** (1g)

If necessary, review some or all of the following: To solve the problem students must determine what portion of 42g is represented by 2.5%. Remind students that they must convert 2.5% into a decimal before they can calculate the mass of the mole-rat's brain. The value of 2.5% can be written as the decimal 0.025. Therefore, the mass of the mole-rat's brain is 0.025 of the mass of its body, or

$$42g \times 0.025 = 1.05g$$

Students might not think of a tooth as being able to sense touch. They may think that a tooth is made of solid, hard material, not nerve cells. Explain that only the outer surface of teeth is hard enamel. But the inner part of a tooth contains nerves and blood vessels. These nerves allow people to feel hot and cold with their teeth. In the mole-rat, these nerves do even more–they allow the mole-rat to distinguish between objects touched with the teeth.

Explain that mole-rats rarely leave their underground tunnels, and that their diet consists of only plant material. **What do you suppose the mole-rats could find to eat underground?** (roots) Tell students that mole-rats eat the roots of plants growing underground.

Check Understanding

Skill: Infer

Remind students that the naked mole-rat is nearly hairless and has small eyes and ears. **Do you suppose a mole-rat could live successfully above the ground?** (Students should infer that the mole-rat, with poor sight and hearing, and no fur to keep it warm, would not do well outside of its tunnel environment.)

Enrichment

Bat Adaptations

Materials research materials on bats

Explain that bats are active in the dark at night. Have students research bats and what adaptations they have for life in the dark. (They use echolocation to navigate when flying and to locate prey: they emit high-pitched sounds that bounce off of objects and come back at them. They use these echoes to judge the distance and location of an object.) Point out that bats have large ears for capturing these echoes.

Have students compare and contrast the mole-rat's adaptation for life in the dark with the bat's adaptation. ***How are the mole-rat's sensitive teeth appropriate for its environment and lifestyle?*** (It runs around in narrow tunnels, so everything new it meets and needs to collect information about is at the front of its face.)

How is echolocation appropriate for a bat's environment and lifestyle? (The bat flies around through the air and uses echolocation to find food, such as flying insects, and to avoid running into objects.)

Look Back

Look at the following two terms from the reading.

Homunculus	Moleratunculus

> **Underline the group of letters that both terms have in common.**

> **What does a "touch map"—or unculus—show?**
> It shows which parts of the body have the most nerve cells and are the most sensitive to touch. Bigger parts have more nerve cells and are more sensitive.

> **What does a homunculus show?**
> It shows which parts of the human body have the most nerve cells and are the most sensitive to touch.

> **What does a moleratunculus show?**
> It shows which parts of the naked mole-rat have the most nerve cells and are the most sensitive to touch.

Science Background

There are eight species of mole rats in the mole-rat family. All are native to sub-Saharan Africa. The naked mole-rat is the smallest species, whose body length is 8–9 cm with a 3.5–4 cm tail. Naked mole-rats have a social structure with colonies of about 100 animals ruled by a queen. Worker naked mole-rats tend to the queen, dig tunnels, and gather food for the colony to eat.

Look Back

Invite students to look back at the reading as needed to answer the first question. After students complete the last two questions, ask: ***What do the two terms have in common? How are they different?*** (They both end in "-unculus," but one begins with "hom-" and the other begins with "molerat-.") Point out that the first part of the term tells what kind of animal the touch map is for. Then have students come up with a list of names for the touch maps of other animals. (Ex: dogunculus, giraffunculus, frogunculus)

Is "moleratunculus" a real word? Where did it come from? (No, homunculus is a real word, and moleratunculus is just a word the scientists doing the experiment made up to describe the touch map of a mole-rat.)

Explore

LOOKING AT THE MOLERATUNCULUS

Look at the photo of the naked mole-rat at right. Now look back at the mole-ratunculus shown on page 21.

Look at the naked mole-rat's body parts in the photo. Now compare the size of these parts to the same parts in the moleratunculus.

> **What do you notice?**
>
> The teeth, feet, and hairs appear bigger in the moleratunculus.

> **According to the moleratunculus, which parts of the naked mole-rat are most sensitive and have the most nerve cells?**
>
> teeth, feet, and hairs

> **Why do you think these parts of the naked mole-rat are the most sensitive to touch? (Hint: Think about how the naked mole-rat moves around in its environment.)**
>
> The naked mole-rat uses its teeth, feet, and hairs to touch the sides of the tunnel and other naked mole-rats it meets. These parts are the most sensitive to touch because they are the parts that are in contact with the environment.

Explore

Looking at the Moleratunculus Do the comparison exercise as a class using overhead transparencies of both the mole-rat photo (p. 23) and the moleratunculus (p. 21).

Encourage students to compare one set of features at a time.

- eyes (about the same size in both)
- ears (about the same size in both)
- teeth (bigger in moleratunculus)
- hairs (bigger in moleratunculus)
- feet (bigger in moleratunculus)
- tail (about the same size in both)
- torso (about the same size in both)

Help students as needed to make the connection between the size of the body part on the moleratunculus and the sensitivity of that part in the mole-ratís body. (Bigger part = more sensitive.)

To help students with the last question, ask them to imagine that they are mole-rats running through the dark, narrow underground tunnels of their home. ***Which parts of your***

Differentiating Instruction

Materials gym mats

Bodily/Kinesthetic In order to help students think about what life in underground tunnels would be like, construct a tunnel using flexible mats from the gymnasium or student desks lined up end-to-end. The tunnel should be large enough for students to crawl through.

Invite students to pretend that they are a naked mole-rat moving through an underground tunnel. Have them close their eyes (mole-rat eyes are very small) and enter the tunnel. Have them note which parts of their bodies are in contact with the tunnel's walls. (In addition to their feet, hands, and knees, the skin and hair of their backs and arms may touch the "walls.")

To model what happens when a mole-rat encounters an object in a tunnel, hang a light object, such as a ping pong ball, head high in the middle of the tunnel. ***Which part of your body first senses the object?*** (head) Discuss how this is analogous to the mole-rat's ability to sense objects with its teeth.

body would be in contact with the objects in the tunnel environment? (The hairs would be touching the sides of the tunnel; the teeth would be touching any object in front that they met in the tunnel; the feet would be touching the ground as they ran.)

Assessment

Skill: Communicate

Use the following question to assess each student's progress.

Explain that one of the laws of nature is that form follows function. That means that the shape or arrangement of an animal's body is related to the job it has to do in its particular environment. *How does the form of the naked mole-rat's body match its function?* (The mole-rat has small eyes and ears because they are not of much use in its tunnel environment. It has very sensitive teeth, feet, and body hairs, which allow it to sense its dark tunnel environment well.)

Review "Find Out" Question

Review the question from the Unit Opener on page 12. *Which parts of a mole-rat's body are most sensitive to touch?* (teeth, feet, body hairs)

Have students use what they learned in the chapter to suggest an answer to the question. Use their responses as the basis for a class discussion.

Explore

DRAWING A HOMUNCULUS

In the human body, the lips, tongue, hands, fingers, and thumbs are the most sensitive to touch.

> **Why do you think these parts of a human are most sensitive to touch?**
>
> Humans touch objects with their hands to feel the objects. So their fingers are very sensitive. The lips and tongue are used when eating, so sensitivity in these parts gives humans information about what they are eating.

> **Use what you have learned about "touch maps" to draw a homunculus. Which parts of the human body are bigger on the homunculus?**

24

Explore

Drawing a Homunculus Help students as needed to draw their homunculuses. Remind them that the most sensitive parts of the body are drawn larger than the other body parts on the unculus. Suggest that students start with the most sensitive parts of the human body and then draw the other body parts around them.

Have students compare their drawing of a homunculus to the molerat-unculus shown on p. 21. *How are the two unculuses similar? How are they different?* (Students should note that both have sensitive areas around the face. In the homunculus, it is the lips and tongue that are most sensitive, not the teeth.) *Why do you suppose the "hands" of the mole-rat are not more sensitive than the feet, as they are in humans?* (Students should suggest that mole-rats do not handle objects with their hands as people do. Both their "hands" and feet have the same sensitivity because they are both used in the same way.)

Chapter 3

Some plants have to get tough to meet their needs.

Like all living things, plants have basic needs that have to be met in order for them to survive. You probably know that plants need water, but water is just one of a plant's basic needs. You will learn about some other needs in this chapter. For example, a plant also needs energy, minerals, and protection from animals that want to eat it.

The environment where a plant grows must supply the plant with all of its needs or the plant will die. Some environments are better than others. Think about a weed growing in a small crack in the sidewalk. The soil is not very deep or rich, and the sidewalk is hot. The weed must be able to deal with the harsh environment where it lives. In places where the environment is not ideal, plants have special ways to meet their needs. In this chapter, you will learn about these types of plants.

Before You Read

A cactus is a kind of plant. Cactuses grow mainly in deserts. The desert environment is very dry because it does not rain very often or very much. Plants that grow in deserts have to store as much water as they can between rainfalls. Desert animals will often eat these plants in order to get at the stored water. A cactus needs to protect itself from animals.

> **Look at the picture of the cactus. What structures protect the cactus from animals?**

The sharp spines of the cactus keep away

animals who might want to eat it.

 Organism's Basic Needs .... p. 76
Adaptations p. 77
Getting and Using Energy .... p. 77
Photosynthesis .... p. 80

 www.scilinks.org
Keyword: Adaptations of Plants
Code: GS5D015

25

Key Idea

Adaptations to their environment help plants meet their needs.

Focus

- Form and function
- Characteristics of organisms
- Organisms and environments
- Structure and function in living systems
- Diversity and adaptations of organisms

Skills and Strategies

- Infer
- Classify
- Interpret scientific illustrations
- Communicate
- *Make a Concept Map (TG)*

Vocabulary*

Before beginning the chapter, make sure students understand these terms.

- digest
- energy
- environment
- minerals
- nutrients
- photosynthesis

* Definitions are in the Glossary on pages 166–172.

Introducing the Chapter

This chapter introduces students to the Venus Fly Trap, a carnivorous plant that meets its special nutritional needs by consuming insects. The Venus Fly Trap is also known as Venus's Fly Trap and Venus's-Flytrap.

To get students thinking about plants and animals and the differences between them, ask: *What makes a plant different from an animal?* (Answer will vary. Students may know that plants make their own food using energy from sunlight, while animals have to eat plants or other animals to get the food they need.) Explain this basic difference to the class.

Before You Read

Before You Read

Materials cactus plant

Show the class the cactus plant. Explain that the spines are actually a special kind of leaf. Point out that, in addition to protecting the cactus from animals that want to eat it, the spines reduce the amount of water that evaporates from the plant and so help to conserve water. Lead students to conclude that spines are a special adaptation that allow a cactus to survive in the desert environment.

More Resources

The following resources are also available from Great Source and NSTA.

A STUDENT HANDBOOK
BLUE BOOK

Reader's Handbook (Yellow Book)

SCI LINKS
THE WORLD'S A CLICK AWAY

www.scilinks.org
Keyword: Adaptations
of Plants
Code: GS5D015

Read

Hosts Don Glass and Yael Ksander discuss the Venus Fly Trap on their radio show, *A Moment of Science.*

"What the Heck Is It?"

Don: Today, on a Moment of Science, it's time for another round of "What the Heck Is It?", that fun and wacky <u>classification</u> game. Please welcome—all the way from Bloomington, Indiana—today's contestant, Yael Ksander.
   [APPLAUSE]

Yael: Thanks, Don. Glad to be here.

Don: Are you ready, Yael?

Yael: Sure am.

Don: Okay, Listen carefully. What the heck is a—Venus Fly Trap?

Yael: Hmm! Is it a type of plant?
   [APPLAUSE]

Don: That's right! You get to move on to the next question! Ready?

Yael: Yes.

Don: Okay! What the heck is a plant?

Yael: Plants are defined as organisms that use photosynthesis to produce their own food. Photosynthesis is the process by which plants use light to convert water and carbon dioxide into simple sugars.

Don: That's 2 out of 3!
   [APPLAUSE] And now, the grand prize question
   [OOO!]
Everyone knows that the Venus Fly Trap catches and <u>consumes</u> small insects. So, how the heck can the Venus Fly Trap be a plant if it's a <u>carnivore</u>?

notes:

> How is a Venus Fly Trap
   classified?
as a plant

> How is a plant defined?
Plants are organisms that
photosynthesize to produce
their own food.

26

classification: system of organizing living things into different groups

consumes: eats
carnivore: an organism that eats animals

Read

Paired Reading If students are unfamiliar with the interview format, take a minute to go over the structure of the reading. ***Who is doing the interviewing?*** (Don) ***Who is being interviewed?*** (Yael) ***How can you tell?*** (Don is asking the questions and Yael is answering them.)

You might want to choose two student volunteers to act out the interview for the rest of the class using their own names instead of the ones used in the reading. Have the volunteers read over the dialogue a few times before the staging. The rest of the class can act as the audience and applaud when signaled by you. Consider presenting the live interview to another class as well.

Ask students to read aloud the "grand prize question." ("How the heck can the Venus Fly Trap be a plant if it's a carnivore?") Hold a class discussion on why these two ideas appear to be in conflict. (Carnivores are animals that eat other animals. Plants are not animals, so they don't fit the definition of carnivore.) Once students have completed the reading, explain that a Venus Fly Trap is not technically a carnivore. It is a plant that consumes insects.

When students have finished the reading, ask: ***What do the insects provide to the Venus Fly Trap plant and what do they not provide?*** (They provide nitrogen and other minerals that most plants get from the soil. Photosynthesis is still their main source of energy.)

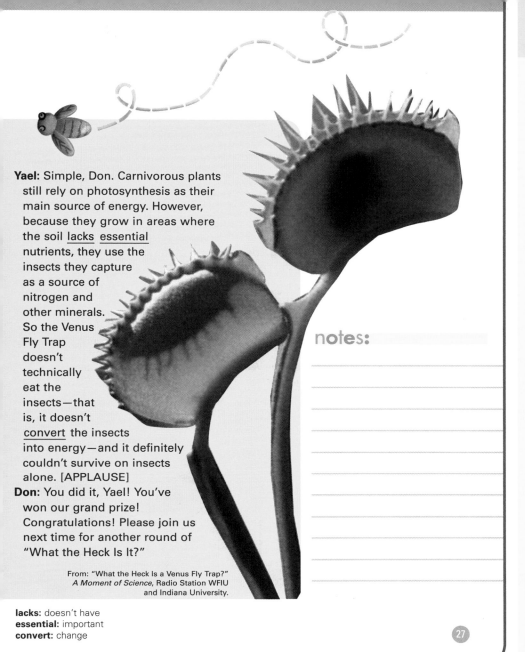

Yael: Simple, Don. Carnivorous plants still rely on photosynthesis as their main source of energy. However, because they grow in areas where the soil <u>lacks</u> <u>essential</u> nutrients, they use the insects they capture as a source of nitrogen and other minerals. So the Venus Fly Trap doesn't technically eat the insects—that is, it doesn't <u>convert</u> the insects into energy—and it definitely couldn't survive on insects alone. [APPLAUSE]

Don: You did it, Yael! You've won our grand prize! Congratulations! Please join us next time for another round of "What the Heck Is It?"

From: "What the Heck Is a Venus Fly Trap?"
A Moment of Science, Radio Station WFIU and Indiana University.

notes:

lacks: doesn't have
essential: important
convert: change

(27)

Connections

Social Studies The survival of plants is affected by many factors, including human activity. Often, such as in the Amazon Rain Forest, the activities of people can be detrimental to plant life. Although temporarily beneficial to the people themselves, the destruction of a rain forest can have long-term consequences to the lives of people.

Have students research the Amazon Rain Forest and the effects development, mining, logging, road building, and farming are having on it.

Students should report on the biological and social consequences of forest clearing. Biological consequences include extinction of species and the greenhouse effect. (The greenhouse effect is produced by a buildup up of carbon dioxide in the atmosphere, which increases world temperatures. Since plants remove carbon dioxide from the atmosphere during the process of photosynthesis, fewer plants mean more carbon dioxide in the air.) Many medicines are harvested from rain forest plants. Students should identify some of these and their uses.

Finally, have students suggest ways to preserve rain forests while not violating the rights of people. Have students propose reasonable governmental actions, laws, and regulations that strike a balance between the needs of people and the preservation of the forests.

Science Background

About 5–12 days after an insect is trapped, the leaf trap reopens and releases the undigested parts of the insect. The trap will only work for 3–5 meals, after which it stops functioning as a trap and simply photosynthesizes for another 2–3 months before finally falling off the plant.

Check Understanding

Skill: Concept mapping

Have students draw a concept map illustrating the relationship between the following terms: carnivorous plants, main source of energy, photosynthesis, insects, nitrogen and other minerals. If students have difficulty understanding what to draw, provide the following template with a few labels included, but others omitted.

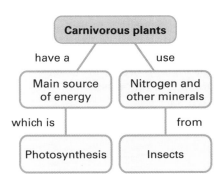

Enrichment

Exploring Sponges

Materials research materials on sea sponges

Have students research an animal that seems to act more like a plant than an animal—the sponge. Sponges are the simplest multi-cellular animal. They live at the bottom of the ocean floor, where they attach themselves to something solid. Specialized cells are used to force water through the sponge. As the water moves through the canals of the sponge, nutrients and oxygen are removed from the water and wastes are carried away. The sponge uses nutrients and oxygen from the water to live.

After student have completed their research, ask: ***How is a sponge like a plant?*** (It does not move, it doesn't have distinct body parts like a mouth or eyes.) ***How is it like an animal?*** (It takes in nutrients and oxygen from its environment and uses them to grow. It does not make its own food.)

Look Back

Like all plants, the Venus Fly Trap uses photosynthesis to get the energy that it needs. Plants also need essential nutrients, such as minerals and nitrogen. Usually plants get these nutrients from soil.

> **How does the Venus Fly Trap get minerals and nitrogen?**

It traps and consumes small insects.

Explore

PLANT OR ANIMAL?

According to the reading, the Venus Fly Trap does some "animal-like" things.

> **Name an "animal-like" thing that the Venus Fly Trap does.**

It catches and consumes small insects.

But scientists still classify the Venus Fly Trap as a plant, not an animal.

> **Why do scientists classify the Venus Fly Trap as a plant if it does "animal-like" things? What makes it a plant?**

It still uses photosynthesis to produce its own food. That makes it a plant.

"My homework ate my dog!"

Look Back

Remind students that most plants get the nutrients they need from the soil. ***What's wrong with the soil that the Venus Fly Trap grows in?*** (It lacks nitrogen and other essential nutrients.)

Explore

Plant or Animal? ***Name some animals that eat insects*** (birds, frogs, lizards, small mammals). Explain that these animals all have systems designed to digest food, absorb nutrients, and get rid of waste.

On the board, draw a simple outline of a bird with a tube running from mouth to stomach, a long intestine stacked in the abdomen, and an exit at the anus. Have students help you trace the path that food takes as it moves through the bird. Explain that the

Venus Fly Trap plant does not have a digestive system. That's another reason why it's not considered an animal.

Explore

EATING INSECTS

You might wonder how the Venus Fly Trap "eats" an insect. It doesn't chew the insect up and swallow it as an animal would. The three steps described below show how a Venus Fly Trap gets nutrients from insects:

1. **Attract:** The Venus Fly Trap has leaves that produce a sweet nectar. This nectar attracts insects that then land on the jaw-like leaf.

2. **Trap:** When an insect steps on the "trigger hairs" inside the leaf, the two halves of the leaf instantly close over the insect. Long spines on the edges of the leaf trap the insect inside.

3. **Digest and Absorb:** Glands in the leaf give off juices that digest the soft parts of the insect, leaving the hard parts. The nutrients from the insect's body are soaked up by the leaf trap.

> Fill in the chart below to show the function of each step and the plant structure that is used to carry out that function. The first box has been done for you.

Step	Function	Plant Structure that Serves this Function
1	Attract insect	leaves that produce sweet nectar
2	trap insect	trigger hairs and long spines
3	digest insect and absorb nutrients	leaves that can digest and soak up nutrients

29

Verbal/Linguistic Have students write a story that describes an imaginary meeting between a Venus Fly Trap and a fly. The story should begin with a short dialogue between the Venus Fly Trap and a fly. The Venus Fly Trap's dialogue should attempt to entice the fly by talking about its sweet-smelling nectar. The fly's dialogue should reflect skepticism and desire at the same time.

After the fly has been captured, students' stories should describe in vibrant language how the plant makes a meal of the fly. Remind students to use the scientific information from page 29 when constructing their stories.

Remind students that, in reality, plants and flies do not have human thoughts as they do in the stories. Fiction writers combine scientific facts and their imaginations to create exciting stories.

Explore

Materials Venus Fly Trap plant

Eating Insects If possible, bring in a Venus Fly Trap so that students can observe each of the steps described in this section. Caution the students not to touch the trap leaves until you give them the signal as it will take a long time for them to reopen.

Before students complete the chart, discuss the idea of structure and function with students. Remind them of what they learned about the naked mole-rat in Chapter 2. (The naked mole-rat had a body structure that was specially suited to its particular environment.)

What would happen if the leaves of the Venus Fly Trap did not have long spines on the edges? (Students should infer that the insect could escape from the trap. As a result, the plant could not get the minerals it needed.) Point out how structure depends on function and function depends on structure.

Assessment

Skill: Communicate

Use the following question to assess each student's progress.

How is the structure of the Venus Fly Trap specially suited to its needs? (It has special leaves, nectar, and glands that allow it to capture insects and get from them the nitrogen and other minerals lacking in the environment where it grows.)

Review "Find Out" Question

Review the question from the Unit Opener on page 12. ***Why do some plants eat insects?*** (The insects provide nitrogen and minerals that the plants need to survive.) Have students use what they learned in the chapter to answer the question. Use their responses as the basis for a class discussion.

Project

CARNIVOROUS BOG PLANTS

Have you ever seen a Venus Fly Trap growing in the wild? You probably haven't. That's because they grow only in bogs found in a few small areas of North Carolina and South Carolina. A bog is an area of land where the soil is very wet and swampy and usually lacks the nitrogen and minerals that plants need to live. The Venus Fly Trap has adapted to life in the bog by being a carnivorous plant. But the Venus Fly Trap is not the only bog plant that "eats" insects.

> **Research another carnivorous plant that grows in bogs. Here are some choices:**

1. Pitcher plant   **2.** Sundew   **3.** Bladderwort

> **How does the plant attract, trap, digest, and absorb insects? What structures does it have to carry out these functions? Record what you find in your research.**

_____

_____

_____

_____

_____

_____

_____

_____

> **Now make a poster showing what you found out about your carnivorous plant. Use pictures and words to describe how the plant captures and digests insects.**

30

Project

Materials research materials on carnivorous bog plants, materials to create posters

Provide students with reference books or web sites that identify and describe other carnivorous bog plants.

The pitcher plant has tube-shaped leaves that collect water. Insects that crawl into the tube drown in the water. A mixture of chemicals then dissolves the bodies of the trapped insects. Finally, the nutrients are absorbed into the plant.

The leaves of the sundew plant are covered with sticky tentacles that trap any insect that lands on them. As the insect struggles, it gets covered with digestive juices that eventually break down the insect's body. The sundew plant then absorbs the nutrients.

The bladderwort is a plant that floats in bog water. It has many special bladders that inflate and suck in passing insects when trigger hairs on the bladder are activated. The insects are then digested and absorbed by the plant.

How can you get at a tasty bug hiding in a narrow crack?

Imagine that you are getting dressed in a hurry one morning. As you grab for your socks, one accidentally slips across your dresser and falls behind it. Uh-oh. The dresser is far too heavy to move. How can you get your sock?

Believe it or not, birds often find themselves facing that same question. Well, they don't wear socks, but they do hunt for insects. These insects are often hiding in hard-to-reach places to protect themselves.

In this lesson, you'll read about a type of bird that found an original way to pick a meal out of a tight space. You'll also learn how sea otters get a meal out of another kind of "tight space."

Before You Read

Can you think of a time when you got something out of a tight space or somewhere that was hard to reach? How did you do it? Did you use another object to help you?

> **Describe your experience with sentences or drawings.**

Adaptations   p. 77
Animal
Behavior ...... p. 93

www.scilinks.org
Keyword:
Behaviors, and
Adaptations
Code: GS5D020

Key Idea

Behavioral adaptations—including the use of tools—help animals meet their basic needs.

Focus

- Evolution and equilibrium
- Characteristics of organisms
- Organisms and environments
- Diversity and adaptations of organisms

Skills and Strategies

- Observe
- Communicate
- Infer
- Compare and contrast

Vocabulary*

Before beginning the chapter, make sure students understand this term.

- adaptation

* The definition is in the Glossary on pages 166–172.

Introducing the Chapter

This chapter introduces students to two different animals that use tools to help them meet their basic need for food. ***Can you think of any animals other than humans that use tools? What do they use the tools for?*** (Students may know that chimpanzees use twigs to pull ants out of ant hills. Accept all answers.)

What tool do you use to open a walnut? (Students will probably say they use a nutcracker, two metal bars joined at one end.) ***How might a bird or a monkey use objects other than their body parts to get a nut open?*** (Accept all reasonable answers. Students might say that a bird could drop the nut from up high onto a hard surface, or that a monkey could use rocks to smash the nut open.)

Before You Read

Have student volunteers share with the class their experiences of getting something out of a tight place. On the board, make a list of tools used to accomplish the task. (Lists will probably include broom handles, bent paper clips, and adhesive tape.) Point out that these objects are not available to animals in the wild. Then ask students to come up with natural substitutes for some of the objects on the list. (twigs or sticks, sap)

More Resources

The following resources are also available from Great Source and NSTA.

SCIENCESAURUS
A STUDENT HANDBOOK
BLUE BOOK

Reader's Handbook (Yellow Book)

SCI**L**INKS.
THE WORLD'S A CLICK AWAY

www.scilinks.org
Keyword: Behavior and Adaptations
Code: GS5D020

Read

Here's a bird that knows how to get what it wants.

"Bird Brain"

notes:

The next time you're tempted to call someone a "bird brain," think twice. Some birds may be craftier than you think. Certain crows can make <u>sophisticated</u> tools. And now, it seems, the birds can even <u>fine tune</u> their designs.

Scientists used to think that humans were the only animals that made and used tools. But in recent <u>decades</u>, chimpanzees, orangutans, Galapagos woodpecker finches, and other animals have been shown to have such skills.

In the mid-1990s, New Zealand researcher Gavin Hunt found that New Caledonian crows snip (twigs) and (leaves) to make tools for <u>digging food out of crevices</u>. The birds use the long, spiky leaves of the pandanus tree to make three kinds of tools with different shapes—wide, narrow, or <u>tapered</u> with a ragged edge.

The crow species on this stamp makes tools (shown at right).

From: "Better Tools for Techno Crows," *Science News for Kids*, March 26, 2

> (Circle) the two objects the crows use to make tools.

> <u>Underline</u> what they use the tools for.

sophisticated: complex
fine-tune: improve
decades: groups of ten years

crevices: narrow spaces, cracks
tapered: pointed

32

Science Background

New Caledonia, home to the New Caledonian crow, is an island in the southwest Pacific, east of Australia. It, along with some neighboring islands, is governed by France.

Read

Paired Reading Invite students to visit researcher Gavin Hunt's web site. (The easiest way to get to the site is to enter the keywords "Gavin Hunt Caledonian Crow" into a search engine.) Mr. Hunt's page is filled with information and photos of the New Caledonian crow and its tools.

Help students as needed to decipher the information on the stamp. Explain that the island of New Caledonia is ruled by France, so the words on the stamp are written in French. Provide the following translations, or have students look them up in an English-French dictionary.

nouvelle—new
outil—tool
feuille—leaf

Look Back

> **What problem did the New Caledonian crows face? What solution did they find? What tool was part of their solution?**

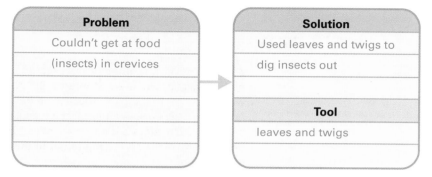

Problem
Couldn't get at food
(insects) in crevices

Solution
Used leaves and twigs to
dig insects out

Tool
leaves and twigs

Explore

WHY USE A TOOL?

Like all animals, crows have basic needs that they have to meet in order to survive. These needs include food, water, air, and shelter.

> **How did the crows use the pandanus leaves to help them get food?**

They snipped the leaves into shapes that were good for digging and then used them to get food out of crevices.

> **Look at the leaf tools shown in the picture on the previous page. Why might these leaves make good tools for digging in crevices?**

They're narrow and have spines.

> **A tool is a device that is used to make a job easier. How do the leaves that the crows cut fit the definition of a tool?**

The crows used the leaves to make getting food easier.

33

Enrichment

Leaf Tools

Materials stiff, narrow leaves or grasses, rice (optional)

Encourage students to recreate some of leaf tools they see in the picture on page 32. Provide students with an assortment of narrow, stiff leaves. Or have them collect leaves themselves on a supervised field trip. They should use only their fingernails to modify the leaves into tool shapes.

Once they have modified their leaves into tools suitable for digging small objects out of cracks, take them outdoors. Have them attempt to use the tools to remove small objects from crevices in tree bark. (You may choose to place single grains of rice inside the bark of nearby trees for students to extract.) If students are not successful at their efforts, ask: *How could you improve your tool?* (Students might suggest reshaping the tool to be more jagged, or using a stiffer leaf.)

Look Back

As needed, explain to students that a "solution" is a way to solve a problem. If they are having difficulty with the word, rephrase the question to read, "How did the crows solve their problem?" The "Solution" part of the diagram should explain the action or behavior of the crows. The "Tool" section should explain the tool the crows used as part of that action.

Explore

Why Use a Tool? Students might not understand that a torn leaf can be defined as a "tool." Explain that while we typically think of hammers and pliers as tools, a tool is any device that makes a job easier. You may choose to explain at this point that the leaf tools of the New Caledonian crows are also considered a type of technology. (Technology is any natural object fashioned to meet a special need.)

Check Understanding

Skill: Communicate

What special behavior allows the New Caledonian crow to meet its need for food? (the use of tools—ripped leaves)

Differentiating Instruction

English-language Learners Have student volunteers who are proficient in English pantomime the actions of the sea otter as described in the reading. Encourage other students in the class to shout out key vocabulary terms (sea otter, floating, oyster, rock, arm pit) as the pantomime is being performed. Write these terms on the board as they are offered.

After the performance, invite English-language learners to write a paragraph describing the action of the sea otter in their own words. Encourage them to make use of all the vocabulary words on the board in their paragraphs.

Partner up English-language learners with native speakers. Have the English-language learners read the story on page 34 again. Ask them to point out any passages or words that they are having trouble with. Have their partners respond to their queries.

Read

Crows aren't the only animals that use tools. Newspaper writer Gary Bogue remembers the time he saw a young sea otter wrestle with a difficult meal.

"A Smashing Idea"

notes:

> (Circle) the first thing the otter did to try to get inside the oyster.

> Why do you think the otter put the stone in its armpit?
to hold onto it while he ate

And I'll never forget the orphan sea otter pup I helped raise down at the Monterey SPCA's wildlife center in the early 1980s. One day he was floating on his back in a big plastic wading pool with several oysters sitting on his chest, (gnawing on the hard shells) and trying to get to the tasty meat inside.

I heard a sudden banging sound and turned to see the otter pounding on one of the oysters with a smooth rock. That was curious because there hadn't been a rock in the pool. I turned my head for a moment and when I looked back, the rock was gone and the otter was eating the oyster.

I checked the pool out thoroughly and no rock. Following up on a hunch, I started to frisk the otter ("Stop, that tickles!"). I found the smooth stone tucked carefully in the otter's right front armpit. He let out a loud chatter until I gave it back.

The sea otter was using the rock as a tool to crack open the shells of the oysters and other shellfish we were feeding him.

From: *Pets and Wildlife* column, Contra Costa Times, April 16, 2003.

SPCA: Society for the Prevention of Cruelty to Animals
oysters: a type of shellfish
gnawing: biting and chewing

34

Science Background

Sea otters belong to a family, the mustelids, which includes weasels, martins, badgers, and skunks. Unlike other members of the family, the sea otter is very well adapted to life in water. The sea otter spends almost of its life in the sea. A layer of air trapped in its thick fur keeps it warm in cold waters, such as those of the Bering Sea.

Read

Independent Reading Point out that the sea otter pup described in the reading was an orphan. As needed, define "orphan" for students. Then explain that most tool-related behaviors are "learned behaviors." That is, the young learn the behavior by watching the elders perform it. Ask: **How do you suppose the orphan pup learned to use the rock to open the oysters?** (Students may suggest that the pup learned the behavior before it was orphaned, or from

other adult otters in the wildlife center.)

Have students compare the tool used in this story to the tool used in the New Caledonian crow story. **What do both tools have in common?** Provide the following hint to guide students. How are these tools different from a hammer, screwdriver, or electric drill? (They are natural objects, or made from natural objects.) Point out that a rock sitting on the ground is not a tool.

Look Back

> **What problem did the sea otter face? What solution did it find? What tool was part of its solution?**

Problem
Couldn't get inside
oyster shell

Solution
Smashed shell with rock

Tool
rock

Explore

MEETING NEEDS

Look at the picture of the sea otter floating in the ocean. Sea otters are able to float on their backs very comfortably for a long time.

> **How does the otter use floating on its back to help it get food?**

By floating on its back, the otter is able to use its body as a sort of table

on which it can work to get the oyster open.

Pill Bug Party

Time 40 minutes

Materials

For each student pair or group:

- 2–3 pill bugs (collected outside or purchased from a biological supply house)
- plastic container (salad bar containers work well)
- paper towel
- water

Pill bugs can be found in moist, dark places, like under flat rocks, logs, piles of decaying leaves, and tree bark. Keep collected pill bugs in a plastic container with holes for ventilation. Add dirt, sticks, decaying leaves, and tree bark. Add a wet paper towel for moisture and a piece of potato for food. Store in a dark place.

Procedure

Have students work in pairs, and give them the following instructions.

1. Tear the paper towel in half. Wet one half.
2. Put the wet towel on one half of the plastic container and the dry towel on the other half.
3. Place 2–3 pill bugs in the middle of the container, right between the wet and dry halves.
4. After two minutes, count how many pill bugs are on each half.
5. Pool the class data in a chart.

- ***Did the pill bugs seem to prefer the dry or moist environment?*** (moist)

Look Back

Once again, if students are having difficulty with the word "solution," rephrase the second question to read, "How did the otter solve its problem?"

Explore

Meeting Needs Ask students to imagine what the sea otter would have to do in order to eat oysters if it couldn't float on its back. (It might have to go onto land to break open the shell and or eat food other than oysters.) Point out that it takes less energy to float that it does to crawl in and out of water. So by floating, the sea otter reduces its energy needs, and thus the amount of food it needs to eat in order to survive.

Check Understanding

Skill: Communicate

What special behavior allows sea otters to meet their need for food? (the use of tools—rocks)

Assessment

Skill: Communicating

Use the following question to assess each student's progress.

In this chapter, you read about a number of different animal adaptations. What does an adaptation help an animal do? (meet one of its basic needs)

Describe two tools used by animals to meet their basic needs. (Certain crows use leaves to dig out insects. Sea otters use rocks to open oysters.)

Review "Find Out" Question

Review the question from the Unit Opener on page 12. *Which animals use tools to help them get food?* (possible answers should include crows and otters) Have students use what they learned in the chapter to suggest an answer to the question. Use their repsonses as the basis for a class discussion.

Put It All Together

Many animals have **adaptations** that help them meet their basic needs. These adaptations can be related to how the animal acts or related to the animal's body. In this chapter, you saw how the adaptations of two animals—the New Caledonian crow and the sea otter—helped them meet one of their basic needs.

> Use what you learned to complete the concept map below. First, describe each adaptation. Then decide whether the adaptation is an action or body part. In the bottom box, name the basic need met by both adaptations.

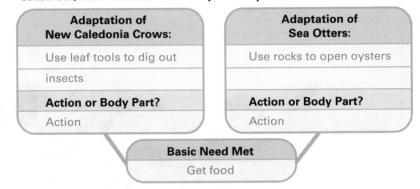

> Now think about the adaptations that help protect insects and oysters from the animals—such as crows and otters—that try to eat them. Use this information to complete the concept map below.

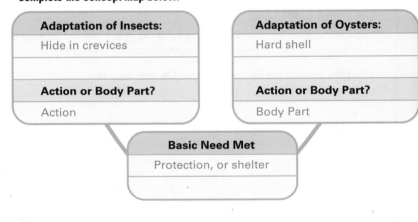

Put It All Together

Point out to students that in this chapter they read about three behavioral adaptations (crows using leaf tools to dig out insects, sea otters using rocks to open oysters, insects hiding in crevices) and one structural adaptation (the hard shell of oysters). As needed, explain the meaning of these terms. (Behavior refers to action, structure refers to physical form.)

Can you think of other examples of structural adaptations that protect animals from other animals that try to eat them? (Students may mention the spiny coat of the porcupine or the pungent odor of the skunk. Make a list on the board.)

Explain that some behavioral adaptations are instinctual. That means that animals are born knowing the behavior. Other behavioral adaptations must be learned. As an example, explain that some tribes of chimpanzees have learned how to use rocks to open nuts. But other tribes of the same species have not learned the behavior. Because they cannot open the nuts, these other tribes do not use them as a food source.

Can you hatch a dinosaur?

Do you know where babies come from? Well, from their parents, of course! All living things come from other living things—their parents. That's why **offspring**, or young, look like their parents.

Adult animals mate and reproduce to make more of their own kind. An animal can mate and reproduce only with another member of its same species, or kind. So, cats cannot mate with dogs and produce some sort of crazy cat-dog animal. They can mate only with other cats and produce baby cats.

In this chapter, you'll read a story about a mother hen and her most unusual offspring.

Before You Read

> **Look at the pictures below. Draw lines matching the offspring with their parents.**

SCIENCESAURUS
A STUDENT HANDBOOK
BLUE BOOK

Reproduction p. 82

SCiLINKS.
THE WORLD A CLICK AWAY

www.scilinks.org
Keyword: Traits
Code: GS5D030

> **What did you base your matches on?**

The parents and offspring look alike.

37

Key Idea

The traits of offspring are similar to those of their parents.

Focus

- Systems, order, and organization
- Characteristics of organisms
- Life cycles of organisms
- Reproduction and heredity

Skills and Strategies

- Infer
- Compare and contrast
- Draw conclusions
- Communicate

Vocabulary*

Before beginning the chapter, make sure students understand these terms.

- mate
- reproduce
- species
- trait

* Definitions are in the Glossary on pages 166–172.

Introducing the Chapter

This chapter introduces the idea that organisms reproduce to make more of their own kind and that a genetic mutation can change a trait in an organism.

You may want to review with students how male and female animals mate and have young. If possible, draw on students' own experiences with family pets. ***Does anyone have a family pet that has had offspring?*** (Students may report family dogs, cats, hamsters, or even livestock that have had young.) Ask student volunteers to describe what the young looked like compared to their parents. (Similar, but not exactly alike.)

Before You Read

Materials pictures of the life cycle of an insect that undergoes complete metamorphosis (butterfly, darkling beetle)

Point out that some insects produce young that don't look anything like their parents at first. These organisms undergo *complete metamorphosis*. That means they go through different physical stages before becoming adults. Show students the life cycle pictures. Point out that the larva and the pupa do not look at all like the adults.

More Resources

The following resources are also available from Great Source and NSTA.

SCIENCESAURUS
A STUDENT HANDBOOK
BLUE BOOK

SCILINKS
THE WORLD'S A CLICK AWAY

www.scilinks.org
Keyword: Traits
Code: GS5D030

Read

For weeks, Nate Twitchell has been helping a tired mother hen take care of her enormous egg. Early one morning, Nate goes to check on the egg in its nest.

"It Can't Be True..."

notes:

I just went over to the nest and put a little grain down for that poor old hen, and started to turn away, when I realized all at once that something had changed. The hen wasn't sitting on the nest anymore. She was walking back and forth with a kind of wild look in her eye, and every time she came near the nest she gave a little hop and fluttered away again. I bent down to look in the nest, and—wow! There was something in there, and it was alive! It was moving around.

I thought at first that it was a rat or something that had busted the egg and eaten it. But after I got a good look I could see that it wasn't any rat. It was about the size of a squirrel, but it didn't have any hair, and its head—well, I couldn't believe my eyes when I saw it. It didn't look like anything I'd ever seen before. It had three little knobs sticking out of its head and a sort of collar up over its neck. It was a lizardy-looking critter, and it kept moving its thick tail slowly back and forth in the nest. The poor hen was looking pretty upset. I guess she hadn't expected anything like this, and neither had I.

> What did the animal in the nest look like? Underline the words that describe its appearance.

38

Read

Paired Reading Have students look at the picture of the hen and egg. *What is wrong with this picture?* (Students should understand that the egg is far too large compared to the chicken.) Point out that young are much smaller than adults. This egg looks like it would produce an adult chicken.

What do you think Nate predicted would hatch out of the chicken egg? Explain your answer. (Students should say that he probably predicted that a chicken would hatch out, because that's what always comes out of chicken eggs.)

What evidence did Dr. Ziemer use when concluding that a dinosaur had hatched from the chicken egg? (observations of the animal's physical traits—how it looked) Remind students that, although this story is fictional, scientists make observations that contradict their predictions all the time. This evidence cannot be ignored, and requires the scientists to rethink their original ideas. Make sure students realize that the story is fiction, not fact.

Point out that, in addition to being a different kind of animal than a chicken, dinosaurs are extinct. Discuss the fact that many movies and books include the idea that an extinct species of animal (dinosaur, wooly mammoth, saber-toothed cat) could somehow reappear in the present day.

Nate telephones rare egg expert Dr. Ziemer, who has asked Nate to call him the minute the egg hatches out.

Dr. Ziemer. . . ran up to the nest and looked in. His eyes opened up wide and he knelt down on the ground and stared and stared and stared. After a long while he said softly, "That's it. By George, that's just what it is." Then he stared for another long time and finally he shook his head and said, "It can't be true, but there it is."

He got up off his knees and looked around at us. His eyes were just sparkling, he was so excited. He put his hand on my shoulder, and I could feel he was <u>quivering</u>. "An amazing thing's happened," he said, in a kind of whisper. "I don't know how to <u>account for</u> it. <u>It must be some sort of freak biological mixup that might happen once in a thousand years.</u>"

"But what is it?" I asked.

Dr. Ziemer turned and pointed a trembling finger at the nest. "Believe it or not, you people have hatched out a *dinosaur*."

From: *The Enormous Egg* by Oliver Butterworth.

quivering: shaking
account for: explain
biological: having to do with living things

notes:

\> Why do you think Dr. Ziemer said "It can't be true…"?
A chicken couldn't produce a dinosaur.

\> What explanation did Dr. Ziemer give for what he saw? <u>Underline</u> the answer.

Review the idea that extinct species are extinct forever, and cannot be brought back, even using their DNA (as was suggested in the *Jurassic Park* movies).

Science Background

Scientists had long thought that dinosaurs were the ancestors of birds. But in the year 2000, paleontologists at Oregon State University reported that they had found a more likely ancestor to birds, and, although it lived around the same time as early dinosaurs (220 million years ago), it was not a dinosaur! It was a small feathered reptile that glided among trees in central Asia.

Enrichment

Dinosaur Hunt

Materials research materials on dinosaurs

Have students do research to find out what kind of dinosaur is depicted in the story *(triceratops)*. To get started, encourage students to observe the picture on page 39 closely and write down some of the physical characteristics of the young dinosaur. (It has a sort of head shield, the beginnings of three horns, a wide stance, a thick neck, and walks on four legs.) Have them use these traits to identify the dinosaur in the resource books.

Have students summarize their research by answering the following questions:

- *What does "triceratops" mean?* (three-horned face)

- *How long was it? How tall? How much did it weigh?* (9 m (30 ft), 2 m (6.6 ft), 6–12 tons)

- *When did it live?* (late Cretaceous, about 72–65 million years ago)

- *Where have its fossils been found?* (Western Canada and Western US)

Check Understanding

Skill: Communicate

Why is what happens in this story impossible? (A chicken couldn't lay an egg that hatched out a dinosaur.)

NSTA Activity

Determine Your Characteristics

Time 20 minutes

Materials paper, pencil

The presence of a "hitchhiker's thumb," the ability to roll the tongue, and the shape of the earlobe are three inherited human traits. This activity has students looking at the frequency of these three traits within their class.

Draw the following sample blank data chart on the board.

Name	Hitchhiker's thumb	Nonhitch-hiker's thumb	Tongue Roller	Non Tongue Roller	Attached Earlobe	Detached Earlobe
Class						
Percentage						

Procedure

Have students work in pairs, and give them the following instructions.

1. Make a similar chart on a sheet of paper.

2. Observe your partner. *Can he or she form a "hitchhiker's thumb" (the thumb can be bent straight out at a right angle to the hand)?* Record data in the chart.

3. *Can he or she roll his or her tongue into a U-shape?* Record data in the chart.

(continued on page 41)

Look Back

Nature is full of surprises. But it follows some basic rules. One rule is that all adult animals (parents) reproduce to make more young (offspring) of their own kind.

> **How do you know that the story you just read isn't really true?**

A dinosaur and a chicken are not the same kind of animal.

Explore

INHERITING TRAITS

Offspring **inherit,** or receive, traits from their parents. You inherited lots of basic traits from both of your parents. For example, you were born with two arms and two legs and two eyes, just like your parents. You don't have feathers or a tail. Neither do your parents.

> **Think about the traits of a chicken. List at least six traits of a chicken below.**

Feathers, beak, two wings, walks on two legs, two eyes, and so on

> **Now list six traits of a dinosaur, like the one shown in reading.**

Bony plate on head, thick tail, smooth skin with no feathers, two eyes, horns on head, walks on four legs, and so on

> **Which traits are unique to a dinosaur? Could it inherit those traits from a chicken?**

Bony plate on head, thick tail, smooth skin with no feathers, horns on head, walks on four legs, and so on. No, a chicken doesn't have dinosaur traits to pass on to its offspring.

40

Look Back

Write "Basic Rules in Nature" on the board. Explain that over time scientists have observed that under the same conditions the same thing happens and this allows scientists to make predictions based on past observations. Start a list of rules, using the example from the chapter as the first rule. (All adult animals reproduce to make more young of their own kind.)

With the class, come up with some other basic rules of nature. (Students may suggest that all living things need energy to survive. Every living thing dies eventually, and so on. Students may suggest the idea that all objects fall to the ground when dropped.)

How does a knowledge of gravity allow us to predict what will happen if we drop something? (Knowing that gravity pulls all objects to Earth allows us to predict that a dropped object will fall to the ground.)

Explore

Inheriting Traits Have students look at the pictures of the chickens on page 41 when answering the first question. Have them look at the drawing of the dinosaur on page 39 when answering the second question. You may want to create a Venn diagram with the class to help them answer the last question. Lead students to realize that a trait is handed down from parents to offspring.

Explore

VARIETY AND MUTATIONS

Offspring look basically like their parents. But that doesn't mean that every offspring looks *exactly* like its parents. Variety among offspring is perfectly normal. For example, the photograph at right shows a mother hen with her six chicks. Notice that they don't all look exactly alike.

Mother hen with chicks

Because offspring inherit traits from both of their parents, they don't look exactly like either parent. Sometimes a mutation can make offspring look even more different. A **mutation** is a change in traits that happens when the traits are being passed from parent to offspring.

Look at the two pictures at right. The first shows a normal chicken. The second shows the same kind of chicken with a mutation known as "frizzles." This mutation causes the chicken's feathers to curve outward.

Normal   *Frizzles*

> **How is the "frizzles" chicken different from the "normal" chicken? How are they alike?**
>
> Its feathers are curved outward; it looks fluffy. It still has the same basic
>
> body shape, feathers, and red comb.

> **Mutations usually change one trait in an offspring, not many traits. Could a dinosaur be a mutant chicken?**
>
> No, a mutation would not produce an offspring that looked totally
>
> different from its parents. They would still have some traits in common.

41

(continued from page 40)

4. ***Does he or she have dangling earlobes, or are they attached to the neck?*** Record data in the chart.

Fill in the data chart on the board that shows the data for all students in the class. Point out that there is variety even among members of a single class.

If all humans are the same species, why do we see variety in these traits? (The individuals in a species are not identical.)

Connections

Materials calculators

Math Have students use the data in the class chart to calculate class percentages for each characteristic. For example, if you have 20 students in your class, and 6 can roll their tongues while 14 cannot, the class percentages of the tongue-rolling trait would be:

$\frac{6}{20} = 0.3 = 30\%$

$\frac{14}{20} = 0.7 = 70\%$

Have students make calculations for each trait observed. Use the data to emphasize the point that variety among individuals in a species is common.

Explore

Variety and Mutations Discuss other kinds of variation among offspring that students might have first-hand knowledge of. As a springboard to discussion, ask: ***Have you ever seen a litter of puppies or kittens? Did each animal in the litter look exactly like its mother or father?*** (Students should report that not all the puppies or kittens had the exact markings of either of the parents.) Then ask: ***How do you look different from your parents? From any brothers or sisters you have?*** (Students should be able to identify a number of physical differences between themselves and their siblings and parents.)

Explain the difference between normal variations in a population and mutations. Normal variations are caused by different combinations of genes being handed down from parents to offspring. A mutation occurs when a single gene in a sex cell, egg or sperm, undergoes a change that produces a new trait in an offspring.

Explain the use of the word "mutant" in the last question. Here, "mutant" is used as an adjective to describe a chicken with a mutation. But "mutant" can also be a noun, especially in science fiction movies. Have students use both forms of the word in sentences.

Help students conclude that, while a mutation may make offspring look slightly different from their parents, no single mutation could produce an animal that looked totally different from its parents.

Assessment

Skill: Communicate

Use the following question to assess each student's progress.

Why couldn't a horse give birth to an animal with an elephant's trunk and a dog's ears? (The horse does not have those traits itself, and so cannot pass them on to its offspring.) ***How are human offspring different and similar to their parents?*** (Human offspring have two legs, two arms, ten fingers and toes, and other traits similar to those of their parents, but they don't look exactly like their parents.)

Review "Find Out" Question

Review the question from the Unit Opener on page 12. ***Can a chicken lay an egg that doesn't contain a chick?*** (No! Chickens only produce other chickens.) Have students use what they learned in the chapter to suggest an answer to the question. Use their responses as the basis for a class discussion.

Science Journal

> Imagine that you have been asked by the author of *The Enormous Egg* to write another version of the story. In the new version, Dr. Ziemer explains to Nate why a dinosaur could not hatch from a chicken egg. Write your explanation in the voice of Dr. Ziemer. Pick up the dialogue after Dr. Ziemer's remark "It can't be true…"

Then he stared for another long time and finally he shook his head and said, "It can't be true …

42

Science Journal

Write Dialogue Remind students that their version of Dr. Ziemer's explanation should be written in the voice of Dr. Ziemer. In order to understand what that voice is, have students read page 39 again, paying close attention to Dr. Ziemer's dialogue. Then review the following questions as a class: ***What tone of voice does Dr. Ziemer use?*** (soft, excited tone) ***How does his voice differ from Nate's?*** (Nate's tone is descriptive, matter of fact) ***What vocabulary seems unique to Dr. Ziemer?*** ("quivering," "account for," "biological") Have students apply these characteristics to their stories.

Have students review the content on pages 40-41 before starting their writing. Student explanations should reflect the fact that it would be impossible for a dinosaur to hatch out of a chicken egg because adult animals only reproduce to make more of their own kind.

Invite student volunteers to read their new stories to the class. Then create a bulletin board display featuring the original story and the students' revised stories.

What's big and green and can take over the whole neighborhood?

If you've ever flipped through an encyclopedia, you know that Earth is home to millions of different species, or kinds, of living things. But not every kind of living thing is found in every place. Each area of the world has its own set of living things. Those living things are part of the area's unique ecosystem. An **ecosystem** is all of the living and non-living things that are found in an area.

For hundreds of years, people have taken plants and animals from one area and brought them to another. Species of plants and animals that have lived in an area for a very long time are called **native** species. Species that have been brought to a new area are called **introduced**, or non-native species. In this chapter, you will learn about what happened when two introduced species—one plant and one animal—were brought to ecosystems where they didn't normally live.

Before You Read

Imagine that you have a large aquarium with several pet goldfish. One day, your friend gives you an angelfish. You put the angelfish in the aquarium, but the next day you realize that the angelfish ate all of your goldfish!

> **In this story, which species of fish is the *native* species?**

The goldfish

> **Which species of fish is the *introduced* species?**

The angelfish

SCIENCESAURUS
A STUDENT HANDBOOK
BLUE BOOK

Species .... p. 128
Ecosystems p. 130
Carnivors .... p. 134

SCILINKS.
THE WORLD'S A CLICK AWAY

www.scilinks.org
Keyword: Changes
in Ecosystems
Code: GS5D035

(43)

Key Idea

The introduction of a new species into an ecosystem may affect the ecological balance that exists there.

Focus

- Evolution and equilibrium
- Characteristics of organisms
- Organisms and environments
- Populations and ecosystems

Skills and Strategies

- Define operationally
- Recognize cause and effect
- Infer
- Draw conclusions
- *Classify (TG)*
- *Predict (TG)*
- *Communicate (TG)*

Vocabulary*

Before beginning the chapter, make sure students understand these terms.

- adaptation
- species

* Definitions are found in the Glossary on pages 166–172.

Introducing the Chapter

This chapter examines some problems that can occur when non-native species are introduced into an existing ecosystem.

Compile a list of plants and animals common in your area (may be available from a local wildlife center)

To get students thinking about native species and their ecosystems, ask: ***Can you name any animals or plants that are native to this area?*** (Students may be able to come up with some of the animals and plants on the list.) Share the list with students. (Be sure to point out any species that may have been introduced.) Invite students to share any experiences they might have had with these plants or animals.

Before You Read

Help students as needed to make the connection between "native species" and the goldfish, and "introduced species" and the angelfish. Point out that, although the goldfish are not really "native" to your area, they show how a species can be affected by an introduced species. ***What effect did the introduced species have on the native species in this example?*** (The introduced species wiped out the native species.) Tell students that introduced species often cause problems in the ecosystems that they enter.

More Resources

The following resources are also available from Great Source and NSTA.

SCIENCESAURUS
A STUDENT HANDBOOK
BLUE BOOK

Reader's Handbook (Yellow Book)

Math at Hand

SCI LINKS.
THE WORLD'S A CLICK AWAY

www.scilinks.org
Keyword: Changes
Code: GS5D035

Read

Read about a Japanese vine that ended up doing more harm than good.

"Kudzu All Over You"

notes:

Often humans don't understand that a change they make in the environment may have a very different result from what they expected. The web of nature is complicated!

In the 1930s the government wanted to control soil erosion in the southern United States. So it hired hundreds of workers to plant fields of kudzu, a beautiful vine that is native to Japan. Big mistake! Without <u>Japan's cooler climate and kudzu-munching beetles</u> to keep the plant <u>in check</u>, kudzu grew out of control. Today it's an expensive problem. Kudzu covers millions of acres of land, <u>smothering</u> native trees and plants.

From: "Big Mistakes!," *ASK* magazine, July/Aug 2003.

> <u>Underline</u> the two factors that keep kudzu under control in Japan.

44

in check: under control
smothering: growing over and killing

Science Background

Kudzu grows and spreads very quickly. Vine runners on the soil's surface can grow up to 1 foot per day in the spring. New plants then grow from every node on the runners. Kudzu also spreads using underground rhizomes. Eradication of kudzu vines often requires a combination of herbicides, burning, grazing, and tilling.

Read

Independent Reading After students have completed the reading, draw their attention to the sentence "The web of nature is complicated!" *What do you think the author of the article meant by this statement?* (Students may suggest that the author was pointing out that living things interact with other living things in many different ways, not just in the limited ways we expect.)

Remind students that the author described the kudzu situation as "an expensive problem." *Why do you think it costs money to fight the kudzu problem?* (Students may know that it takes costly chemicals and many hours of labor to get rid of kudzu where it's not wanted.)

Look Back

What was the original problem faced by people in the United States? What solution did they find? What new problem did this solution create?

> Complete the graphic organizer based on information from the reading.

Original Problem	Human Solution	New Problem
soil erosion	Plant fields of kudzu.	Kudzu smothered native plants.

Explore

STAYING BALANCED.

All living things in an ecosystem interact with one another in a balanced way. That means that one group of living things does not grow out of control and destroy other groups of living things. This balance exists because they have lived together for many generations.

> **Why didn't the kudzu grow out of control in Japan? Describe the balance that existed between kudzu and the ecosystem where it grew.**

The cooler climate and the beetles kept the kudzu under control.

> **Why was the kudzu able to grow out of control in the new ecosystem?**

The new ecosystem had a warmer climate and did not have kudzu-eating beetles.

> **Why would it not be a good idea to bring in kudzu-eating beetles to control the kudzu?**

The kudzu-eating beetles may cause other problems. Also, that does not solve the problem of the warmer climate.

(45)

Materials research materials on the Civilian Conservation Corps (CCC)

Social Studies Explain that the workers hired by the government to plant kudzu around the southern United States were part of the Civilian Conservation Corps (CCC). Have students research the CCC and find out the answers to the following questions:

- *When was the CCC established?* (1933)
- *Who established it?* (President Franklin D. Roosevelt and the U.S. Congress)
- *Why was it established? What problem was the nation facing?* (to provide employment for young unemployed men; the nation was facing widespread unemployment due to the Great Depression)
- *What sort of projects did the CCC workers do?* (all sort of environmental projects, including planting trees, building public parks, draining swamps to fight malaria, and working on flood control.)

Have students focus on one CCC project they find particularly interesting and create a storyboard that shows the history of the project. Was the project a success, or an environmental disaster like the kudzu project?

Look Back

If students are having trouble with the word "solution," rephrase the second question to say "How did they solve the problem?"

Explore

Staying Balanced As needed, go over the definition of "generation" with students, using their families as an example: grandparents are one generation, parents are another, they are another, their children will be another.

Explain that letting local cattle graze on kudzu vines has actually worked in some places to eliminate the plants (where 80% or more of the vegetation is continuously consumed for 3-4 years). *Why would using local cattle to control the kudzu be better than using the beetles?* (Students should recognize that since the cattle are not recently introduced species, they are less likely to create an ecological imbalance than introduced beetles.)

Check Understanding

Skill: Classify

Where is kudzu a native plant? Where was it introduced? (Japan; southern United States)

Enrichment

Australian Pests

Materials research materials on animals introduced into Australia, materials to create posters

Have students research animals introduced to Australia as biological controls (cane toad, mosquito fish, starling). ***What pests were they brought in to control? How did they become pests themselves?***

(The cane toad was brought in to control two insect pests of cane sugar fields. The cane toad reproduced and spread rapidly and because it is poisonous harmed many local predators that ate it.)

(The mosquito fish was brought in to control mosquito larvae in dams. Unfortunately, it also attacked native fish and competed with them for food, greatly harming their populations.)

(The starling was brought in to control insects, but soon became an agricultural pest. It also stole many nesting spots from local birds.)

Have students present their finding in a poster or other visual display.

Read

It is not just introduced plants that can cause problems for native species. Read about an animal whose eating habits created serious problems for a native bird.

"Mongoose on the Loose"

notes:

In the late 1880s someone brought (mongooses) to Hawaii to control the (rats) (which had also been brought by humans). Nice try! But mongooses hunt during the daytime, while rats are active at night. So what's a hungry mongoose to do? Prey on birds, including the nene, a wild goose that is Hawaii's state bird. Once there were 25,000 nenes on Hawaii. Now, thanks to human interference, there are less than 500 nenes left in the wild.

Those nenes! They're just the thing when a mongoose gets the munchies.

From: "Big Mistakes!," *ASK* magazine, July/Aug 2003.

> Underline the native species named in the reading.

> (Circle) the species that were introduced by humans.

mongooses: small mammals that feed on other animals
prey on: eat
interference: changes

Science Background

The small Indian mongoose (*Herpestes javanicus*) discussed in this article was introduced to many different places (West Indies, Jamaica, Fiji) in the late 1800s to control rat and snake populations. In each new place, the mongoose expanded its diet to include other native species that were not meant to be targeted.

Read

Independent Reading After students have completed the reading ask: ***Why didn't the plan to have the mongooses eat all the rats work?*** (The mongooses hunt during the daytime and the rats are active at night.) Then ask: ***How could scientific observations of the mongoose and rat populations have allowed people to avoid making the mistake described in the reading?*** (Observations of mongoose and rat activity could have shown people that the mongooses were not active at the same time as the rats.) Point out how scientific research helps people understand more about the natural world so that they can make informed decisions.

Look Back

What was the original problem faced by people in Hawaii? What solution did they find? What new problem did this solution create?

> **Complete the graphic organizer based on information from the reading.**

Original Problem		Human Solution		New Problem
too many rats	→	Introduce mongooses.	→	Mongooses ate lots of nenes.

Explore

STAYING BALANCED

In every ecosystem, there are animals that eat other animals for food. The animals that eat other animals are called **predators**. The animals that are eaten are called **prey**. The humans who brought the mongooses over to Hawaii were hoping that the animals would eat the rats as their prey.

Relationships between predators and prey within an ecosystem are balanced so that, normally, one group does not wipe out another group. But if a new species is introduced, the balance can be upset.

One of the reasons why predators don't wipe out prey is because the prey are often able to avoid predators. The ability to avoid predators is an adaptation that develops over thousands of years of living in the same area. It cannot be developed over just a couple of generations.

> **Why do you think the nenes are so easily hunted by the mongoose?**

The nenes are easily hunted by the mongooses because the nenes have not lived with the mongooses for many generations. They are not adapted to avoid the mongooses.

47

Look Back

If students are having trouble with the word "solution," rephrase the second question to say "How did they solve the problem?"

Explore

Staying Balanced Discuss with students animal adaptations for avoiding predators. ***What adaptation do gazelles have for avoiding lion predators?*** (Students will probably know that gazelles are very fast runners and agile jumpers.) Invite students to come up with their own examples. (porcupines—quills; skunks—spray; "stick" insects—camouflage; and so on)

Point out that nenes are flightless birds. ***How would being flightless make the nene more vulnerable to the mongooses?*** (Students should infer that flying would allow the birds to escape the predators more easily than running away, as geese are not great runners.)

Assessment

Skill: Communicate

Use the following question to assess each student's progress.

Why is the balance in an ecosystem thrown off when introduced species are brought in? (Native species are not adapted to the introduced species. As a result, many native species may die off.)

Review "Find Out" Question

Review the question from the Unit Opener on page 12. ***What if the solution to one environmental problem creates another?*** (The new problem must be solved.) Have students use what they learned in the chapter to suggest an answer to the question. Use their responses as the basis for a class discussion.

Put It All Together

Look over the past pages. Think about what the kudzu story and the mongoose story have in common. In both cases, humans faced a problem with their local ecosystem.

> **What solution did the humans come up with in both cases?**

introduce a new species

> **What went wrong with their solution?**

The new species caused a new problem by harming other species.

> **What can you conclude about introducing species into a new ecosystem?**

Students should say that new species often cause as many problems as

they solve and introducing them is not a good idea.

Introduced species don't have to come from another country. Any species that is brought into an area where it doesn't normally live can cause problems.

Imagine that your friend Trisha is planning on setting her two pet goldfish free in a local pond where many native plants and animals live. Goldfish are not native to the pond ecosystem. In the space below, explain to Trisha why letting the fish go would not be a good idea. (Hint: What kinds of problems might the goldfish cause for native species?)

Students might say that if the goldfish live, they may cause problems

that could kill off many of the native plants and animals. For example,

the fish may eat all of a certain kind of plant that other native fish need

to survive. The fish may reproduce and crowd out the native animals,

and so on.

Put It All Together

Help students as needed to make the connection between the kudzu story and the mongoose story. ***What do the two species have in common?*** (Both were taken from one area and introduced to a new area.) Lead students to understand that in both the kudzu and the mongoose story, native species were harmed as the result of introduced species.

Many students may think that releasing pets back into the wild is a good idea because the animals would be most happy there. Explain that pets are used to being protected and fed by their owners and most would have a very difficult time surviving in the wild where competition for resources and the dangers of predation are very real.

If students have a pet that they no longer feel they can take care of, they should contact their local Humane Society and get information about people or organizations that might help them relocate the pet. Under no circumstances should they release a pet into the wild.

UNIT 1: Life Science

What Did We Learn?

What traits do scientists look at when classifying ladybugs?
number of spots on the ladybug

Why are a mole-rat's teeth so sensitive to touch?
because as it moves through its underground tunnels, its teeth are what touch other animals and objects it meets in the tunnels

Why are insect-eating plants often found in bogs?
The plants in the bog eat the insects to get nutrients not found in bog soil.

What do the New Caledonian crow and the sea otter have in common?
Both use tools to help them get food.

Why couldn't a dinosaur hatch out of a chicken egg?
They are different species.

Why is it dangerous to bring plants and animals from one ecosystem to another?
They may disrupt the balance in the new ecosystem.

49

What Did We Learn?

The questions on this page complement the questions in the Unit Opener on page 12. Discuss the questions as a class. Invite students to share their ideas about the chapters they have completed. What new questions do they have after completing these chapters?

Bulletin Board Have students create a bulletin board display showing the main ideas of each chapter in this Unit. Then have them look for connections between units. For example, ask: *What structural adaptations can you identify in the naked mole-rat?* (Small eyes and ears, narrow body, sensitive teeth) *How are the teeth of the mole-rat like the trap leaves of the Venus Fly Trap?* (They are both specially designed for a specific function.) *What do the sea otter and the sundew plant have in common?* (They both need to meet their nutritional needs—one does it by eating shellfish, the other by photosynthesizing and consuming insects.) *How would the chicken be classified within the animal kingdom?* (as a bird)

UNIT 2: Earth Science

A major goal of the *Science Daybooks* is to enrich science instruction through reading selections that promote critical thinking skills as well as reading and writing fluency. The chart below describes science content and process skills and also includes the reading and writing skills used in each chapter.

Chapter Title	Science Concepts	Science Skills	Reading & Writing Skills
7. **Earthquakes on the Edge**	• Earthquakes • Ring of Fire • Plate boundaries	• Compare and contrast • Interpret data • Apply knowledge • Interpret scientific illustrations	• Making inferences • Read for details • Read a map • *Compare and contrast* • *Write a paragraph*
8. **Caverns Are Cool**	• Slow changes in Earth's surface • Caverns • Weathering • Erosion • Deposition	• Apply knowledge • Use numbers • Construct models • Observe • Create and use tables • *Classify*	• Connect prior experiences and ideas to text • Read a diagram • Evaluate information sources • *Write an article*
9. **A Hiding Place**	• Landforms • Weathering • Erosion • Relief maps	• Infer • Recognizing cause and effect • Interpret scientific illustrations • *Apply knowledge*	• Visualize • Read a map • Read a diagram • *Read for details* • *Retell*
10. **Caught in the Act?**	• History of Earth • Observations and inferences • Fossil formation • Nature of scientific investigation	• Understand that scientific findings undergo peer review • Compare and contrast • Understand that scientists change their ideas in the face of experimental evidence • *Generate ideas*	• Read for details • Distinguish fact and opinion • *Read critically* • *Make predictions* • *Write letters* • *Evaluate sources of information* • *Write a paragraph*
11. **It's a Twister!**	• Tornadoes • Tornado safety	• Infer • Construct models • Apply knowledge • *Interpret data* • *Compare and contrast*	• Read for details • Demonstrate comprehension • *Compare and contrast* • *Write and follow directions*
12. **Eclipsed!**	• Motions of Earth and moon • Lunar eclipses	• Construct models • Compare and contrast • Use numbers • Infer • *Define operationally*	• Evaluate information sources • Read a diagram • *Locate information* • *Write a paragraph*

Skill appears only in Teacher's Guide
Skill appears in Teacher's Guide and Student Book

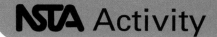

The following activity and other NSTA activities throughout this *Science Daybook* are adapted from NSTA publications with the permission of the National Science Teachers Association. The activity below is best used with Chapter 7.

Real Earthquakes, Real Learning

Time two class sessions, followed by 10-minute sessions for small groups of students 2-4 times per week, for 3 or more months

Materials
For the class:
- wall-sized world map
- bulletin board for several months
- box of small push pins in 5 colors

For each student pair:
- copy of Outline Map for Plotting Earthquake Locations Copymaster, page 176
- list of earthquakes for the past week from web site (www.earthquake.usgs.gov)
- Before starting Part 1, go to the web site listed above. Click on the link "List of Latest Earthquakes World-wide." Print the list from the web site, cross off any earthquake less than magnitude 3.0, and make enough copies for each student or pair.
- Make a copy of Copymaster page 176, Outline Map for Plotting Earthquake Locations for each student pair
- Post the world map on a bulletin board.

Procedure
Part 1
1. Introduce the project by telling students that earthquakes happen somewhere on Earth daily. For the next several months, the class will be recording earthquakes by marking where they occur.
2. Point out the wall map and briefly go over the names of the continents and oceans. Then review or introduce latitude and longitude. Demonstrate how to locate a specific point on a world map. Choose an earthquake from the list. Show students how to find the location of an earthquake.
3. Give a copymaster map and earthquake list to each student pair.
4. Have students plot the location of several earthquakes from the list.

Part 2
Before beginning Part 2, assign one color of pin to each magnitude of earthquake in this list.

Pin Color	Earthquake Magnitude	Description
	7-7.9	Major
	6-6.9	Strong
	5-5.9	Moderate
	4-4.9	Light
	3-3.9	Minor
(do not plot)	less than 3	Very minor

5. The next day, tell students that they will take turns plotting earthquakes on the wall map.
6. Ask for two student volunteers to plot the earthquakes from the outline maps onto the wall map.
7. Set up a schedule for students to plot earthquakes.
   - Group students into pairs.
   - Print out one copy of the earthquake list from the Earthquake Hazards site at the start of each week. Divide the list of earthquakes by the number of school days in that week. Note how many earthquakes each student pair should plot so the whole list is plotted by week's end.
8. When a student pair has located an earthquake, have them mark it on the world map using the correct color of pin for its magnitude.

Ask the following questions:
- ***Does every part of Earth get the same number of earthquakes?*** (No)
- ***Do earthquakes occur on land, under the ocean, or both?*** (Both.)
- ***Do earthquakes happen more under the middle of continents, or at the edges?*** (Mostly at the edges, but sometimes in the middle,)

As more and more earthquakes are plotted, the pins will outline the edges of the plates that make up Earth's crust. Introduce the idea of these plates as students start to recognize the regular pattern of earthquakes.

Chapter 7   Earthquakes on the Edge

Key Idea: Seismic waves can be used to determine the location of earthquakes, which usually occur at the edges of the plates that make up Earth's crust.

A passage from the historical novel *Dragonwings* by Laurence Yep introduces students to the rapid changes that take place during an earthquake.

Materials

Enrichment (p. 53):
• long coiled spring, such as a Slinky (one for a demonstration, one for each student pair for a class activity)

Differentiating Instruction (p. 54), for class demonstration:
• box of dominoes

NSTA Activity (pp. 49B and 55), for the class:
• wall-sized world map
• push pins in 5 colors
• bulletin board
• access to Internet

For each student pair:
• copy of Outline Map for Plotting Earthquake Locations Copymaster, page 176
• list of world earthquakes from web site (see p. 49b)

Explore (p. 55), for the class:
• wall map or globe of world

Assessment (p. 56), for the class:
• wall map of world

Chapter 8   Caverns are Cool

Key Idea: Like many processes at Earth's surface, the formation of interesting shapes in a limestone cavern happens very, very slowly.

A newspaper description of a show-cave tour introduces students to the slow processes of weathering, erosion, and deposition that form limestone caverns.

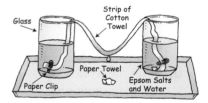

Materials

Enrichment, (p. 59), for the class:
• research sources about cave-dwelling animals

Activity (p. 60), for each group:
• large bowl
• 250 mL (1 cup) Epsom salt
• 2 glasses or glass jars
• 2 big paper clips
• strip of cotton towel about 1-2 cm wide and 45 cm long
• warm water
• spoon
• tray
• paper towel

Safety Tip

Review this safety tip with students:

• Do not taste any substance in the laboratory unless you are instructed to do so.

Chapter 9   A Hiding Place

Key Idea: A relief map can show many different types of landforms, including those that result from weathering and erosion.

A passage from the historical novel *Sing Down the Moon* by Scott O'Dell describes the land in Canyon de Chelly, Arizona.

Materials

Connection (p. 64):
• Copy of *Sing Down the Moon* by Scott O'Dell (*for each student*), or research sources on *The Long Walk* (*for the class*)

NSTA Activity (p. 66), for each student pair:
• 2 copies of Relief Map copymaster, p. 175
• piece of corrugated cardboard about 20 cm x 25 cm
• additional sheets of corrugated cardboard or box (to cut up)
• markers, colored pencils, and crayons
• glue
• scissors

Project (p. 68), for each student pair or group:
• relief map of your local area, or Relief Map copymaster, p.175 (Relief maps can be obtained by calling 888-ASK-USGS or from www.nationalmap.usgs.gov.)

Chapter 10   Caught in the Act?

Key Idea: Scientists draw conclusions based on the observations they make, but new observations can change those conclusions dramatically.

The story of a misnamed dinosaur introduces students to fossils and gives an example of how ideas change in science.

Materials

Connections (p. 71), for the class:
- Book, In the *Days of the Dinosaurs* by Roy Chapman Andrews

Enrichment (p. 72), for the class:
- VHS or DVD of "Dinosaur Hunters: Secrets of the Gobi Desert" © 1997 National Geographic Society
- equipment to show movie

NSTA Activity (p. 73), for each student pair or group:
- wooden 3-D dinosaur skeleton model (may be ordered from a science or museum supply catalog or bought at local science stores)
- deep plastic tray or dishpan filled with sand
- 2-3 toothpicks or skewers
- dry paintbrush
- newspapers
- plain paper and pencil

Chapter 11   It's a Twister!

Key Idea: Tornadoes are powerful storms that form quickly and can move and destroy even heavy objects.

In this chapter, students consider the speed with which a tornado develops and moves, and create a model tornado in a bottle.

Materials

Before You Read (p. 75), for each student:
- Copy of Beaufort Wind Scale (optional)

Differentiating Instruction (p. 76), for the class:
- video footage of a tornado
- equipment to show video

Connections (p. 77), for interested students:
- Book, *Night of the Twisters* by Ivy Ruckman

Activity (p. 78), for each pair or group:
- 1–2 liter plastic bottle with straight sides, flat bottom, and secure cap
- water
- 2–3 drops dish soap
- pinch of glitter
- 2–3 pieces aquarium gravel

Enrichment (p. 78), for each student:
- matched set of 1-liter clear plastic bottles
- water
- pinch of glitter
- 2–3 pieces aquarium gravel
- tornado tube connector OR heavy waterproof tape and a washer of same outside diameter as mouth of bottles

Science Journal (p. 80), for each student:
- copy of floor plan of your school (optional)

Safety Tip
Review this safety tip with students:
Activity (p. 78) and Enrichment (p. 78):
- Wipe up spills immediately to reduce the risk of slips and falls.

Chapter 12   Eclipsed!

Key Idea: Scientists can use lunar eclipses to measure the motions of Earth and the moon.

A transcript of a radio show describes what an observer would see during a lunar eclipse, and tells how scientists use Earth's shadow to time the motions of Earth and the moon.

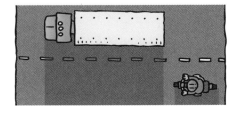

Materials

Explore (p. 83), for teacher demonstration:
- toy truck
- toy motorcycle
- large ball (such as playground ball)
- small ball (such as tennis ball)
- source of bright light

Differentiating Instruction (p. 83), for the class:
- large flashlight

Connections (p. 84), for the class:
- research sources about the ancient Maya civilization

Assessment (p. 86), for the class:
- overhead projector or other light source
- large ball (such as playground ball)
- small ball (such as tennis ball)

The following sources are used in this unit.

www.scilinks.org
Keyword: Developing
Classroom Activities
Code: GSSD05

UNIT 2: Earth Science

Chapter 7
Earthquakes on the Edge
Find Out: Why do some places have so many earthquakes?

Chapter 8 Caverns Are Cool
Find Out: Can a stalactite grow in your lifetime?

Chapter 9 A Hiding Place
Find Out: Can you find a mesa by looking at a map?

Chapter 10
Caught in the Act?
Find Out: How did a dinosaur get named after something it didn't do?

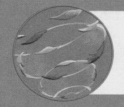

Chapter 11 It's a Twister!
Find Out: Should you go home if a tornado is coming?

Chapter 12 Eclipsed!
Find Out: What shadow are you seeing during an eclipse of the moon?

50

Introducing the Unit

To generate interest in the chapters, use the questions on the student page. Invite students to read the questions, but explain that they do not have to answer them right now. Ask students what they think they will find out in each chapter, based on the questions and images on this page. Accept all answers at this point.

Earthquakes on the Edge Chapter 7

Have you ever experienced an earthquake?

If you have seen waves on an ocean or large lake, then you know what one kind of wave looks like. **Earthquakes** produce waves that pass through the earth instead of water. Usually when an earthquake wave passes, the ground shakes and so does everything on it. The shaking from an earthquake lasts only a few minutes. But while it is happening, the earthquake can cause a lot of changes to Earth's surface and anything that is on it.

What are the chances that you will experience an earthquake? It depends on where you live. In some parts of the world, every school has a plan for what to do in case of an earthquake. That's because they are common in those areas. In other places, a major earthquake is so rare that no person alive today has ever experienced one there. Where do earthquakes happen? Why do they happen in some places, but hardly ever in others?

In this chapter, you will read a description of what happens during an earthquake. Then you will find out why they happen more often in certain places.

Before You Read

Look around the room you are in. Imagine what would happen to the room and to the people and things in it if everything started shaking. Describe five specific changes that you can imagine happening in the room.

People falling down, things falling off of

shelves, furniture falling over, windows

breaking, walls cracking, floor cracking

open, etc.

 Earth's Moving
Plates .... p. 176
Earthquakes
.... p. 180

 www.scilinks.org
Keyword:
Plate Tectonics
Code: GS5D040

Key Idea

Seismic waves can be used to determine the locations of earthquakes, which usually occur at the edges of the plates that make up Earth's crust.

Focus

- Changes in earth and sky
- Structure of the earth system
- Natural hazards
- Evidence, models, and explanation

Skills and Strategies

- Compare and contrast
- Interpret data
- Interpret scientific illustrations

Vocabulary*

Before beginning the chapter, make sure students understand these terms.

- earthquake
- eruption
- plate
- wave

* Definitions are in the Glossary on pages 166–172.

Introducing the Chapter

This chapter focuses on earthquakes and on the reason that earthquakes are more common in some places than in others. Find out what ideas students have about earthquakes. **What happens during an earthquake?** (The ground shakes, buildings crash, cars go off the road. Accept all reasonable answers.) Tell students that although we usually think of major earthquakes, many small earthquakes that do not make the news occur every day. However, the cause of major and minor earthquakes is the same. **What causes an earthquake?** (Movement of rock along a fault. But for now, accept all reasonable answers.) Tell students that in this chapter they will read a description of an earthquake, learn about earthquake waves, and find out where earthquakes are most common.

Loss of life from earthquakes in the United States is relatively low, but victims can number in the thousands in countries with poorly-enforced or no building codes, especially for private homes.

Before You Read

Students who live in earthquake-prone areas are more likely to be aware of the changes that an earthquake can cause. Students who have never experienced an earthquake may need help understanding what can happen. **Think of picking up and shaking a doll house full of furniture. What would the house look like afterward?** (The furniture would be moved or tumbled over.)

More Resources

The following resources are also available from Great Source and NSTA.

*SCI*LINKS.
THE WORLD'S A CLICK AWAY
www.scilinks.org
Keyword: Plate Tectonics
Code: GS5D040

Read

Moon Shadow, age 11, is a Chinese-American living in San Francisco, California in the early 1900s. Here, we see the great earthquake of 1906 through his eyes.

"The Earth Turns Fluid"

notes:

I had gotten dressed and gone out to the pump to get some water. The morning was filled with that soft, gentle twilight of spring, when everything is filled with soft, dreamy colors and shapes; so when the earthquake hit, I did not believe it at first. It seemed like a nightmare where everything you take to be the rock-hard, solid <u>basis</u> for reality becomes unreal.

Wood and stone and brick and the very earth became <u>fluidlike</u>. The <u>pail beneath the pump jumped and rattled</u> like a spider dancing on a hot stove. The <u>ground deliberately seemed to slide right out from under me</u>. I landed on my back hard enough to drive the wind from my lungs. The whole world had become unglued. Our <u>stable and Miss Whitlaw's house and the tenements to either side heaved and bobbed up and down</u>, riding the ground like ships on a heavy sea....

San Francisco before the earthquake

> <u>Underline</u> all the phrases on this page that tell how things moved during the earthquake.

52

basis: base, or foundation
fluidlike: like moving water
deliberately: on purpose

tenements: crowded apartment buildings
heaved: moved up and down

Read

Paired Reading *The Earth Turns Fluid* is a work of historical fiction. In this type of book, the author sets fictional characters in a real place and time in history. Part of the author's task is to make events seem real to the reader, even though neither the author nor the reader were there. One way that the author does this is through the use of details. For example, in the reading, the author does not just say that the earth moved, and that it was noisy. **What details about the earth-**

quake does the author use to help the reader "experience" it? (Pail jumped and rattled, house and tenements heaved and bobbled, city bells ringing, metal tearing, bricks crashing, cracking of wood, tinkling of glass, screams of people.)

Science Background

Earthquakes in the San Francisco area are related to the boundary between two of the plates that make up Earth's crust. At this boundary, two plates are moving past each other and as a result, cracks, or faults, in the rock are very common. Stress builds up at the faults until the rocks on either side of the fault suddenly slip, allowing them to move and causing an earthquake.

Not all faults occur at plate boundaries. For example,

San Francisco after the earthquake, April 18, 1906

Moon Shadow's father comes running out in bare feet. He has just enough time to say a few things to Moon Shadow and put on his shoes when something more happens...

[Father] started to get to his feet when the second <u>tremor</u> shook and <u>he fell forward flat on his face</u>. I heard <u>the city bells ringing</u>. They were rung by no human hand—the earthquake had just shaken them in their steeples. The second tremor was worse than the first. From all over came an <u>immense</u> wall of noise: <u>of metal tearing, of bricks crashing, of wood breaking free from wood nails</u>, and all. Everywhere, what man had built came undone. I was looking <u>at a tenement house to our right and it just seemed to shudder and then collapse</u>. One moment there were solid wooden walls and the next moment it had fallen with the cracking of wood and the tinkling of glass and the screams of people inside.

From: *Dragonwings* by Laurence Yep.

bobbed: moved
tremor: earthquake wave
immense: huge

notes:

_____

_____

_____

_____

_____

_____

_____

_____

_____

_____

_____

_____

> <u>Underline</u> all the phrases on this page that tell how things moved during the second tremor.

 53

Earthquake Waves

Time 10–15 minutes

Materials long coiled spring, such as a Slinky (one for a demonstration, one for each student pair for a class activity)

Two of the types of waves associated with an earthquake are called P and S waves. The P wave, or primary wave, arrives first. It is a compression wave, which means that it moves the earth forward and back as it travels through it. The S wave, or secondary wave, travels more slowly than the P wave and arrives second. The S wave moves the earth side to side as it travels through it.

Have students explore the difference between a P wave and an S wave through this activity. Two students each hold one end of the spring and gently stretch it across a bare floor so that the coils are separated but not stretched to the limit.

To make a P wave, one student pushes the spring forward and back sharply, just once. Observe the coils as the wave moves through the spring. To demonstrate an S wave, one student sharply pulls one end of the spring from side to side, just once. For each type of wave, observe the coils as the wave moves through. Students should compare the motions of the spring in each case and identify which represents a P wave and which an S wave.

earthquakes in both the central United States and in central China occur at fault regions in the middle of plates. These fault regions are thought to result from stress due to compression of the plates.

Science Background

Each earthquake event has multiple waves. Earthquake waves move the matter through which they travel. The matter itself ends up in the same place, but the wave moves the matter as it goes by. How the matter moves depends on the type of wave. The first wave to arrive is the P wave, also called the Primary wave or comPression wave. The P wave moves the earth forward and back, parallel to the direction the wave is traveling. The second wave to arrive

is the S wave, also called the Secondary wave or Shear wave. The S wave moves the earth side to side.

A third kind of earthquake wave, the L wave, arrives even later than the S wave. It causes the earth to move up and down, and causes most of the damage during an earthquake.

In addition to the P, S, and L waves, smaller earthquakes called aftershocks are common for several days after a major earthquake.

Differentiating Instruction

Time 10 minutes

Materials dominos

Bodily/Kinesthetic The effects of earthquakes are strongest in the places they begin. But earthquakes can cause destruction at a distance, as well.

Involve students in a demonstration of this concept. Have students use dominos to build structures on a table, or on their desks if the desks are arranged so they are touching each other. (Students may wish to set the dominos on edge, but stacking them flat is better for the purpose of the demonstration.)

Have one student cause an earthquake by pounding with his or her fists on the table or on one of the desks. (Ten to fifteen seconds of pounding should be enough.)

Students will observe that even structures at a distance from the earthquake can be damaged. Invite students to compare damage to the "buildings" closer to the earthquake with damage to those that are farther away.

Look Back

The story is fictional but describes a real earthquake that took place in San Francisco, California on April 18, 1906. The reading describes the results of two different earthquake waves. Both waves were part of the same earthquake, but the second wave arrived a little while after the first.

> **The waves started out at the same place and at the same time. But they moved at different speeds. Which wave moved faster? How can you tell?**

The first wave moved faster. I can tell because it got there first.

Explore

TIMING EARTHQUAKE WAVES

Vibrations show up as zigzag marks on a seismograph printout.

The shaking from an earthquake wave is very strong close to the place where the earthquake first occurs. As the wave travels away from the original location, the shaking in each new location that the wave passes gets less and less. People in places that are far away from the original location cannot even feel the earthquake wave that is passing. Scientists must use a machine called a **seismograph** to detect the tiny vibrations from far away earthquakes.

Scientists can use a seismograph to measure the amount of time that takes place between earthquake waves. They use this time to determine where the earthquake originally took place. The farther away the earthquake took place, the longer the amount of time between waves.

> **Imagine that a scientist in Denver measures the time in between two earthquake waves to be 3 minutes and 10 seconds. A scientist in San Diego measures the time in between waves to be 1 minute 50 seconds. Which scientist is closest to the place where the earthquake originally took place? Explain your answer.**

The scientist in San Diego is closest, because the amount of time

between waves was shortest in San Diego.

(54)

Look Back

Once students have identified which earthquake wave moved faster, ask: ***Which tremor did more damage, the first or the second?*** (the second) Have students revisit their answers to the questions in the margins on pages 52-53. Compare and contrast the effects of the two tremors in a class discussion.

Explore

Timing Earthquake Waves

Encourage students to relate the information in this section with the description of the two tremors in the reading on pages 52-53. Only a short time passes between the first and second tremors in the reading. ***Do you think the earthquake happened close to San Francisco, or far away?*** (close) ***Was the earthquake right underneath the city? Explain.*** (Probably not, because there was some time between the two waves.)

Explore

THE RING OF FIRE

Scientists can pinpoint exactly where an earthquake occurs using the data that they collect on earthquake waves. On the map below, the red dots show places where major earthquakes or volcanic eruptions have occurred.

> **Are earthquakes just as common everywhere on Earth? Explain, using examples from the map.**

No, they are more common in some places than in others. The map

shows lines with many red dots, which are places where they are common.

Other places don't have any red dots.

> **The land on the edges of the Pacific Ocean is sometimes called the Ring of Fire. Why do you think this area is given a special name?**

There are a lot of destructive volcanoes and earthquakes there, and not

as many in other places.

55

NSTA Activity

Real Earthquakes, Real Learning

See page 49B for an NSTA activity in which students plot earthquakes on a world map. Tie this activity in with the Explore sections on this page and on page 56. This activity will reinforce students' understanding of the Ring of Fire as well as provide clues to the location of plate boundaries.

Write to Learn

Descriptive paragraph Have students write a descriptive paragraph about the Ring of Fire. Paragraphs should include a description of where the Ring of Fire is located, the events that occur there, and the meaning of the phrase. Tell students that someone who has not read the chapter should be able to describe the Ring of Fire after reading the paragraph.

Explore

Material Wall map or globe of the world; overhead projector

The Ring of Fire Make a transparency from the map on page 55. Project the image. Have students identify the Ring of Fire (strings of red dots). Have students identify the approximate location of their community. Based on this identification, ask: *What is the likelihood of a volcanic eruption or earthquake in or near our community?* (The likelihood is greatest near the ring of fire.) Point out that volcanic eruptions along the Pacific Coast of North America are much more rare than are earthquakes in the same areas.

Check Understanding

Skill: Apply Knowledge

Have students reread their answers to the question at the bottom of the page. *Which scientist is more likely to see damage from the earthquake, the one in Denver or the one in San Diego? Why?* (The one in San Diego, because that is closer to where the earthquake took place, and the shaking is very strong close to the place where the earthquake starts.)

Assessment

Materials wall map of world

Skills: Apply knowledge, recognize cause and effect

Use the following questions to assess each student's progress.

Ask students to find the approximate locations of Canada and Mexico on the map on page 56. ***Which person is more likely to experience an earth quake, someone in the middle of Canada, or someone in the middle of Mexico? Explain.*** (middle of Mexico; This area lies near a plate boundary and is more earthquake-prone than the middle of Canada, which lies farther from a plate boundary.) Point to the location of Los Angeles and ask: ***If an earthquake occurred here, would the middle of Mexico or the middle of Canada receive the seismic waves first? Why?*** (middle of Mexico, because it is closer to the earthquake than the middle of Canada)

Review "Find Out" Question

Review the question for Chapter 7 from the Unit Opener on page 50. ***Why do some places have so many earthquakes?*** (Earth's plates are moving, or slipping, relative to each other. Earthquakes happen more often where these plates meet.)

Explore

THE EDGES OF EARTH'S PLATES

Earth's surface, or crust, has huge cracks in it. The cracks divide the crust into large pieces, called **plates**. The whole crust is broken up into about ten major plates of different sizes. Even though you can't feel it, these plates are always moving. Sometimes the movement of these plates can cause earthquakes, which are more common at the edges of the plates. The map below shows some of the major plates that make up Earth's crust.

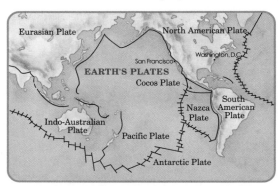

EARTH'S PLATES

> **Compare the map of Earth's plates with the map of the Ring of Fire on the previous page. Where does the Ring of Fire lie in relation to the plates?**

It lies on the edges of plates.

> **Why are earthquakes more common along the Ring of Fire than in other places?**

Earthquakes are more common at the edges of plates. The Ring of Fire is on the edge of the Pacific plate.

> **Find San Francisco and Washington, D.C. on the map. In which city do you think it's more common to have earthquakes? Explain your answer.**

Earthquakes are more common in San Francisco, because it lies on the edge of a plate. There are more red dots there.

 56

Explore

The Edges of Earth's Plates Help students to understand that Earth's crust is broken into plates by asking them to think about a jigsaw puzzle. ***How are the pieces shown on the map like the pieces of a jigsaw puzzle?*** (They fit together.) ***How are the pieces shown on the map different from the pieces of a jigsaw puzzle?*** (They fit together snugly the way most jigsaw puzzle pieces do. They can move against each other, or pull away from each other, which jigsaw puzzle pieces do not.)

Caverns Are Cool

Chapter 8

What wonders lie down under?

Imagine that tomorrow is your big family reunion. To get ready, you go for a haircut. The next day, you see your family. An uncle who hasn't seen you in a year says, "Wow! You've grown taller!" But an aunt who sees you every weekend says, "Oh, you got your hair cut." Your aunt notices that your hair has been cut, because that was a sudden change. She hasn't noticed how much you've grown, because she sees you a lot, and growing taller is a slow change.

Some Earth events, like earthquakes, cause big changes very quickly—kind of like a hair cut, which changes how you look in just a few minutes. But other events take place so slowly that it is hard to see them happen—like the way that you grow taller, day by day.

In this chapter, you will explore how amazing rock formations are created in caverns underground. All it takes is the dripping of water and many thousands of years.

Before You Read

Close your eyes and think about caves. After one minute, open your eyes. On the lines below, write five or more words that describe the caves you imagine. In the box below, draw a small sketch of what you imagine when you think of a cave or cavern.

SCIENCESAURUS
A STUDENT HANDBOOK
BLUE BOOK

Weathering .... p. 171
Erosion and Deposition ... p. 172

SCi LINKS.
THE WORLD'S A CLICK AWAY

www.scilinks.org
Keyword: Caverns
Code: GS5D045

dark, cold, bats,

stalactites, stalagmites,

wet, dripping, etc.

Drawings may show

cave formations,

bats, darkness, etc.

(57)

Key Idea

Like many processes at Earth's surface, the formation of interesting shapes in a limestone cavern happens very, very slowly.

Focus

- Properties of earth materials
- Changes in earth and sky

Skills and Strategies

- Apply knowledge
- Classify
- Compare and contrast
- Construct models
- Create and use tables
- Infer
- Observe

Vocabulary*

Before beginning the chapter, make sure students understand these terms.

- cavern
- dissolve
- evaporate

* Definitions are in the Glossary on pages 166-172.

Introducing the Chapter

Sudden, dramatic earth events such as earthquakes grab our attention because they cause major changes in a very short time. But other changes to Earth's surface take place very slowly. ***How quickly does Earth's surface change during an earthquake?*** (Almost instantly) ***Can you think of some changes at Earth's surface that take place slowly?*** (Answers may include trees growing, rocks wearing away, formation of canyons and caverns. For now, accept all

reasonable answers.) Tell students that in this chapter they will read a description of a limestone cavern, then create a working model of how stalactites and other cavern shapes form.

Before You Read

Ask for a show of hands of those students who have been on a tour of a limestone cavern. Depending on where you live, this may be something that many students have done, or it may be something that only a few students have done while visiting another part of the country. After students have completed Before You Read, you may wish to invite one or two students who have visited a cavern to read aloud their descriptions.

More Resources

The following resources are also available from Great Source and NSTA.

SCIENCESAURUS
A STUDENT HANDBOOK
BLUE BOOK

Reader's Handbook (Yellow Book)

Math at Hand

Writers Express

SCI LINKS
THE WORLD'S A CLICK AWAY

www.scilinks.org
Keyword: Caverns
Code: GS5D045

Read

In this newspaper article, Deborah Owen tells readers what to expect on a tour of Grand Caverns in Grottoes, Virginia.

"A Visit to Grand Caverns"

notes:

Grand Caverns might be called the granddaddy of <u>show caves</u>. Discovered in 1804, it's been open to the public continually since 1806, making it America's oldest show cave....*Parade Magazine* has rated Grand Caverns second only to Carlsbad Caverns in New Mexico.

...Caverns are cool—about 55 degrees [F] year-round. It's a good idea to take a sweater or jacket, and to wear comfortable walking shoes with good <u>traction</u>. The same <u>dripping and seeping water</u> that makes the stunning formations inside the caverns can make for slippery spots underfoot.

One of the first things our tour guide, Katie Brown, pointed out was that the formations extending down from the ceiling are called stalactites and the ones rising from the floor are stalagmites. They are formed by the <u>mineral deposits in the water</u> building up over long periods of time. It can take from 100 to 150 years to form one cubic inch of a stalactite.

> Underline the words that describe what makes the cavern formations.

Stalactite ——
Column ——
Stalagmite ——

show caves: caves or caverns with paid tours
traction: grip on slippery surfaces

mineral deposits: rock that was dissolved and then set down by water

Read

Independent Reading Call students' attention to the purpose of the article. *What is the purpose of this newspaper article? Is it mainly to explain about the science of caverns?* (No) *Then what is its main purpose?* (To tell readers what to expect on an outing to a cavern.) *Is there science information in it?* (Yes, there are descriptions of how structures formed in Grand Caverns.) *Does this make it a science article?* (Students may disagree on whether having science in it makes it a science article.)

This is a good opportunity to point out that, although there are science facts in this article, its main purpose is to tell people about something fun to go do with family and friends. Because science was not the main purpose, the writer would not have any reason to double-check the science information, but the science in the excerpt has been checked out and it is reliable. Thus, although it is a good article, it would not be a good reference for a science report on caverns. When researching science topics, students need to use sources written for the purpose of

explaining the science of a topic.

Students may ask about the difference between a cave and a cavern. The two terms mean the same thing: an underground hole or cavity that formed naturally.

Caves can be formed by several different processes. How did Grand Caverns form? (by water dissolving the rock) Point out to students that many other caves formed this way. Caves can also be formed by lava flows, earthquakes, or by a pile-up of giant boulders left behind by glaciers.

Flowstone and draperies in Hurricane Crawl Cave, Sequoia National Park, California

Grand Caverns is known for having a large number of shield formations. Round and flat like a clamshell, shields have geologists <u>stumped</u> as to exactly how they are formed. Other types of formations typically found in caverns are columns, in which stalactites and stalagmites meet in the middle, <u>flowstone</u> and <u>draperies</u>. One unusual example we saw was in an area known as the Bridal Chamber. The Bridal Veil combines a <u>shield formation</u> with the rippling and <u>cascading</u> of flowstone and draperies.

...Brown entertained the youngsters on our tour with lighting tricks, ghost stories...and funny <u>anecdotes</u>....Don't be surprised if you work up an appetite on a cavern tour. It's good exercise, and many formations—a cheeseburger here, an ice cream cone there, a pizza hanging from the ceiling—resemble food.

From: *"In Grottoes' Grand Caverns; Form a Line for Stalactites, Stalagmites, Flowstone and Draperies"* by Deborah Owen, Richmond (VA) Times-Dispatch, August 14, 2003.

stumped: puzzled
flowstone: rock formation that looks like a frozen waterfall
draperies: rock formation that looks like hanging cloth
cascading: waterfall-like
anecdotes: stories

notes:

_____

_____

_____

_____

_____

_____

_____

_____

_____

_____

> <u>Underline</u> the type of formation that is still a mystery to scientists.

59

Life in Caves

Time 1–2 library periods

Materials research sources about cave-dwelling animals

Animals that live in caverns have developed some truly amazing adaptations to this perpetually dark environment. Have interested students investigate the kinds of animals that live in caves. Which animals live in caves, but also spend time outdoors? Which animals spend all of their time in caves? Do these animals live in water, or on the rocks? What do cave-dwelling animals eat, since very few plants grow underground? Many species that live in caves, such as certain fish and insects, are related to animals that live on the surface. How do the cave-dwelling animals differ from their above-ground relatives?

Connections

Social Studies Grand Caverns was discovered fairly early in U.S. history, and as a result has played a part in that history, however small. Famous historical figures visited the show cave in its early days, and during the Civil War quite a few soldiers left their mark on its walls. Invite interested students to research the history of Grand Caverns. An online search including these keywords produces good results: Grand Caverns, Confederate, Stonewall Jackson.

Science Background

The formation of limestone caverns, such as Grand Caverns, occurs in two stages. During the first stage, groundwater fills natural cracks in the limestone, dissolving the

surrounding rock. Over time, more and more rock is dissolved, and the cracks become larger and larger, turning into water-filled cavities. The cavities will continue to grow as long as groundwater fills them. But various events can cause this process to stop. For example, if the groundwater level drops below the

cavities, they will fill with air and the second stage of cavern formation will begin. This stage, which is described in the reading, involves the build-up of stalactites and stalagmites. As water seeps down through the ceiling of the cavities, it dissolves more limestone. When the water reaches the air in the cavity, it evaporates, and mineral deposits are left behind as stalactites and stalagmites.

Check Understanding

Skill: Apply knowledge

What are all the different cavern formations made out of? (mineral deposits) ***How did these minerals get there?*** (They came from dissolved limestone, and were carried by seeping water that dripped and evaporated.)

Connections

Physical Education Caves host a sport all their own. Cavers (or spelunkers, as they are sometimes called) enjoy exploring the world of underground landforms.

Because caving can be dangerous, cavers always explore in groups. Responsible cavers have proper equipment and are trained how to use it; they expect the same of their fellow explorers.

Invite a caver to your school to give a talk and demonstration about the sport. The National Speleological Society promotes the study, conservation, and safe exploration of caves. Local chapters (called Grottoes) of this organization exist across the United States, and some can help arrange for guest speakers. Contact information for a Grotto in your area is available at the National Speleological Society web site (www.caves.org).

Look Back

The drawing at right shows what a cubic-inch looks like.

> **How long does it take a cubic inch of stalactite to form?**
>
> 100 to 150 years

> **About how many cubic inches could have been added to a stalactite since Grand Caverns first opened in 1806?**
>
> about 1 to 2 cubic inches

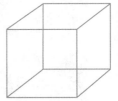

1 cubic inch

Activity

CREATING CAVERN FORMATIONS

Why do stalactites look like rock icicles?

What You Need:
- large bowl
- Epsom salts (about 250 mL, or 1 cup)
- warm water
- spoon
- 2 glass glasses or jars
- tray (to catch the extra solution)
- strip of cotton towel (about 1–2 cm wide and 45 cm long)
- 2 big paper clips (to weigh down the ends of the strip)
- small piece of paper towel

Cavern formations look like frozen water for a very good reason—they are made up of rock, but the rock is formed by water! First, water runs down through cracks in the limestone rock above the cavern. The water dissolves some of the rock along the way. Second, the water drips out of cracks in the cavern ceiling. Third, the water evaporates (turns from liquid to gas). The dissolved rock material is left behind as part of a new stalactite. In this activity, you will model two of these three steps.

What to Do:
1. Put the Epsom salts in the bowl. Add about 400 mL (1 to 2 cups) warm tap water. Stir with the spoon to dissolve the Epsom salts.
2. Place the two glasses on the tray about 30–40 centimeters apart. Pour half the liquid into each glass. *(continued on next page)*

 60

Look Back

As needed, help students estimate the time since Grand Caverns first opened as a show cave (about 200 years). Refer students to their answers in this section when reviewing the "Find Out" question (page 62).

Activity

Time 40 minutes, followed by brief observations over the next two days
Materials For each student pair or group: large bowl, Epsom salt, warm water, spoon, 2 glass glasses or glass jars, tray, strip of cotton towel, 2 big paper clips, paper towel

What You Need
- Jars or glasses should be at least 10 cm (4 in.) tall. It helps if pairs of jars or glasses are matched in size.
- Epsom salt (magnesium sulfate) is available inexpensively at most drug stores. About a 1.4 kg (3-pound) carton is enough for 6 or 7 groups.
- This activity can be done using a cotton string instead of a strip of towel, but the string must be cotton (not hemp or a synthetic fiber).

What to Do
- Epsom salt is safe, but remind students not to taste any materials, nor allow them near their eyes.
- Explain to students that the crumpled piece of paper towel on the tray gives the stalagmite a place to start.
- If you begin the activity in the afternoon, have students change the entries in the Time column on page 61 to read: immediately, morning of day two, afternoon of day two, morning of day three.

(continued from previous page)

3. Put one paper clip on each end of the strip of towel. Put the strip into one of the glasses to get it soaking wet. Then pull it out again.

4. Put one end of the wet strip into each glass. Make sure each end is underwater. Let the strip hang down in the middle, between the two glasses. Make sure that the bottom part of the hanging strip is below the level of the liquid in the glasses.

5. Place a small piece of crumpled paper towel under the bottom part of the hanging strip where the dripping water falls.

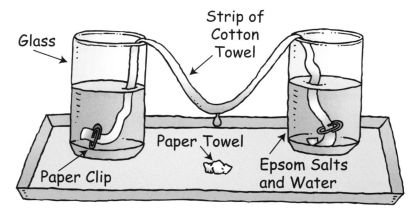

Glass · Strip of Cotton Towel · Paper Towel · Paper Clip · Epsom Salts and Water

6. Observe the setup right away and then at the times listed in the table below. Record what you see each time in the second column. Use the words *stalactites*, *stalagmites*, and *columns*, if you see these features.

Time	Observation
immediately	water drips off strip onto tray
afternoon of day one	small stalactite hanging off strip
morning of day two	longer stalactite
afternoon of day two	column formed

61

Visual/Spatial Invite students to sketch the progress of their cavern formation models, as well as describing them. If your school owns an inexpensive digital camera, these same students may be able to document the progress of their models through snapshots that can then be included in a report.

Write to Learn

Promotional piece Have students write a promotional piece encouraging people to visit their class to view their models. Just as the reading on pages 58-59 makes Grand Caverns sound inviting while teaching something about the science involved, the students' promotional pieces should make their models sound exciting while describing something about how they formed.

• If the water is not dripping, move the glasses closer together so that the lower curve of the towel is below the level of the water in the glasses.

• If no stalactite is visible by the time of the second observation, the water is dripping too quickly to evaporate. Move the glasses farther apart so the bottom curve of the towel is closer to the level of the water in the glasses.

Make sure students understand that cavern formations, unlike icicles, are not frozen water. They look like icicles because, like icicles, they are formed by a process that involves dripping water.

Formations occur on the sides of the glasses or jars because some of the Epsom salt solution runs down the outside of the glass, instead of going down through the towel. The walls of many caverns are covered with formations similar to the ones that student will see growing on the sides of the glasses or jars.

Science Background

You may wish to explain to students the chemistry behind the changes they are observing. When Epsom salt is added to the water, it dissolves to form a solution. That is, the particles that make up Epsom salt are evenly dissolved in the water. The solution moves up through the towel until it drips off the towel, or down the side of the glass. Once the solution is exposed to air, the water evaporates, and Epsom salt is left behind to form a stalactite.

Assessment

Skill: Classify

Use the following task to assess each student's progress.

On the board, write the following list of events that take place at or near Earth's surface.

- earthquake
- hurricane damage
- glacier moving
- river valley forming
- rock breaking up
- volcano erupting

Ask students to classify each event as a "rapid change" or a "slow change." Suggest that students think in terms of time frames such as minutes, hours, and days for rapid changes and years, hundreds of years, thousands of years, and millions of years for slow changes. (Rapid changes include earthquakes, hurricanes, volcano erupting. Slow changes include glacier moving, river valley forming, and rock breaking up.)

Review "Find Out" Question

Review the question for Chapter 8 from the Unit Opener on page 50. *Can a stalactite grow in your lifetime?* To answer the question, have students use what they learned in the chapter, especially their answers to the Look Back question on page 60. (It takes a century to grow just one cubic inch of stalactite.)

Explore

ANALYZE A MODEL

There are three processes that take place in the making of cave formations. When the rock dissolves, that's called **weathering**. When the water takes the rock material with it, it's called **erosion**. When the water evaporates and leaves the rock material behind, it's called **deposition**.

> **In setting up your model of a cavern formation, you dissolved the Epsom salts in water. This is like the weathering of rock. Which part of the model is like erosion?**

the part where the water takes the dissolved Epsom salts with it

through the cloth strip

> **Look at your model of a cavern formation. Which part of the model is like deposition?**

the part where the water drips and evaporates, leaving behind the

Epsom salts

Science Journal

Look for examples of slow changes in your neighborhood over the next two weeks. How do permanent things change slowly over time? Slow changes include weathering, erosion, deposition, melting, and freezing. Copy the chart below onto a separate sheet of paper. Look for the kinds of examples suggested in the chart. An example is done for you.

Slow Change	Date and Place	What it looks like	What might have caused it
icicles forming or changing	February 10, edge of roof at home	long, bumpy spikes hanging down	snow melting and water freezing again
crack in paved road or sidewalk			
rut in dirt road			
garden soil washing away			
metal rusting			

Explore

Analyze a Model Help students to understand that models are limited in what they show about a process or object. After reviewing student answers to the questions on the page, ask: *How is the time it takes your model to form different from the time it takes a real stalactite to form?* (Student models took a couple of days to produce. Real stalactites take many years to produce.) *How is the way that Epsom salts dissolve in your model different from the way limestone dissolves in a real cavern?* (I dissolved the Epsom salts in a lot of water, and stirred it. Limestone dissolves in a little water that seeps through cracks, as described on page 60.)

Science Journal

Evidence of weathering, erosion, and deposition are visible wherever students live, in rural, suburban, or urban settings. In addition to the changes listed in the table, you may suggest that students look for weathering and erosion on these surfaces.

- brick buildings
- headstones in cemeteries
- brick or stone steps
- iron railings
- cars
- painted houses
- farm fields
- farm equipment

A Hiding Place

Chapter 9

How do you hide outside?

Imagine that your next-door neighbor is pounding on your door. She shouts that an enemy army is on the way! Everyone in the neighborhood has to go into hiding right now or be taken prisoner. Because there isn't much time, you need to hide somewhere nearby. Where would you go? What would you do?

Today, most North Americans are not used to events like this. Unfortunately, it is more common in some parts of the world. And, it has happened before in what is now the United States.

In this chapter, you will read part of a novel. It describes a village of Navajo, a Native American people, as they go into hiding. Their knowledge of the land near their home helps them to hide for a while. But it is impossible for them to hide forever.

Before You Read

Think about landforms in the place that you live. **Landforms** are features of Earth's surface. On the lines below, write three or more sentences that describe the shape of the land in and around your town. Are there any hills or mountains? Are there flat places? What does the shape of the land look like?

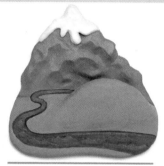

Answers will vary.

 Weathering ... p. 171
Erosion and
Deposition ... p. 172
Parts of a
Map .... p. 404

 www.scilinks.org
Keyword: Erosion
Code: GS5D050

(63)

Key Idea

A relief map can show many different types of landforms, including those that result from weathering and erosion.

Focus

- Properties of earth materials
- Changes in earth and sky
- Populations, resources, and environments

Skills and Strategies

- Infer
- Recognize cause and effect
- Interpret scientific illustrations
- *Compare and contrast (TG)*
- *Construct models (TG)*

Vocabulary*

Before beginning the chapter, make sure students understand these terms.

- landform
- weathering

* Definitions are in the Glossary on pages 166–172.

Introducing the Chapter

The shape of Earth's surface has played an important role in human history. After students have read the introduction, ask: **Have you ever played hide and seek?** (Answers will vary but students will probably remember playing the game when they were younger, even if they do not play it any more.) **If you are playing hide and seek at a friend's house, who has the advantage, you or your friend? Why? (Your friend, because it's your friend's house and** *he or she will know the best hiding places.)* Tell students that in this chapter they will read about Native Americans who hid from soldiers. Students will then learn something about the forces that shaped the land these people lived in, and they will explore how the landforms of this area look on a map.

Before You Read

When they begin this exercise, some students may think of features built by people, such as landmark buildings. Let students know that although buildings are noticeable features of a landscape, they should be describing the natural lay of the land in your area. If you live in a heavily-developed area, such as a city, suggest that students think about the land under the streets and buildings. Is the land flat or hilly? Do the streets follow any natural features, such as rivers?

More Resources

The following resources are also available from Great Source and NSTA.

SCILINKS. THE WORLD'S A CLICK AWAY

www.scilinks.org
Keyword: Erosion
Code: GS5D050

Read

Bright Morning, a Navajo girl, is living in Canyon de Chelly [de SHAY], Arizona, in the 1860s. She tells how her people hid when soldiers came to drive them away.

"Up River, Uphill, into Hiding

notes:

> What did the people use for a trail when they first left the village? How did that help which way they went?

They used the river as a trail. It washed away their footsteps.

When the sun was high we <u>filed</u> out of the village and followed the river north, walking through the shallow water. At dusk we reached the trail that led upward to the south <u>mesa</u>....

The soldiers could not follow our path from the village because the flowing water covered our footsteps as fast as they were made. But when we moved out of the river our steps showed clear in the sand. After we were all on the trail some of the men broke branches from a tree and went back and swept away the marks we had left. There was no sign for the soldiers to see. They could not tell whether we had gone up the river or down.

The trail was narrow and steep. It was mostly slabs of stone which we scrambled over, lifting ourselves from one to the other. We crawled as much as we walked. In places the sheep had to

Canyon de Chelly

filed: walked in a long line   **mesa:** flat-topped land with cliffs at the edges

64

Read

Paired Reading After students have finished the reading, have them compare the reading to the photo on page 64. ***When the people were walking in the river, was the land mostly level or mostly steep?*** (mostly level) ***What was the trail like as they climbed up to the mesa?*** (The trail was very steep.) ***What is the land like at the top of the mesa where they make camp for the night?*** (It is level.) Point out to students that this landscape has mostly level land and

steep cliffs. There are no gently rolling hills here, nor are there mountains with sharp peaks. Tell students that the shape of the land depends on the forces in Earth's crust that formed it. The area in the reading was formed when flat, level layers of rock were eroded by water, leaving steep cliffs behind.

Students may wonder what happens next to the people in the story. The soldiers wait, holding them under siege until their provisions run out. Then the soldiers force them to walk a couple of hundred miles to a reservation.

Science Background

Canyons and mesas are found in the same landscape because they are formed by the same processes—weathering and erosion, which are defined on page 66. All rocks get weathered, but some kinds of rock are harder than others. Harder rocks resist being worn away, while softer rocks wear away relatively quickly.

Canyons form where a layer of harder rock lies over layers of softer rock. Water flows through cracks in the hard rock layer and weathers the

Navajo woman with her sheep, 1943

be carried and two of them slipped and fell into a <u>ravine</u>. The trail upward was less than half a mile long, but night was falling before we reached the end.

We made camp on the rim of the mesa, among rocks and <u>stunted</u> piñon trees. We did not think that the soldiers would come until morning, but we lighted no fires and ate a cold supper of corn-cakes. The moon rose and in a short time shone down into the <u>canyon</u>. It showed the river winding toward the south, past our peach orchards and <u>corrals</u> and <u>hogans</u>. Where the tall cliffs ended, where the river wound out of the canyon into the flatlands, the moon shone on white tents and <u>tethered</u> horses.

"The soldiers have come," my uncle said. "They will not look for us until morning. Lie down and sleep."

We made our beds among the rocks but few of us slept. At dawn we did not light fires, for fear the soldiers would see the rising smoke, and ate a cold breakfast. My father ordered everyone to gather stones and pile them where the trail entered the mesa. He posted a guard of young men at the trail head to use the stones if the soldiers came to attack us.

From: *Sing Down the Moon* by Scott O'Dell.

ravine: deep, narrow, valley
stunted: poorly-grown
canyon: steep-sided river valley

corrals: animal pens
hogans: houses
tethered: tied

notes:

> How do the people get ready to defend themselves against the soldiers?

They gather a pile of stones to throw, at the trail entrance.

> Where did Bright Morning's father expect the soldiers to attack from?

He expected the soldiers to attack from the trail that climbed the canyon.

65

Differentiating Instruction

Intrapersonal The reading on these two pages describes the journey that Bright Morning takes, but it does not describe her feelings during the trip. Encourage students to write a journal entry as if they were waiting on the mesa after taking this journey with Bright Morning. Student entries should include descriptions of what it was like for the people to carry everything they needed for several days, how they managed to get animals and small children up to the mesa, and how the various landforms affected the difficulty of the trip. Entries should also include descriptions of their physical and emotional feelings throughout their imagined journey.

Connections

Materials Copy of *Sing Down the Moon* by Scott O'Dell, or research sources on The Long Walk

Social Studies In 1864, United States soldiers, led by Kit Carson, rounded up thousands of Navajo people and forced them to walk hundreds of miles to a reservation at Bosque Redondo, New Mexico. This event, which the Navajo remember as The Long Walk, figures prominently in the action of *Sing Down the Moon*. Invite students to read the entire novel, or to do research into this chapter in American history.

soft rock layers below. When rain falls again, the water erodes the weathered rock. As the process repeats over many thousands of years, the crack widens into a steep-sided canyon of soft rock walls, topped by a harder capstone layer. The river flowing at the bottom continues to carve the canyon deeper, while rainfall weathers and erodes its sides.

Mesas are left anywhere that the hard rock layer is still protecting the soft rock layers beneath. As the

harder rock is worn away, the softer rock beneath is exposed to erosion, and the mesa itself is gradually removed by the very process that led to its formation.

Write to Learn

Write a short paragraph Ask students to imagine using a hose to clean a chalk drawing off pavement. Have students write a short paragraph comparing and contrasting how water weathers and erodes the chalk.

NSTA Activity

What a Relief!

Skill Construct models

Time 2–4 class periods

Materials

For each student pair:

- copies of Relief Map copymaster, p. 175
- sheet of corrugated cardboard about 8 x 10 inches
- additional sheets of corrugated cardboard or box (to cut up)
- markers, colored pencils, and crayons
- glue • scissors

The United States contains a vast range of landforms. Creating a three-dimensional model of a relief map helps students visualize landforms outside their town.

Procedure

Have students work in pairs, and give them the following instructions:

1. Tell students that they will convert the relief map into a relief model.

(continued on page 67)

Look Back

> At first, the people in the story are walking in the river. Then they go up a trail to a mesa. What words and phrases in the reading describe the journey up this trail?

steep, scrambled, lifting, crawled, upward, sheep slipped and fell

> Contrast the land the river flows through with the land leading up to the mesa. How are they different?

The land around the river is flat; the land going up the mesa is very steep.

> What is the land at the top of the mesa like? It is flat.

Explore

FORMATION OF LANDFORMS

Canyons and mesas are formed by weathering and erosion. **Weathering** is the wearing away of rock. **Erosion** is rock being worn away and moved to another place. Wind, water, and ice are the most common causes of weathering and erosion.

> What do you think was the cause of the weathering and erosion that formed the canyons and mesas in the area described in the reading?

water from the flowing rivers

> Look at the picture of the mesa below. Mesa is the Spanish word for "table." Why do you think that mesas have this name?

Mesas have steep sides and are flat on top, like tables

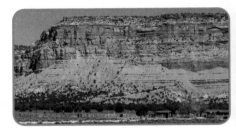

Look Back

The questions in this section are intended to help students think about the character's experience as she travels through the landforms of Canyon de Chelly. Students will expand on their understanding of these landforms in the rest of the chapter.

Explore

Formation of Landforms Explain to students that although weathering and erosion are different processes, they are caused by the same agents: wind, water, and ice. Although water is the most common agent of weathering and erosion, other agents can also be important, depending on the area. *Where would ice be an agent of weathering and erosion?* (in places where it is cold enough for water to freeze; near glaciers) *Where could wind be an agent of weathering and erosion?* (in places where wind blows freely, either because the land is flat or because there are few trees)

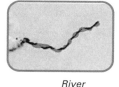

Explore

USING A RELIEF MAP

A **relief map** shows features of the land, such as hills and valleys, by showing the shadows that they cast. The shaded areas give you an idea of about how tall or how deep a feature is. For example, the pictures below show how a river, a canyon, and a mesa might appear on a relief map.

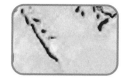

River

Canyon

Mesa

> The relief map below shows Canyon de Chelly. Look closely at the map. Find one example of a river, a canyon, and a mesa. Then, label each feature with its name (River, Canyon, Mesa).

> Compare the relief map to the description of where the people in the reading traveled. The reading said that they walked north along a river and then hiked up a steep cliff wall to the top of a mesa. Use a pencil to draw one possible route that the characters could have taken. Answers will show a route that includes going north along a river and then up a steep cliff wall to the top of a mesa.

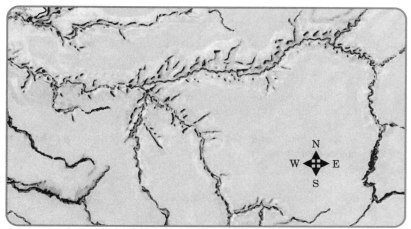

Relief map of Canyon de Chelly

67

(continued from page 66)

They will keep one copy of the reference, and use the other as a pattern. Likewise, they will use one piece of cardboard as the model's base, and cut the others into shapes that build up the model.

2. Tell students to insert a piece of cardboard under one map and trace the lowest contour line hard enough to make an impression on the cardboard.

3. After tracing the lowest contour, have students cut along the impression they made.

4. Have students glue the shape onto the piece of cardboard that is serving as the base.

5. Tell students to insert another piece of cardboard under the map that they are using as a pattern. Have them trace around the next highest contours, cut out along the impressions, and glue the resulting shapes onto the model.

6. Have students continue in the same way until they have completed a model of all the landforms in the relief map.

7. Students may may decorate their models using markers or colored pencils.

Have students compare their models with the flat map, and ask the following questions:

- *How does the model show the shape of the land?* (The model is raised where the land is raised and flat where the land is flat.)

- *How does the original map show the shape of the land?* (It shows this in two ways: through shading, and through contour lines.)

Explore

Using a Relief Map   The shape of Earth's surface is called its relief. Thus, a relief map shows the shape of all or part of Earth's surface. Help students to relate the shapes of landforms to their appearance on a relief map. *Which of the landforms shown in the three sketches is also shown in the map of Canyon de Chelly (at the bottom of the page)?* (river, canyon, and mesa)

Have students compare the relief map of Canyon de Chelly on this page with the photo of this area on page 64. *Which level area looks wider in the photo, the floor of the canyon or the tops of the mesas?* (the floor of the canyon) According to the map, which area is wider? (the tops of the mesas) Lead a class discussion on the relative value of a photo versus a map. *Which view do you think explains the landscape more accurately, the photo or the map?* (Student answers will vary. The map shows the overall lay of the land more accurately, but the photo gives a better view of the steep cliffs and flat canyon floor.)

Check Understanding

Skill: Apply knowledge

What landforms are common in Canyon de Chelly? (canyons and mesas) *What processes formed these features?* (weathering and erosion)

Assessment

Skill: Recognize cause and effect

Use the following task to assess each student's progress.

On the board, copy the chart below (omitting the answers in parentheses). Tell students that throughout history, humans have changed Earth's surface to make it easier for them to travel around. For each landform in the chart, list at least one thing that people have built to get around, through, over or under that landform.

Landform	Human Structure
River	(bridge, tunnel)
Mountain	(tunnel, road)
Small hill	(road cut)

After students have completed this activity, ask: *How would a relief map help engineers to design the structures you have identified?* (Accept all answers that focus on problems associated land elevations.

Review "Find Out" Question

Review the question for Chapter 9 from the Unit Opener on page 50. *Can you find a mesa by looking at a map?* To answer the question, have students point to a mesa on page 67.

Project

THE LANDFORMS IN YOUR AREA

Your teacher will provide you with a relief map of your area. Look at the map. Can you find where your school is located on the map? Can you find your neighborhood? Choose a small area on the map that has at least one interesting landform, such as a mountain, hill, flatland, canyon, river valley, mesa, or cliff. Sketch that area of the map in the box below. Label any interesting landforms that you see.

Imagine what the area you chose used to look like before there were houses, buildings, and roads. Are there any landforms that would have been hard to climb or cross?

> **How would you choose to travel from one side of the map to the other? Draw the path that you would take on the map above.**

> **Describe what it would have been like to journey along this path before there were any modern structures.**

Answers will vary.

Project

Materials *(for each pair or group)* relief map of your local area, or Relief Map copymaster, p. 175

Students will gain the most from this project if they use a relief map of your local area. Ideas for obtaining a local relief map are listed below. If, however, you are unable to find a satisfactory relief map, use copies of the relief map of an imaginary island on page 175 of this Teacher's Guide. (This map also includes topographic lines for use in the NSTA activity on page 66 of this Teacher's Guide.)

The United States Geological Survey (USGS) has for many years produced topographic maps, on which are drawn parallel lines called contours. These contour lines reveal elevations of the land. Topographic maps are readily available; however, they require practice to learn to read. You may order topographic maps (and keys for reading them) through the USGS web site (www.mapping.usgs.gov). Many other suppliers, including local stores that sell hiking and camping equipment, also carry topographic maps.

Shaded relief maps, such as the map on page 67, are easier for students to understand. Maps that present land this way, or as a combination of shaded relief and contour lines, are available through the DeLorme company (www.delorme.com). DeLorme offers software for creating relief maps of any location in the United States. It also provides printed relief map atlases of specific areas.

For every observation, there can be many explanations!

Imagine this: Your little brother leaves toys all over the yard. He says that if you pick them up, he'll give you his allowance and take out the trash for you. So you start picking them up. Your mother sees you and says, "What are you doing playing with your brother's toys? You don't let him play with yours!" Of course, you can explain what you were doing. But what if you couldn't? What if you were suddenly buried by a sandstorm at that exact moment? You and the toys are trapped, and you all become fossils in a rock. Millions of years from now, what would people think you were *really* doing?

Scientists try to figure out puzzles like this all the time. They use the best information that they have to explain what they see. But in science, new discoveries can change old explanations.

In this chapter, you will learn about a famous fossil find—the discovery of fossil dinosaur eggs! Next to the eggs lay a fossil of a mysterious new dinosaur. What was it doing there?

Before You Read

Think about a time when you *thought* you saw or heard someone doing something, but it turned out they were really doing something else. What made you believe they were doing something other than what they were really doing? Why did you think that?

Answers will vary. A student might say they

saw someone trying on a costume for a play

and thought they were going to wear

the weird outfit to a party.

 Making Scientific
Observations
.... p. 11
BLUE BOOK Making
Inferences ..... p. 18
Fossils .... p. 185

 www.scilinks.org
Keyword: Fossils
Code: GS5D055

69

Key Idea
Scientists draw conclusions based on the observations they make, but new observations can change those conclusions dramatically.

Focus
- Earth's history
- Evidence, models, and explanation
- Life cycles of organisms
- Understandings about scientific inquiry

Skills and Strategies
- Compare and contrast
- Create and use tables
- Infer
- Understand that scientific findings undergo peer review
- Understand that scientists change their ideas in the face of experimental evidence that does not support existing hypotheses

Vocabulary*
Before beginning the chapter, make sure students understand these terms.
- dinosaur
- dissolve
- fossil

* Definitions are in the Glossary on pages 166–172.

Introducing the Chapter
In this chapter, students will be reading about two exciting fossil discoveries made 70 years apart, in the same part of the world. Introduce the topic by asking: ***What is a dinosaur?*** (Student answers may include references to movies, television, and theme parks, as well as fossils and museums.)

Make sure students understand that dinosaurs are animals that have been extinct for millions of years. ***Has anyone ever seen a living dinosaur?*** (No) ***How do we know about dinosaurs?*** (We have found fossils of their bones, tracks, nests.) Reinforce that everything we know about dinosaurs comes from observing and interpreting fossil evidence.

Before You Read
Some students may have trouble thinking of a time when they misinterpreted an event. Be prepared to stage a scene that can be interpreted multiple ways. For example, you could have a student stand with his or her back to you, then freeze in position while reaching out to pat the student's head. ***What am I doing? Am I trying to get his attention? Am I touching him? Am I swatting a mosquito on his head?*** (Students should recognize that there is more than one way to interpret the scene.)

More Resources

The following resources are also available from Great Source and NSTA.

SCIENCESAURUS
A STUDENT HANDBOOK
BLUE BOOK

Reader's Handbook (Yellow Book)

Writers Express

SC/LINKS.
THE WORLD'S A CLICK AWAY

www.scilinks.org
Keyword: Fossils
Code: GS5D055

Read

The Gobi is a huge desert in central Asia. It was there, in 1923, that fossils of dinosaur eggs were discovered by scientists, including George Olsen and Roy Chapman Andrews.

"In the Gobi, 1923"

notes:

At first sight, Andrews thought the dinosaur eggs looked like [rock formations] or maybe bird eggs. ...But judging by the shape, size, and crinkled texture of the eggs, the scientists were quite sure they were dinosaur eggs. They also agreed that the eggs probably belonged to *Protoceratops* because these small dinosaurs were so common.

As Olsen continued to scrape away sand and loose rock around the nest, he uncovered parts of a skeleton of a small, clawed dinosaur a few inches from the eggs. From the position of the bones, it looked as though this dinosaur had been buried by a sudden sandstorm just as it was about to rob the eggs from the nest....

Back in the laboratory..., Dr. Osborn...agreed with the scientists on the expedition that [the fossil eggs] must be from *Protoceratops*. His decision, like theirs, was based on little more than the abundance of these dinosaurs at the site.

[He also] agreed that [the dinosaur found near the eggs] probably had been...robbing the nest. Osborn gave that ostrich-size dinosaur the scientific name *Oviraptor*.... *Ovi* means "egg," raptor means "robber...."

> Underline the name of the dinosaur that probably laid the eggs.

> Circle the name of the dinosaur found near the eggs.

From: *Tracking Dinosaurs in the Gobi*, by Margery Facklam.

expedition: trip   **abundance:** large number

70

Read

Independent Reading   Point out to students that scientists work in teams, and that they work in different places. *How many scientists are named in the reading? Where was each scientist working?* (Three scientists: Andrews and Olsen were on the expedition, Dr. Osborn was back in the laboratory.) Tell students that there were other scientists involved in the expedition and in the lab, as well, who are described in the book that is the source of the reading.

What did the scientists think the dinosaur was doing? (Stealing eggs.) *Did all three scientists agree about that?* (Yes.) *If the scientists agreed, does that mean they were correct?* (Maybe not.)

Invite students to revisit page 69. What hints are there that the dinosaur might have been doing something other than stealing eggs? (The introduction talks about new discoveries changing old explanations; both the introduction and Before You Read describe actions being misinterpreted.)

Science Background

The lack of bones in the fossil eggs found in 1923 is discussed on pages 72–74 of the student book. In fact, a few bone fragments were discovered in two eggs found in the 1920s. But the fragments did not add up to a complete skeleton, and could not be used to determine the type of dinosaur that was in the egg.

Protoceratops

Explore

MAKING INFERENCES

An **observation** is something that you note using your senses. Everybody who makes the observation generally agrees about it, because there is no guessing about what they see, touch, hear, or smell.

> **What observations led the scientists to believe the fossil eggs were dinosaur eggs?**

They made observations about their size, shape, and crinkled texture.

An **inference** is an idea that explains an observation or answers a question. An inference is based on an observation. Often, more than one inference can be made for the same observations. The scientists in 1923 made some inferences about the eggs and about the dinosaurs. Fill in the chart below, based on the reading.

Question	Inference	Observation that the inference was based on
Which kind of dinosaur laid the eggs?	*Protoceratops*	*Protoceratops* fossils are common in the area.
What was the *Oviraptor* dinosaur doing near the eggs?	robbing them	The position of the bones made it look like the dinosaur was about to rob the eggs.

(71)

Explore

Making Inferences Reinforce the distinction between observation and inference by giving an example of each. For example, tell students that one day you came home and your dog was not on the screened porch, where she belonged. ***If I say that my dog is not on the porch, is that an observation or an inference?*** (observation) ***What if I say that she opened the door and let herself out? Is that an observation or an inference?*** (inference) ***What would***

make it an observation? (If you saw the dog do it.)

Is that a good inference, that my dog opened the door? Why or why not? (It depends. It is if you have seen the dog open the door before. If you have not seen her do it, then it is not a good inference.) Tell students that a good inference is based on observations. ***Was the inference the scientists made about the oviraptor a good one?*** (Yes, because it was based on observations of the dinosaur's position.)

Differentiating Instruction

Analyzing a Video

Time 60 minutes total (can be done over multiple days)

Materials VHS or DVD of "Dinosaur Hunters: Secrets of the Gobi Desert" ©1997, in libraries or buy from the National Geographic Society (shop.nationalgeographic.com); equipment for showing it (VHS or DVD player and monitor)

This fine documentary follows the paleontologists from the reading on page 72 on an expedition, and into the lab. As you show the video, ask students to look for answers to these questions: *Why were scientists disappointed when a large fossil turned out to be an* **Ankylosaur?** (Ankylosaurs are very common, so it wasn't an important fossil.) *What inference did the scientists make about the two dinosaurs found near each other?* (That they were traveling together, perhaps they were a mated pair.)

⌐Read

Seventy years later, a new group of scientists discovered more fossil dinosaurs and eggs in the same desert.

"In the Gobi, 1993"

notes:

> How were the new fossil eggs like the ones found in 1923?

They were the same size, the same shape, and they had the same crinkled surface.

> How was the fossil egg Mark Norell found different from the others?

It had fossil bones of an embryo dinosaur inside. The other fossil eggs were solid rock.

After lunch that first day, Mark Norell found a <u>concentration</u> of dinosaur eggs and nests. ...[H]e saw one that had broken open, <u>revealing</u> the tiny bones of an <u>embryo</u> dinosaur. The seven-inch-long egg was oval shaped, and its surface was crinkled— the same kind of egg George Olsen had found at the Flaming Cliffs seventy years before. These were just like the eggs from the dinosaur named *Protoceratops*. But no one had ever seen [a complete] embryo in one of those eggs.

...Each new find seemed more exciting than the last, but one discovery sent a shock through the camp. Luis Chiappe and Amy Davidson were chipping away at an *Oviraptor* skeleton when they found eggs under it. They knew immediately that it was a major scientific discovery, but they had to wait until they could examine it in the lab before they made an announcement. ...

During the winter of 1993–1994, Davidson spent more than four hundred hours cleaning the bones of the tiny embryo in its eggshell. The seventy-year-old mistake was finally corrected. The embryo was not *Protoceratops*, but an *Oviraptor*. The *Oviraptor* found in 1923 at the Flaming Cliffs was not an egg robber. She was probably protecting her own nest.

From: *Tracking Dinosaurs in the Gobi*, by Margery Facklam.

concentration: large number in a small area
revealing: showing

embryo: body of an unhatched animal

⌐Read

Independent Reading Invite students to compare the 1993 team with the 1923 team. How many 1993 scientists are named in this reading? Where were the scientists working? (Three: Norell, Chiappe, and Davidson were on the expedition; Davidson also worked back in the lab.) Tell students that, as in the 1923 expedition, there were other scientists involved. Point out that the approach of the two teams was similar: collect specimens in the field, then return them to the lab for careful preparation and study.

⌐Look Back

Why was a fossil skeleton in a dinosaur egg such an important find? (It showed what kind of dinosaur was in the eggs; or, it showed that the dinosaurs in the eggs were the same kind as the adult dinosaur nearby.)

⌐Explore

How a Fossil Forms Review the process of fossilization described on the student page. Make sure students understand that the fossil dinosaur eggs contain none of the original material. Rock material has replaced the original material, as happens in the case of petrified wood. However, when this happens, many of the original features are still visible.

Look Back

> **What made the fossil eggs found in 1993 more useful to the scientists than the fossil eggs found in 1923?**

One of the 1993 fossil eggs had a complete fossil skeleton of an embryo inside. They could tell that the skeleton was definitely an Oviraptor embryo. The 1923 fossil eggs did not have complete skeletons, so they could not tell for sure what type of dinosaur they belonged to.

Oviraptor

Explore

HOW A FOSSIL FORMS

When a dead animal is buried, the soft parts of its body decay leaving the hard parts, such as the bones and teeth. These hard parts can become fossils over very long periods of time. Water carrying dissolved minerals slowly replaces the bone material with the minerals, making a rock shaped exactly like the bone material. This rock is a fossil. The hard shells of eggs can also become fossils by this process.

If the embryo inside an egg has a hard skeleton, it too can become a fossil.

> **What part of the adult *Oviraptor* became a fossil?**

its skeleton

> **What parts of the eggs described in the readings became fossils?**

the eggshells and one of the embryo skeletons.

An Oviraptor embryo.

73

NSTA Activity

Digging Science

Skills Construct models, infer

Time 40–60 minutes

Materials

For each student pair or group:

- wooden 3-D dinosaur skeleton model
- deep plastic tray or dishpan filled with sand
- 2–3 toothpicks or skewers
- dry paintbrush   • newspapers
- plain paper and pencil

To prepare a "fossil" for each team, separate the pieces of each model and bury them in a tray of sand. Tell students that they will excavate the fossil from the rock, then put it together.

Procedure:

1. Using the toothpicks and brushes, remove the sand from around the fossil.
2. As you uncover its parts, infer what type of animal it is.
3. When you have uncovered all the parts, work together to reconstruct the animal.
4. Compare your model to a picture of the completed model.

Ask the class the following question:

- ***How close was your reconstruction to the correct model?*** (answers will vary)

Point out that paleontologists do not have a picture of a model to look at. Their reconstructions are based on careful observation of the fossils, and on information about dinosaurs.

Ask students to think about a chicken developing in an egg. ***Why would some fossil eggs have bones, and others not have bones?*** (The bones might not have been petrified when the fossil formed. Or the egg might not have had bones in it, if it were in a very early stage of development.)

Science Background

The 1993 dinosaur egg with the *Oviraptor* embryo inside was not found in the nest under the *Oviraptor* skeleton. Nevertheless, all the fossil eggs, including the ones found in 1923, were confirmed as being *Oviraptor* because of their characteristic properties: crinkled shell, oblong shape, and size.

Check Understanding

Skills: Observe, infer

What observation did the scientists make in 1993? (They observed fossil eggs under an Oviraptor skeleton.)
What inference did the scientists make about the eggs being under the Oviraptor? (The dinosaur was protecting the eggs like a bird does.)

Assessment

Skills: Generate ideas, Infer

Use the following task to assess each student's progress.

Tell students that in 1993, the fossil skulls of two baby *Velociraptors* were found in the nest with the *Oviraptor* eggs. Have students write a paragraph that describes this observation and at least two inferences about what the baby *Velociraptors* were doing in an *Oviraptor* nest.

   Remind students that a good inference is based on observations. Tell them they may base their inferences on the fossils themselves, and on observations of modern animals that are related to dinosaurs, such as birds. (Paragraphs should include the observation that two different kinds of young dinosaurs were found in the same nest.)

Review "Find Out" Question

Review the question for Chapter 10 from the Unit Opener on page 50. *How did the dinosaur Oviraptor get named for something it did not do?* Have students use what they learned in the chapter to answer to the question.

Explore

NEW OBSERVATIONS, NEW INFERENCES

The scientists in 1993 and 1994 made some observations and inferences about the fossil eggs and dinosaurs they found. Fill in the chart below, based on the second reading.

Question	Inference	Observation that the inference was based on
Which kind of dinosaur laid the eggs?	*Oviraptor*	An *Oviraptor* fossil was found in one of the eggs.
What was the *Oviraptor* dinosaur doing near the eggs?	protecting them	The eggs were of the same kind of dinosaur she was.

Put It All Together

> **Look back over the past few pages. What information about the fossil eggs did the scientists have in 1993 that the scientists in 1923 did not have?**

The 1993 scientists knew what kind of dinosaur was in the eggs.

> **How did this new information change the identification of the fossil eggs?**

It changed the identification of the fossil eggs from *Protoceratops* to *Oviraptor*.

> **How did the inference made about the *Oviraptor* change from 1923 to 1993?**

Instead of stealing another dinosaur's eggs, the *Oviraptor* was most likely protecting its own eggs.

Explore

New Observations, New Inferences
Some students may ask why they are answering the same questions they already answered on page 71. Remind them that this time they are answering the questions from the perspective of the scientists on the 1990s expeditions. Their answers should be different this time, because they are based on observations of different fossils.

Put It All Together

Help students to recognize that scientists on both expeditions made good scientific inferences, based on the information available to them. *Did the scientists in the 1920s use observations to make their inferences?* (Yes) *Were their inferences scientific?* (Yes) *Did the scientists in the 1990s make scientific inferences?* (Yes) *What made their inferences scientific?* (The inferences were based on observations.)

It's a Twister!

Chapter 11

You've seen clouds shaped like many different things, but what about a cloud shaped like a spinning funnel?

A gentle breeze is a pleasant part of a spring day. But spring can also bring fierce storms called **tornadoes**. A tornado is a funnel-shaped storm cloud caused by rotating, high-speed winds. The winds have such high speeds that they can cause serious damage to buildings and property. Tornadoes can happen anywhere, at any time of the year. But in some parts of the country, they are most common in the spring.

In this chapter, you will read about a tornado that raged through a town on an April afternoon. You will also make a model of a tornado and figure out the safest place for you to go if a tornado has been seen in your area.

Before You Read

Think about the wind where you live. Is it always windy? What is the wind usually like? What is it like on a very windy day? How strong does wind have to be to pick something up and move it? Describe at least three different winds you have observed. Include the strongest wind you have ever experienced.

Answers will vary. A light breeze picks up feathers and dry leaves. A brisk wind picks up papers and sand. The strongest wind I've ever seen picked up deck furniture and trash cans.

SCIENCESAURUS
A STUDENT HANDBOOK
BLUE BOOK

Tornadoes ... p. 213

SC/LINKS
THE WORLD'S A CLICK AWAY

www.scilinks.org
Keyword:
Tornadoes
Code: GS5D060

75

Key Idea

Tornadoes are powerful storms that form quickly and can move and destroy even heavy objects.

Focus

- Changes in earth and sky
- Natural hazards

Skills and Strategies

- Infer
- Construct models
- Apply knowledge
- *Interpret data (TG)*
- *Compare and contrast (TG)*

Introducing the Chapter

Your students have probably heard of tornadoes, but depending on where you teach, they may or may not have experienced one. Find out what your students already know, or what they think they know, about tornadoes. **What do you know about tornadoes?** (Students may have experienced these storms, or they may have seen them on television news broadcasts or movies.) Tell students that in this chapter they will read about a real tornado that struck a school in Ohio. They will also make a

model tornado, and learn how to stay safe if tornadoes are predicted for their area.

Before You Read

Materials Copy of Beaufort Wind Scale for each student (optional)

You can extend your students' appreciation of wind by comparing their wind observations to the Beaufort Wind Scale. All versions of the Beaufort Scale describe wind by its visible effects on objects, and rank these winds on a scale of 0-12.

Printable versions of The Beaufort Wind Scale are widely available on the Internet; web sites maintained by the National Weather Service (NWS) and the National Oceanographic and Atmospheric Administration (NOAA) are good places to search. Examples include the following:

http://www.crh.noaa.gov/gjt/beaufort.htm

http://www.spc.noaa.gov/faq/tornado/beaufort.html

More Resources

The following resources are also available from Great Source and NSTA.

SCIENCESAURUS
A STUDENT HANDBOOK
BLUE BOOK

Writers Express

SCiLINKS.
THE WORLD'S A CLICK AWAY

www.scilinks.org
Keyword: Tornadoes
Code: GS5D060

Read

Xenia, Ohio was one of many towns hit hard during a huge outbreak of tornadoes on the afternoon of April 3, 1974.

"No School Tomorrow"

notes:

> Underline the sentence that describes the tornado forming.

...Of the town's twelve schools, six <u>sustained</u> severe damage or were <u>reduced to rubble</u>. Fortunately, most of the students had already left for the day, but not all.

Ruth Venuti, 18, was waiting at Xenia High School for a friend to give her a ride home. <u>In the distance she noticed an immense black cloud change into a gigantic, rotating funnel.</u> Ruth realized a tornado was headed her way. She raced to the auditorium to <u>alert</u> drama club members rehearsing for an upcoming performance of *The Boyfriend*. Bursting in on the rehearsal, Ruth asked if anybody wanted to see a tornado.

A tornado is a huge funnel-shaped cloud.

sustained: experienced
reduced to rubble: smashed into small pieces

immense: huge
alert: tell about a risk

76

Read

Paired Reading As students read the passage, encourage them to note words that the author uses to suggest the size of the storm, and words and phrases that she uses to convey the urgency of the situation. Your students may highlight the terms using colored markers on the page, or organize them in lists, as shown at right.

Size
immense
gigantic
enormous

Urgency
raced
bursting in
jumped
dashed
seconds later

Science Background

Scientists still have not unraveled all the mysteries of tornadoes, but they have a good understanding of the conditions in which they form. Warm, moist air at ground level combined with cool, dry air in the upper atmosphere leads to severe, long-lasting thunderstorms called supercells. Like all thunderstorms, supercells include powerful updrafts of air. When winds in the upper atmosphere start an updraft spinning, a funnel cloud is born.

Mossy Grove, Tennessee, after a tornado, 2002

David Heath, an English teacher and the club's director, jumped off the stage and told the students to follow. They dashed to the hallway, where through the windows they <u>spied</u> an enormous funnel <u>writhing</u> just 200 feet (61 m) away. Terrified, the group took cover in the school's central corridor. Seconds later the tornado struck. For four minutes, mud, wood, dirt, broken glass, and other chunks of <u>debris</u> swirled above the students, who were now lying on the floor.

None of the students were killed or seriously injured. But the twister had <u>obliterated</u> the top floor of the school and partially caved in the auditorium roof. <u>Sprawled</u> across the stage where students had rehearsed only minutes earlier was an upside-down school bus.

From: *Nature's Fury: Eyewitness Reports of Natural Disasters,*
by Carole G. Vogel.

spied: saw
writhing: twisting
debris: broken pieces

obliterated: completely destroyed
sprawled: spread out

notes:

> How long was the tornado over the school?

four minutes

> How did the tornado change the school during that time?

It destroyed the top floor,

caved in the auditorium roof,

and put a school bus upside-

down on the stage.

Connections

Literature The children's novel *Night of the Twisters* by Ivy Ruckman is a thrilling tale of a 12-year-old boy who must act quickly to save himself, his best friend, and his baby brother from tornadoes that are tearing through his town. The book is available in many children's libraries and in book stores. The characters are imaginary, but details of the storm are based on the author's own experience surviving a tornado.

Encourage interested students to read *Night of the Twisters*, then report on this book to the class. Lead a discussion comparing this book, which is realistic fiction, with the account of tornado survivors on pages 76-77, which is nonfiction. How are the actions of the characters alike? How are their hiding places similar?

Differentiating Instruction

English Language Learners Still photos do not adequately show what a tornado is. Before students read the material on pages 76–77, show video footage of a tornado to help students understand the topic of the chapter. Educational videos of severe weather are available through many public libraries. A link on the NOAA Weather Partners Public Affairs web site (www.norman.noaa.gov/publicaffairs) provides information about obtaining public-domain footage of severe storms.

Because supercells contain many updrafts, a single thunderstorm can have several funnel clouds associated with it, although single funnel clouds are also common.

Conditions for tornado formation occur most often in the Great Plains states. For this reason, the area has earned the nickname "Tornado Alley." In the spring and early summer months, warm, moist air from the Gulf of Mexico moves north into the Great Plains states. At the same time, cool, dry air flows in from the west off the higher-altitude Rocky Mountains. When these masses meet they create an unstable situation and the ingredients for the supercells that lead to tornado formation.

While tornadoes are most common in the Midwest in spring and early summer, they can and do occur in many other places and at other times of year. It is helpful for students living anywhere to know what to do in case of a twister. Page 80 gives some helpful hints about tornado safety.

Enrichment

Model Tornado

Time 20 minutes

Materials For each student pair: matched set of 1-liter clear plastic bottles, water, pinch of glitter, 2-3 pieces aquarium gravel, tornado tube connector OR heavy waterproof tape and washer with same outside diameter as mouth of the bottles

Procedure

Another version of the activity on pages 78–79 involves making a vortex using two plastic bottles attached together.

1. Fill one bottle most of the way with water. Add glitter and gravel. (No dish soap is needed.)

2. If you have a tornado tube connector, attach it to the full bottle first, then screw the empty bottle into the other end of the connector.

3. If you do not have a tornado tube, place the washer on the mouth of the full bottle. Turn the empty bottle upside-down on top of the first one. Have one partner hold the bottles in place while the other tapes them securely together. Tape the bottles securely enough that they do not wiggle. Use enough tape to avoid leaks.

(continued on page 79)

Look Back

Some weather events build up slowly. Others build up very quickly. A tornado forms when a thunderstorm meets cool winds high in the atmosphere. The winds cause a rapid, spinning cloud movement in the thunderstorm. Under certain conditions, tornadoes can develop suddenly and move very quickly.

> **Do you think the tornado in the reading built up slowly or quickly? Give examples from the reading to explain your answer.**

The tornado built up quickly. The reading says the cloud turned into a funnel while the girl was watching. Everybody ran out quickly but they barely got to safety in time.

Activity

BOTTLED TWISTER

How does a tornado move things?

What You Need:
- ¹/₂ liter (20-oz) plastic bottle with straight sides
- cap for the bottle
- water
- 2 or 3 drops dish soap
- pinch of glitter
- 2 or 3 pieces aquarium gravel

A tornado is a kind of vortex. A **vortex** is a swirling, twirling, moving shape in water or air. It takes energy to get a vortex started. But once it's started, it can keep going for awhile before it slows down. In this activity, you will make a vortex in a bottle. Then you will observe how the motion of a vortex can move things that are caught in it.

What to Do:
1. Fill the bottle most of the way with water. Add 2 or 3 drops of dish soap. Do not add more than 2 or 3 drops! If you do, empty the bottle, rinse it, and start over again.

2. Add a pinch of glitter and two or three bits of gravel.
(continued on next page)

Look Back

Students who have read pages 76–77 should have no trouble recognizing that the tornado formed quickly. Make sure they list specific passages from the reading to support this conclusion.

Activity

Time 20 minutes

Materials For each student pair or group: ½-liter plastic bottle with cap, water, 2–3 drops dish soap, pinch of glitter, 2–3 pieces aquarium gravel.

What You Need
- Bottle sizes and shapes vary, depending on local beverage distributors. A 2-liter bottle is probably too large for students to easily handle. A straight-sided bottle with a flat, undimpled bottom works best, such as a water bottle. Test the activity ahead of time, using a sample bottle.
- Make sure that each bottle has its correct cap, and that the caps fit snugly.
- Consider putting dish soap in small cups with medicine droppers, to help control the amount of soap used. Do not use for than 2–3 drops!

What to Do
- More than 2–3 drops of dish soap will create so many suds that a

(continued from previous page)

3. Put the cap on the bottle. Seal it tightly!
4. Hold the bottle sideways in both hands so that the length of the bottle is parallel to the ground. Move the bottle so it makes circles in the air, as shown in the picture on the left. Move it fast! Do this for 10–15 seconds, then IMMEDIATELY turn the bottle upside-down, as shown in the picture on the right. Watch what happens inside the bottle.

Move the bottle in a circle.   *Quickly turn bottle upside-down.*

NOTE: Making the vortex takes practice. Be patient and keep trying. A common mistake is moving the bottle in a bigger circle at one end than the other. Another common mistake is turning the bottle in your hands as if it were rolling. Hold the bottle sideways, and move your arms quickly to make circles in the air.

> **Describe what is happening in the bottle.**

Everything inside is spinning. The glitter is whirling around.

> **Make the vortex again. Describe what the gravel pieces do.**

The gravel pieces jump up and down.

> **How is the vortex in the bottle like a tornado? How is it different?**

It is like a tornado because it is spinning like one and it can pick things

up. It is different because it is in water, while a tornado is moving air.

79

(continued from page 78)

4. To form a vortex, turn the two bottles upside down so the full bottle is on top. Quickly rotate the top bottle until a vortex starts to form. Stand the empty bottle on a table and watch the vortex as the water pours from the top bottle into the bottom bottle.

Tell students that scientists use models to help understand objects and events. A vortex is a model that can be used to understand tornadoes. Encourage students to compare the one-bottle vortex to the two-bottle vortex. ***How are the two models alike?*** (Both have spinning water, both last for only a little while.) Which model does a better job of showing the empty space in the middle of a tornado? (the two-bottle model) ***Which model does a better job of showing that objects are picked up and put down by a tornado?*** (the one-bottle model) ***How are both models different from a tornado?*** (The vortex does not form the same way, they are much smaller, they are in water, not air.)

vortex may not form and will not be visible even if it does.
• As noted on the student page, making the vortex takes practice. Encourage student partners to take turns and help each other until both make a vortex.
• Remind students not to pour gravel in the sink when they are cleaning up.

Check Understanding

Skill: Compare and contrast

If the vortex in the bottle were a real tornado, what would the gravel and glitter be? (rocks and debris picked up by the tornado)

✏ Write to Learn

Safety pamphlet Have students prepare a tornado safety pamphlet. Pamphlets should include information about where go and what to do in the event of a tornado.

Assessment

Skill: Apply knowledge

Use the following question to assess each student's progress.

What is a tornado, and why should you seek a safe place to stay right away if you ever see one? (A tornado is a powerful, swirling, fast-moving storm that can tear apart houses and lift cars. It moves so fast that you have very little time to find a safe place to stay, so you do not have any time to waste if you see one.)

Review "Find Out" Question

Review the question for Chapter 11 from the Unit Opener on page 50. ***Should you go home if a tornado is coming?*** (If you are away from home when a tornado strikes, do not go home. Seek shelter where you are.)

⌐Science Journal

In the reading, the student asked if anybody wanted to see the tornado. But you should never try to watch a tornado. Instead you should quickly find a safe place to stay until the tornado is gone. During a tornado, the strong winds can cause windows to shatter, objects to fly about at high speeds, and walls and roofs to be torn apart or collapse. To avoid being hurt by these things, follow this list of tornado safety tips.

> **Tornado Safety**
>
> • Get out of cars, buses, and other vehicles. If you cannot find shelter, lie flat in a ditch or underneath an overpass and cover your head.
> • Go indoors and into the basement. If there is no basement, go to the lowest floor.
> • Go to a room or hallway near the middle of the building. It should have no outside walls, windows, or skylights. Bathrooms are often a good choice.
> • Avoid cafeterias, gymnasiums, and auditoriums. Most are unsafe during a tornado.
> • Lie face–down and cover your head with your arms.

Source: National Weather Service Web Site

> **Look back at the reading. Where did the students go when the tornado arrived? Was this a good place to go, according to the safety information above?**
>
> They went to the school's central corridor (hallway). It was a good place to go because it was not the auditorium and because it did not have outside walls or windows.

> **Think about your school. What is the safest place to go if a tornado is coming? Explain why that place is safest.**
>
> Answers will vary.

> **Think about your home. What is the safest place to go there if a tornado is coming? Explain why that place is safest.**
>
> Answers will vary.

Science Background

The National Weather Service (NWS) issues two types of tornado forecasts.

• A **tornado watch** means that weather conditions in a particular area may lead to the formation of tornadoes. If a tornado watch is issued, people in the area should be on the lookout for tornadoes and should plan activities wisely to avoid unnecessary risks.

• A **tornado warning** means that a funnel cloud has been seen in the area, either on radar or by eye. If a tornado warning is issued, everyone should seek shelter immediately, following to the guidelines on the student page.

• When a tornado watch has been issued, people should monitor TV and radio broadcasts to discover whether the "watch" has been changed to a "warning."

⌐Science Journal

Materials floor plan of your school

If possible, provide students with a floor plan of your school to help them answer the second question. Have them mark your classroom on the map, and then identify the closest place where they would be safe from a tornado. (Remind student to use the Tornado Safety information as a guide.) In a similar manner, have students figure out where they should go if they are in the cafeteria, gymnasium, or other large room.

Eclipsed!

Chapter 12

What happens when the moon is eclipsed?

Imagine yourself at a movie theater. A person stands up to go for popcorn. The light from the projector hits the person, and the person's shadow is seen on the screen. Please move out of the way! That area of the screen is dark until the person moves away.

When the person's shadow is seen on the screen, it is kind of like what happens during an **eclipse**. What is an eclipse? It's a shadow passing across an object in space. In an eclipse of the moon, the moon moves through Earth's shadow. There is a shadow because light from the sun is blocked by Earth. The light that would normally make the moon appear bright in the night sky doesn't reach the moon during the eclipse.

In this chapter, you will learn what to expect during an eclipse of the moon. You'll also find out one reason that eclipses are important to scientists.

Before You Read

What do you imagine an eclipse looks like? An eclipse of the moon happens at night. If you have seen an eclipse of the moon, describe what you saw. If not, describe what you imagine an eclipse of the moon would look like.

Answers will vary.

Eclipses ...... p. 224

BLUE BOOK

www.scilinks.org
Keyword: Eclipses
Code: GS5D065

81

Key Idea

Scientists can use lunar eclipses to measure the motions of Earth and the moon.

Focus

- Objects in the sky
- Earth in the solar system
- Position and motion of objects
- Evidence, models, and explanation
- Change, constancy, and measurement

Skills and Strategies

- Construct models
- Compare and contrast
- Interpret scientific illustrations
- Use numbers
- *Infer (TG)*
- *Define operationally (TG)*

Vocabulary*

Before beginning the chapter, make sure students understand these terms.

- phases (of the moon)
- telescope
- binoculars

* Definitions are in the Glossary on pages 166–172.

Introducing the Chapter

Imagining the movement of objects in space can be challenging for students, and even for many adults. In this chapter, students will discover that an eclipse of the moon—an event that sounds mysterious and may be difficult to comprehend—is really nothing more than the moon passing through a shadow.

Check to make sure students understand the difference between sunlight and moonlight. **What makes the sun shine?** (It produces its own light. Some students may add that sunlight is produced by nuclear reactions.) **What makes the moon shine?** (It reflects light from the sun.) **What would happen if the moon did not reflect sunlight?** (The moon would be dark.)

Before You Read

The purpose of this exercise is to find out what students know and don't know about eclipses. Chances are that few, if any, of your students has seen a lunar eclipse. If they are not sure what to write, refer them to the definition of an eclipse in the introduction, and have them imagine what one looks like. Assure students that there are no wrong answers for this section.

More Resources

The following resources are also available from Great Source and NSTA.

SCI LINKS.
THE WORLD'S A CLICK AWAY

www.scilinks.org
Keyword: Eclipses
Code: GS5D065

Read

Ira Flatow hosts a radio show called "Science Friday." In this transcript, he talks with scientist Derrick Pitts about an upcoming eclipse of the moon.

"A Lunar Eclipse"

notes:

> Did astronomers really plan the eclipse?

No

> Underline when a lunar eclipse happens.

During a lunar eclipse, the moon appears red.

IRA FLATOW, host: [W]e're going to talk about astronomy because tomorrow is International Astronomy Day. ... And to help celebrate that event, astronomers have arranged for a lunar eclipse later in the week. Isn't that something? OK. Now they didn't exactly arrange for the eclipse, but they can help us figure out when to look for it .... Joining me to talk more about it...is Derrick Pitts. He's the chief astronomer for The Franklin Institute in Philadelphia. ...Welcome back to SCIENCE FRIDAY, Derrick.

DERRICK PITTS: Thank you very much, Ira. It's great to be here.

FLATOW: First, tell everybody what this kind of eclipse is....

PITTS: ...[T]his is a lunar eclipse.... The lunar eclipse happens at full moon phase. So in this part of the world, everyone, as long as the sky is clear, will be able to see the moon as it is full, and they'll be able to watch and see as the moon starts to change color. And in this particular instance, it's going to develop into a very deep, rich red.

FLATOW: So it's not going to go away; it's just going to get dark red, and you can see it....

PITTS: You'll be able to see it without any problem at all.

From: *Talk of the Nation: Science Friday*, May 9, 2003, second hour, National Public Radio.

astronomy: study of stars, planets, moons, and other things in space

arranged for: planned
lunar eclipse: eclipse of the moon
phase: stage, or time period

Read

Paired Reading Students may not have read a transcript before. Make sure they understand what they are reading. *Where did this information come from? A magazine? A book?* (a radio show) *How many people are talking, and who are they?* (two people: Ira Flatow is the host and Derrick Pitts is the guest)

Remind students that the moon's appearance changes. These changes are called phases, and the phases repeat about every four weeks. *What does the moon look like during the full moon phase?* (a big, bright circle) Try to avoid a discussion of why the moon goes through phases. For now, just get students to think about their own experiences seeing the full moon, so they have a context for what the astronomer is saying.

Science Background

During a lunar eclipse, the moon is in Earth's shadow. However, sunlight that passes through Earth's atmosphere is bent, causing it to change direction. (The same process, called refraction, bends light as it passes through a glass of water.) Enough sunlight is bent through Earth's atmosphere to light the moon dimly during an eclipse. But Earth's atmosphere also filters the sunlight, leaving only the red part to reach the moon. This is why the moon appears red during an eclipse.

Explore

THE MOON AS A MOTORCYCLE

In the pictures below, a motorcycle is passing a truck on the road at sun rise. The sun is shining from the right (East). In the first box, the shadows of the motorcycle and truck fall to the left (West), away from the sun.

> **Shade in the shadows of the truck and the motorcycle in the other two pictures.**

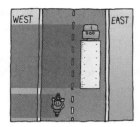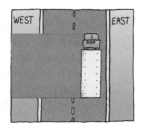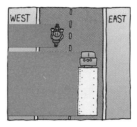

In the pictures below, the moon is traveling in its orbit around Earth. The sun is shining from the right. The first box shows the shadows of the moon and Earth, which point away from the sun. (They are not to scale.)

> **Shade in the shadows of Earth and the moon in the other two pictures.**

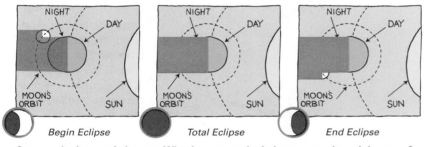

| Begin Eclipse | Total Eclipse | End Eclipse |

> **Compare both sets of pictures. What happens to both the motorcycle and the moon?**

Both the moon and the motorcycle move through a shadow.

(83)

Explore

Materials For teacher demonstration: toy truck, toy motorcycle, large ball, small ball, source of bright light

The Moon as a Motorcycle Use a toy tractor-trailer truck and a toy motorcycle to demonstrate the situation shown on the page, or invite students to demonstrate it for the class. (Your students may be able to lend you the toys.) If you have a sunny window, perform the demonstration there; otherwise darken the room and use a bright light, such as the light from an overhead projector. ***What happens to the motorcycle as it passes by the truck?*** (It gets dark.) ***Does the motorcycle stay in the dark for very long?*** (No) ***How is the motorcycle passing by the truck like the moon during a lunar eclipse?*** (Both the motorcycle and the moon are passing through the shadows of larger objects.) Reinforce this comparison by repeating the demonstration, this time using the large ball as Earth and the smaller ball as the moon.

Write to Learn

Write a transcript A transcript is a written record of spoken language, which is why a transcript does not read like most written material. Challenge students to rewrite the first half of the transcript on page 84 as a paragraph, up through the sentence about watching the shadow cross craters. (Leave out the crater timings.) Paragraphs should include a topic sentence, main body with information, and a closing statement.

Connections

Materials *(for the class)* Research sources about the ancient Maya civilization

Social Studies The Maya civilization flourished from about 900 B.C. until about 900 A.D. in what is now eastern Mexico. The Maya were very advanced in astronomy and mathematics, and used their knowledge to devise a calendar more accurate than the one we use today. Among other events, the Mayan calendar correctly predicted solar and lunar eclipses for centuries in advance. Have students use the library and internet resources to do research on Mayan astronomy and mathematics, and report their findings to the class.

Read

Lunar eclipses are more than just fun to watch. They're also useful. Flatow and Pitts talk about how lunar eclipses help scientists observe motions of Earth and the moon.

"Timing Earth's Shadow"

notes:

_____

_____

_____

> Underline what the scientists use to time Earth's motion and the moon's motion.

FLATOW: Now getting back to the lunar eclipse, we don't need any special equipment to look at the moon here—Right?—and see the eclipse.

PITTS: No, you don't.

FLATOW: But if you have a small telescope or a pair of binoculars, is it fun to watch the shadow move across the moon if you can look at the moon a little closer?

PITTS: You sure can. And it is fun to watch the shadow move across because if you wanted to, you could actually watch it as it passes over specific craters. There are crater timings that you can look for on the Web that will tell you when the shadow is going to move over particular craters. And scientists actually use this to time the Earth's motion and the moon's motion, by looking at how quickly the shadow moves across particular craters....

From: *Talk of the Nation: Science Friday*, May 9, 2003, second hour, National Public Radio.

crater timings: times that the edge of Earth's shadow will pass across certain craters

Read

Paired Reading Encourage your students to observe a lunar eclipse the next time one is visible in your area. Eclipse dates are known well in advance. Many almanacs publish this information, and upcoming eclipses are often included in weather reports on the news. NASA maintains a general-interest web site, its "Eclipse Home Page," which includes information about upcoming eclipses and where they are visible.

Science Background

Lunar eclipses occur only during the full moon phase. The full moon is the only phase when the moon is on the opposite side of Earth from the sun, and therefore the only phase when the moon can pass through Earth's shadow. Although there is a full moon about every four weeks, lunar eclipses cannot occur every month. The moon's orbit around Earth is tilted slightly compared with Earth's orbit around the sun. Most months, the full moon passes "above" or "below" Earth's shadow in space, and there is no eclipse.

Explore

Interpreting Photos A series of photos, such as the one on this page, captures the changes that take place as an eclipse progresses. The time it takes for those changes to occur is less apparent.

After students have calculated the elapsed time between the photos, help them to relate the length of time to a familiar event. ***About what part of an hour is 32 minutes?*** (a half-hour) ***Can you think of something else that takes about the same length of time?*** (Answers will vary, but may

Explore

These three photos were taken in Iceland during a lunar eclipse in January, 2001.

| 7:00 P.M. | 7:16 P.M. | 7:32 P.M. |

> **How much time passed between the first and the second photo?**   16 minutes

> **Between the second and the third?**   16 minutes

> **Between the first and the third?**   32 minutes

> **How does the shadow on the moon change from one photo to the next?**
> The shadow covers more of the moon from one photo to the next.

Look at the first photo. Arrows are pointing to two dark, round areas on the moon's surface.

> **Look for the same two dark areas in the second photo. What happened to the dark areas and the shadow of Earth between the first and second photos?**
> The shadow has moved closer to the dark areas.

> **Look at the third photo. Where are the dark areas now?**
> The dark areas are under the shadow.

> **Find the dark area near the edge of the moon in the third photo. Predict how long it will take for the shadow to cover that area.**
> Answers will vary from just a few more minutes to 16 minutes.

(85)

Enrichment

Eclipsing the Moon and Sun Students may be interested in the difference between an eclipse of the sun and an eclipse of the moon. In an eclipse of the sun, the moon passes between Earth and the sun, blocking the sun from viewers on Earth. Because the moon's shadow is so much smaller than Earth's, an eclipse of the sun is much quicker than an eclipse of the moon, and far fewer people can see it.

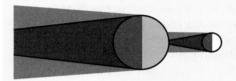

Challenge students to draw the motorcycle and truck to demonstrate the positions of Earth and moon during an eclipse of the sun. Student drawings should show the motorcycle passing the truck on its sunny side. The motorcycle casts a small shadow on the side of the truck as it passes by. The shadow of the motorcycle moves rapidly along the truck. As the shadow moves over an area on the truck, that area "experiences" an eclipse.

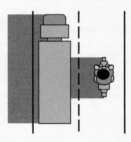

---

include a school event such as recess, a television show, or half of a team practice.)

When students have completed the questions on the page, tell them that these photos were taken early in the eclipse. ***What will the moon look like when the shadow is completely covering it?*** (It will look red, or dark, as described on page 82.) Tell students to turn to page 82 for a picture of the moon when it is completely eclipsed.

Science Background

The dark areas visible on the moon's surface are called maria (MAR ee uh), which is Latin for "seas." They were named by Galileo, who thought they looked like oceans when he first viewed the moon through a telescope. These areas are actually vast plains of hardened lava, and do not contain any water.

Check Understanding
Skill: Infer

During an eclipse of the moon, what is the main cause of the eclipse?
(The moon is moving into Earth's shadow.)

Assessment

Skill: Define operationally

Materials overhead projector or other light source, large ball, small ball

Use the following task to assess each student's progress.

Hand the student the two balls. Tell the student that the large ball stands for the Earth and the small one stands for the moon. The overhead projector stands for the sun. Say to the student: ***Move the two balls in the light to show the moon and the Earth during an eclipse of the moon.*** (Students should hold the larger ball nearer to the light, and move the smaller ball into the shadow of the larger ball.)

Review "Find Out" Question

Review the question for Chapter 12 from the Unit Opener on page 50. ***What shadow are you seeing during an eclipse of the moon?*** (Earth's shadow) Have students use what they learned in the chapter to answer the question. ***Can you see Earth's shadow any other time?*** Use their responses as the basis of a class discussion. (Technically, you can see Earth's shadow every night, because night happens when you are in Earth's shadow.)

Put It All Together

Look back at the truck and motorcycle pictures on page 83. On each picture, draw a *tiny* bug on the shady side of the truck.

Imagine that you are the bug riding on the shady side of the truck. You are so small, and the truck is so big, that you can't tell that the truck is moving. (Pretend you can't feel the wind.) But you can tell that the motorcycle is moving. You watch the motorcycle turn dark as it goes into the shadow of the truck. You watch it pass in the shadow. Then you watch it become light again as it moves back into the sunshine.

> **How can the changes from light to dark to light again help you see how fast the motorcycle is moving past the truck? (Hint: Think about how quickly the light-dark-light change happens if the motorcycle moves quickly. Does the change happen as quickly when the motorcycle moves slowly?)**

The light-dark-light change would happen quickly if the motorcycle is moving quickly past the truck. The change would happen slowly if the motorcycle is moving slowly past the truck.

> **Now compare the bug on the truck to a person watching an eclipse while standing on the shady side of Earth—the part of Earth where it is night. How is the bug watching the motorcycle like a person watching the eclipse?**

The person can watch the moon pass through Earth's shadow like the bug watches the motorcycle pass through the truck's shadow. Both can tell something about how quickly the objects are moving by how quickly they move into the shadows.

Put It All Together

When students have answered the questions in this section, refer them again to the photos on page 85, which show the moon as it moves into Earth's shadow. ***What do you think you would see as the moon moves out of Earth's shadow?*** (I would see the edge of the shadow move across the moon in the direction opposite to the moon's movement, until the moon was completely bright again.)

Science Background

Unlike a motorcycle, the speed of the moon does not change much. However, the length of time that the moon spends in Earth's shadow does vary with each eclipse. Earth's shadow is a very large circle. When the moon passes through the middle of the shadow, the eclipse lasts longer. When the moon passes through an edge of the shadow, the eclipse takes less time. Lunar eclipses generally last between one and three hours from the time the shadow first touches the moon to the time the moon is completely out of Earth's shadow.

UNIT 2: Earth Science

What Did We Learn?

CHAPTER 7

What causes so many earthquakes along the Ring of Fire?
Earth's plates are moving, which can cause earthquakes along the edges of these plates. The Ring of Fire is located along the edges of these moving plates.

CHAPTER 8

Why can't a stalactite form in your lifetime?
Stalactites take thousands of years to form.

CHAPTER 9

How do rivers form canyons and mesas?
River water forms canyons and mesas by weathering and eroding rock.

CHAPTER 10

How did the dinosaur *Oviraptor* get the wrong name? What happened to correct the scientists' mistake?
Scientists thought it was stealing eggs. But later, they found fossils that showed it was in fact protecting them.

CHAPTER 11

Why shouldn't you go home if you see a tornado? What should you do instead?
Tornadoes move too quickly for you to get home in time safely. Instead, seek shelter where you are.

CHAPTER 12

What do scientists use Earth's shadow for during a lunar eclipse?
to time the motions of Earth and the moon

87

UNIT 2 Wrap Up
Earth Science

Create a poster Help students to look for common threads among the chapters in the unit. For example, ask: **What do earthquakes and tornadoes have in common?** (Both happen very quickly, both cause rapid changes at Earth's surface, both are natural hazards and can cause injury and damage.) **What is similar about the way caverns and canyons form?** (Both form through the slow, gradual processes of weathering and erosion.) **Which of the things we learned about in this unit take millions of years to form?** (caverns, canyons, fossils) **Which things take less than a day?** (earthquake, tornado, eclipse)

Invite interested students to create a poster display summarizing the similarities among the topics in this unit.

What Did We Learn?

The questions on this page complement the ones in the Unit Opener on page 50. Discuss the questions as a class. Invite students to share their ideas about the chapters they have completed. What new questions do they have after completing these chapters?

UNIT 3: Physical Science

A major goal of the *Science Daybooks* is to enrich science instruction through reading selections that promote critical thinking skills as well as reading and writing fluency. The chart below describes science content and process skills and also includes the reading and writing skills used in each chapter.

Chapter Title	Science Concepts	Science Skills	Reading & Writing Skills
13. Frog Chemist	• Chemical compounds • Chemical properties	• Infer • Draw conclusions • Conduct investigations • Interpret data • *Communicate*	• Distinguish cause and effect • Cite supporting evidence • *Concept map* • *Write a hypothesis*
14. Secret Messages	• Chemical changes of matter	• Compare and contrast • Conduct investigations • Interpret data • Draw conclusions • *Communicate*	• Compare and contrast • Extract appropriate information • *Write a rap* • *Write a letter*
15. Electricity Bike	• Energy conversions • Generating electricity • Technology	• Communicate • Interpret scientific illustrations • Conduct investigations • *Concept map*	• Demonstrate comprehension • Connect to own experience • *Draw a picture* • *Write a letter*
16. Magic Machine?	• Stored energy • Energy of motion • Conservation of energy • Friction	• Concept map • Interpret scientific illustrations • Communicate • Apply knowledge	• Connect prior experiences and ideas to text • *Share information* • *Write an interview dialogue* • *Write a report*
17. Desert Refrigerator	• Heat energy • Movement of heat energy • Technology	• Make and use scientific illustrations • Infer • Conduct investigations • Generate ideas • Design an experiment • *Compare and contrast* • *Communicate*	• Connect prior experiences and ideas to text • Extract appropriate information • *Write an outline* • *Write a hypothesis*
18. Light Tricks	• Reflection • Refraction	• Infer • Draw conclusions • Conduct investigations • Interpret scientific illustrations • *Communicate* • *Compare and contrast*	• Demonstrate comprehension • *Draw a picture* • *Write a journal entry* • *Write a report*

*Skill appears only in Teacher's Guide
Skill appears in Teacher's Guide and Student Book

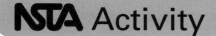
The following activity and other NSTA activities throughout this *Science Daybook* are adapted from NSTA publications with the permission of the National Science Teachers Association. The activity below is best used with Chapter 18.

Bouncing Light

Time 30–40 minutes

Materials

For each group:
- flashlight
- tennis ball
- large mirror
- powder puff with talcum powder
- pencil
- paper

This activity demonstrates how light reflects off of an object at the same angle it strikes the object.

Safety Notes:

- Make sure students use care around the mirrors. Remind them never to step on the mirrors. If a mirror does break, have the students let you know immediately. Instruct them not to try and pick up the pieces themselves.
- Remind students to use the talcum powder as instructed
(and not for plying around). Talcum powder may cause some students to sneeze.
- Remind students that the tennis balls are not for playing. Direct students to only use as instructed.

Procedure

Have students work in small groups and give them the following instructions.

1. Do this activity in a clear area with a hard and smooth floor surface.

2. Have two people stand one meter apart and bounce the tennis ball between them.

3. Draw a picture showing the angle of the ball's path as it approaches the floor and the angle of its path as it leaves the floor.

4. Darken the room. Now place the mirror face up on the floor and "bounce" the light beam from the flashlight off of the mirror at an angle. Shake the powder puff over the light beam to help you see the path of the light.

5. Draw a picture showing the angle of the beam's path as it approaches the mirror and the angle of its path as it leaves the mirror.

Have small groups of students talk about their observations. Ask the following question:

- ***How do the angles of the light beam approaching and leaving the mirror compare with the angles of the bouncing ball approaching and leaving the floor?*** (In both cases, the incoming angle is the same as the outgoing angle.)

Explain that the law of reflection states that light rays bounce off of surfaces at the same angle they strike the surfaces.

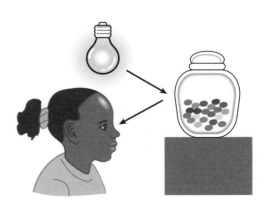

Chapter 13   Frog Chemist

Key Idea: Some frogs use toxic chemical compounds from insects in their diet to produce their own, more powerful, toxins.

A science article about poison dart frogs introduces students to the idea of chemical compounds.

Materials

Read (p. 90), for the class:
- paper clips

Enrichment (p. 92), for the class:
- research materials on bees and wasps, black widow spiders, jellyfish, scorpions, coral snakes, skunks

Connections (p. 93), for the class:
- pictures of poisonous animals
- materials to make posters

Activity (pp. 93-94), for the class:
- small paper cups
- water
- cream of tartar
- measuring spoons
- paper towels
- purple cabbage
- baking soda
- vinegar
- toothpicks
- safety goggles (optional)

Chapter 14   Secret Messages

Key Idea: Chemical changes often involve a change in color and can therefore be used to reveal secret messages.

Students read about invisible inks and how they have been used by spies throughout history.

Materials

Introducing the Lesson (p. 95), for the class:
- invisible ink puzzle books

Enrichment (p. 97), for the class:
- alum
- cotton swabs or paint brushes
- eggs
- white vinegar
- pot of boiling water

Connections (p. 99), for the class:
- lined paper
- lemon juice
- pens
- toothpicks

Activity (p. 99), for the class:
- lemon juice
- cotton swabs or toothpicks
- white paper
- paper towels
- small paper cups
- lamp

Chapter 15   Electricity Bike

Key Idea: Generators convert mechanical energy to electrical energy, which can be used to power light bulbs.

Students read about a high school student in Peru who used a bicycle and a generator to power a household appliance.

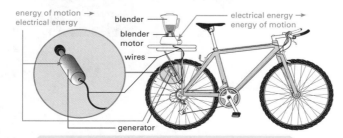

energy of motion → electrical energy
blender
blender motor
wires
electrical energy → energy of motion
generator

Materials

Introducing the Lesson (p. 101), for the class:
- research materials on how electricity in generated in your area
- local maps

Connections (p. 104), for the class:
- electricity bill showing kWh

Explore (p. 104), for a teacher demonstration:
- drum
- uncooked rice grains

Activity (p. 106), for the class:
- hand-crank generators
- light bulbs with stands

Chapter 16 Magic Machine

Key Idea: Heat energy produced by friction makes the dream of perpetual motion machines impossible.

Students read about a man who tried to create a perpetual motion machine in the 1600s.

Materials

Enrichment (p. 111), for each pair or group:
- rubber ball
- graph paper
- meter stick
- pencil

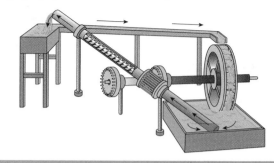

Chapter 17 Desert Refrigerator

Key Idea: People in hot, rural areas can use evaporation to keep perishable items fresh.

Students read about a "desert refrigerator" that uses evaporation to keep food cool and fresh.

Materials

Introducing the Lesson (p. 113), for the class:
- cotton ball
- water

Read (p. 114), for the class:
- world map

NSTA Activity (p. 117), for each pair or group:
- empty clear glass bottle
- small plastic tub
- balloon
- ice

Activity (p. 117), for each student pair or group:
- clay pot
- sand
- dish towel
- lettuce leaves
- smaller clay pot (same shape)
- water
- thermometer

Chapter 18 Light Tricks

Key Idea: Reflection and refraction are two different behaviors of light.

Two different classic children's stories describe the behavior of light and how it can trick the eye.

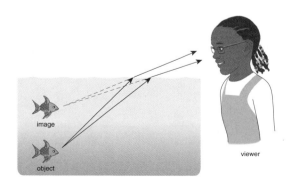

image

object

viewer

Materials

Before You Read (p. 119), for the class:
- polished metal spoons

Read (p. 120), for the class:
- abalone shells

Science & Children Activity (p.121), for each pair or group:
- see page 87B

NSTA Activity (p.122), for each pair or group:
- drinking glass, empty
- drinking glass, half-full of water
- pencil

Connections (p. 123), for the class:
- research materials on free diving and SCUBA diving

Activity (p. 123), for each student pair or group:
- shallow bowl (not see-through)
- penny
- pitcher (optional)
- water
- masking tape (optional)

The following sources are used in this Unit.

Chapter 13
Magazine Article
"Frog Chemist Creates a Deadlier Poison" from *Science News for Kids*, September 10, 2003

Chapter 14
Magazine Article
"Jimmy + the Bug" from *ASK* magazine, January/February 2003

Chapter 15
"Tinkering with the Basic Bike," from *Science News for Kids*, August 27, 2003

Chapter 16
Magazine Article
"Something for Nothing?" from *Muse* magazine, May/June 2003

Chapter 17
Radio Transcript
"A Cooler for the Sahara" from the radio show *A Moment of Science*, WFIU and Indiana University

Chapter 18
Fiction
Island of the Blue Dolphins by Scott O'Dell

Fiction
Call It Courage by Armstrong Sperry

www.scilinks.org
Keyword: Mentoring
Code: GSSD06

UNIT 3: Physical Science

Chapter 13 Frog Chemist
Find Out: How does a frog use chemicals to protect itself?

Chapter 14 Secret Messages
Find Out: Why do spies need to know about chemicals?

Chapter 15 Electricity Bike
Find Out: How can you use your bike to blend up a tasty smoothie?

Chapter 16 Magic Machine?
Find Out: What do all machines need in order to run?

Chapter 17
Desert Refrigerator
Find Out: How can you keep food cool in the middle of the desert?

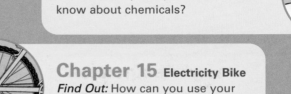

Chapter 18 Light Tricks
Find Out: How can light trick your eye?

88

Introducing the Unit

To generate interest in the chapters, use the questions on the student page. Invite students to read the questions, but explain that they do not have to answer them right now. Ask students what they think they will find out in each chapter, based on the questions and images on this page. Accept all answers at this point.

Who would want to eat poisonous insects?

What do you think of when you hear the word "chemical"? Do you think of a person in a white coat with glasses and test tubes full of purple liquid? The purple liquid would be a chemical, but so are the plastic in the glasses and the fabric in the white coat. Actually, everything around you is made up of chemicals—your desk, the floor, the light bulb above your head, and even your own body.

When people say "chemicals," they usually mean chemical compounds. A **chemical compound** is a substance made up of two or more **elements** that are chemically joined. An element is the most basic kind of matter. Oxygen is an element. Water, which is made up of oxygen and hydrogen, is a chemical compound.

In this chapter, you will learn about an animal that makes a special kind of chemical compound, one that helps protect it from other animals. You will also learn how to identify chemical compounds based on their abilities to change when they meet other chemical compounds.

Before You Read

Can you think of any animals that use a chemical compound to attack other animals or to protect themselves? For example, some stinging insects inject their victims with a venom, which is a chemical compound. List at least four animals that are poisonous or that can sting other animals.

Students should be able to come up with bees, wasps, some spiders, scorpions, snakes, jellyfish.

SCIENCESAURUS
A STUDENT HANDBOOK
BLUE BOOK

Physical and Chemical Properties ... p. 246
Elements ..... p. 250
Compounds p. 256

SCILINKS.
THE WORLD'S A CLICK AWAY

www.scilinks.org
Keyword: Chemical Properties of Matter
Code: GS5D070

89

Key Idea

Some frogs use toxic chemical compounds from insects in their diet to produce their own more powerful toxins.

Focus

- Systems, order, and organization
- Properties and changes of properties in matter

Skills and Strategies

- Infer
- Draw conclusions
- Conduct investigations
- Interpret data
- *Communicate (TG)*

Vocabulary*

Before beginning the chapter, make sure students understand this term.

- experiment

* A definition is in the Glossary on pages 166–172.

Introducing the Chapter

This chapter examines some species of frogs that use chemical toxins to discourage predators. To get students thinking about predator-prey relationships, ask: ***What animal do you think might want to eat a frog?*** (Students may guess that birds and snakes and small mammals may feed on frogs.) Draw the following simple food web on the board to show some of the feeding relationships that exist in a North American ecosystem.

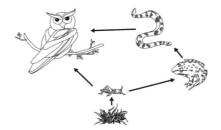

How do you suppose a frog defends itself from predators? (Students may answer that a frog can hide, swim away, or climb a tree. They may also know that some taste bad and many are camouflaged.)

Before You Read

Invite students to share any experiences they might have had with stinging insects or other venomous animals. ***Why do you suppose this animal stung you?*** (Answers will vary.) Lead students to see that they can be perceived as predators by animals and that stinging is often used as a defense against predators.

More Resources

The following resources are also available from Great Source and NSTA.

SCIENCESAURUS
A STUDENT HANDBOOK
BLUE BOOK

www.scilinks.org
Keyword: Chemical
Properties of Matter
Code: GS5D070

SCI**LINKS**
THE WORLD'S A CLICK AWAY

Read

Scientists have been wondering how poisonous frogs are able to make their poisons. Here's what the scientists found out.

"Poison Frog"

notes:

Talk about playing with your food.

Scientists have discovered a poisonous frog that takes up a toxin from its food and makes the chemical even deadlier. It's the first example of a frog using chemistry to make a poison for its own defense stronger.

Several types of frogs from South America, Australia, and Madagascar carry deadly poisons in their skin. When raised in zoos and aquariums, however, most of the frogs grow up to be totally harmless.

About 10 years ago, researchers... figured out that many poison dart frogs take up toxins from the food they eat, including

> Underline the words that describe what happens to most of the poisonous frogs raised in zoos and aquariums.

90

toxin: poison
chemistry: the science of elements and chemical compounds
defense: protection

aquariums: a kind of zoo for plants and animals that live in water
poison dart frogs: a group of frogs that all produce poisons

Science Background

"Poison dart frogs" are so named because they are used by some tribes to make poison darts. For example, the Choco Indian tribe of Columbia, South America, uses toxins from the Golden Poison Frog to hunt animals that live in the trees of the rainforest.

Read

Read Aloud

Materials paper clips

After students complete the first page of the reading, have them imagine that they are the scientists that completed the research on poison dart frogs ten years ago. Challenge students to come up with a hypothesis about how poison dart frogs become poisonous, and an experiment to test the hypothesis. For example:

Hypothesis—Frogs that do not eat toxic ants and other toxic insects will not store toxins in their skin.

Experiment—Feed non-toxic insects to one group of poison dart frogs and toxic insects to another group of poison dart frogs for a period of time, then test their skins for toxins.

Review some of the variables in this experiment with students (frogs in each group must be the same species, quantities of insects fed to each group of frogs must be equal, and so on). **How would you control these variables?** (Answers will vary.)

Dendrobates auratus is only about 4 centimeters long, but it can still defend itself.

ants and other insects. If such <u>prey</u> isn't available, the frogs get no toxins to store in their skins.

Scientists later found out that the frogs weren't just storing the toxin in their skin. They were also improving it....

More recently, scientists were working with a toxin...often found on the skin of the...green poison dart frog *(Dendrobates auratus)*. The scientists sprinkled the toxin on termites and fruit flies, which they then fed to the <u>captive</u> [poison dart] frogs.

Later <u>analyses</u> of the frogs' skins showed that about 80 percent of the [toxin] had been <u>converted</u> to a different toxin.... The new toxin was five times more poisonous to mice than the original chemical.

Scientists were surprised by their findings. Any creature that tries to eat a wild *Dendrobates* would get an even bigger surprise. It's quite possible that its frog-leg dinner would be its last!

From: "Frog Chemist Creates a Deadlier Poison." *Science News for Kids,* Sept 10, 2003.

prey: an animal that is eaten for food
captive: caged
analyses: studies
converted: changed

notes:

> How was the new toxin different from the original toxin?

It was five times more poisonous to mice than the original chemical.

Differentiating Instruction

Visual/Spatial The reading describes how a poison dart frog uses toxic chemicals contained in its food to produce new toxins. Have students construct a concept map showing how a poison dart frog makes toxic chemicals. Maps may vary. They may be linear:

or more complex:

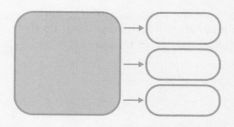

Accept all maps that show relationships accurately.

Help students as needed with the math in the second-to-last paragraph of the reading.

"...about 80 percent of the [toxin] had been converted to a different toxin."

Remind students that 80% is $\frac{80}{100}$ or $\frac{8}{10}$. Have students use paper clips to show you 80% of 10, 20, and 40 clips (8, 16, 32). You may also want to inform students that 80% can be expressed as "almost all" or "most of."

"The new toxin was five times

more poisonous to mice than the original chemical."

Remind students that "five times more" means multiplied by 5. Have students use paper clips to find 80% of 10 (8) and then multiply this number by 5 (40). This multiple can also be expressed more generally as "way more than double."

Check Understanding

Skill: Infer

Why didn't the toxin that the scientists sprinkled on the termites and fruit flies harm the frogs that ate these insects? (The toxin was found in the skin of the frogs. Students should infer that a toxin produced by a frog may be toxic to other animals, but will not be toxic to the frog itself.)

Enrichment

Chemical Defenses

Materials information on bees and wasps, black widow spiders, jellyfish, scorpions, coral snakes, skunks

Invite students to research other animals that make use of poisonous or noxious chemicals.

Students should address the following questions: ***Are the chemicals used to protect the animal against predators? If so, which predators? How are the predators warned that the poisonous animals are dangerous?***

Are the chemicals used to hurt prey? If so, which prey? What do the chemicals do to the prey?

Have students present their findings in the form of a report.

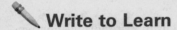

Write to Learn

Write a poem Have students write a poem in the voice of the zoo frogs, who have no toxic insects to eat and therefore no toxins in their skin to protect them. The frogs should be longing for their days in the wild and their former meals.

Look Back

The reading describes a lab experiment with green poison dart frogs and insects sprinkled with a toxin. The experiment demonstrates what happens in the wild with the poison dart frogs and the toxic insects they normally eat.

> Look at the chart below, which shows the poison dart frogs in three different situations. Decide whether the frog is poisonous or not poisonous and circle the correct word. Look back at the reading to help you.

Frogs in the wild that eat wild insects	Frogs in the lab that eat normal insects	Frogs in the lab that eat insects sprinkled with toxin
(Poisonous) or Not Poisonous?	Poisonous or (Not Poisonous?)	(Poisonous) or Not Poisonous?

> **What can you conclude about how the frogs in the lab get the toxins in their skins?**

They get the toxin in their skins from the toxin sprinkled on their food (the original toxin).

> **What can you conclude about how the frogs in the wild get the toxins in their skins?**

They get the toxin in their skins from the toxin in the wild insects that they eat.

> **Why didn't the frogs raised in zoos and aquariums have toxins in their skins?**

They weren't eating the wild ants and other insects that had the original toxin. Without the original toxin, they couldn't make the toxin they stored in their skins.

Look Back

Help students as needed to understand that the insects sprinkled with toxin in the lab were meant to simulate the toxic insects the poison frogs would eat in the wild. ***Where do you suppose the wild ants and other insects get their toxins from?*** (Students may guess that they get them from the foods they eat, or make them themselves.)

Ask students to predict what they think would happen if a wild poison dart frog was brought into a pet store and it lived there for several months eating non-toxic insects. ***Would this frog have toxins in its skin? Explain your answer.*** (No, because it would not have been eating wild toxic insects.)

Lead students to draw connections between the frogs' diet and their toxicity. ***Why is the expression "You are what you eat" really true when it comes to poison dart frogs?*** (Students should explain that poison dart frogs are only poisonous when they eat the poisons as part of their diet.)

Explore

CHEMICAL PROPERTIES

The world is made up of many different kinds of chemical compounds. Different compounds contain different combinations of elements. These elements give each compound its own unique set of chemical properties. **Chemical properties** describe the ability of a chemical compound to react with other compounds.

How can you determine the chemical properties of a compound? By seeing how it reacts with other compounds. For example, you can see how a chemical compound affects an animal when it interacts with the compounds found in the animal's own body.

Look back at the reading. The original toxin sprinkled on the frog's food was changed by the frog's body into a new toxin found on the frog's skin.

> **Think about how the two different toxins affected the mice. How were the chemical properties of the new toxin found on the frog's skin different from the chemical properties of the original toxin?**

The new toxin was five times as strong as the original toxin. It was

more poisonous to the mice.

Activity

OBSERVING CHEMICAL PROPERTIES

Can you identify a chemical property?

What You Need:

- 4 small paper cups
- 2 tablespoons purple cabbage juice
- $\frac{1}{2}$ teaspoon baking soda
- $\frac{1}{2}$ teaspoon cream of tartar
- 2 tablespoons vinegar

If you see a change in the appearance of chemical compounds when they are added together, you might be observing a chemical property of those compounds. Try it out in this activity. *(continued on next page)* 93

Explore

Chemical Properties Review some other chemical reactions with students. Point out that burning is simply a chemical reaction between oxygen in air and a material that can burn. Rusting is also a chemical reaction between oxygen in the air and a material that can rust. The ability to burn is a chemical property of paper, wood, and other natural fibers. The ability to rust is a chemical property of iron and materials that contain iron (like steel).

Help students see that every chemical has its own unique set of properties. ***How do you know that carbon, the main chemical in coal and oil, is a different chemical than iron?*** (Students should see that one, carbon, can burn and one, iron, cannot. One, iron, rusts and one, coal, does not.)

Connections

Materials pictures of poisonous animals, materials to make posters

Art Have students look back at the photos of the poison dart frogs on page 90. Point out that poison dart frogs possess chemicals that make them, or parts of them, very brightly colored. Students may have also noticed that many of the poisonous animals they researched as part of the Enrichment activity (p. 92) also were distinctly colored.

The bright colors, which are produced by chemical reactions in the animals, serve as a warning to predators that might want to eat the animals.

Compile with a class list of the animals students researched and their color patterns.

Poison dart frogs: striking patterns and colors, including bright green, yellow, red, blue

Bees/wasps: black and yellow

Black widow spider: black and red

Coral snake: red and yellow

Skunk: black and white

Have students choose one animal from the list and find color pictures that show the animal. Have them use colored markers or crayons to draw pictures of the animal on a poster. Then have them label the poster with safety information about where the animal is found and how the animal can be avoided.

Activity

Time 30–40 minutes

Materials small paper cups, purple cabbage, water, baking soda, cream of tartar, vinegar, measuring spoons, toothpicks, paper towels, safety goggles (optional)

- Prepare the purple cabbage juice indicator as follows: cut up half a head of purple cabbage into 1-inch strips. Boil the cabbage for about 5

(continued on page 94)

Assessment

Skill: Communicate

Use the following questions to assess each student's progress.

How do green poison dart frogs get the chemicals they need to make their poisons? (from the insects they eat)

What evidence was found that showed that the toxin produced by the frogs and the toxin produced by the insects might not be the same? (They affected the mice differently.)

Review "Find Out" Question

Review the question from the Unit Opener on page 88. *How does a frog use chemicals to protect itself?* (Predators learn that eating a poisonous frog is dangerous. Experience teaches them not to eat poisonous frogs.) Have students use what they learned in the chapter to suggest an answer to the question. Use their responses as the basis for a class discussion.

(continued from previous page)

What to Do:

1. Label four paper cups 1–4.
2. Put 1 tablespoon of purple cabbage juice into cups 1 and 2.
3. To cup 1, add $\frac{1}{4}$ teaspoon of baking soda. To cup 2, add $\frac{1}{4}$ teaspoon of cream of tartar.
4. What happens in cups 1 and 2? Write your observations in the chart.
5. Put 1 tablespoon of vinegar into cups 3 and 4.
6. To cup 3, add $\frac{1}{4}$ teaspoon of baking soda. To cup 4, add $\frac{1}{4}$ teaspoon of cream of tartar.
7. What happens in cups 3 and 4? Write your observations in the chart.

What Do You See?

Cup	Liquid	Powder	Observation
1	Purple cabbage juice	Baking soda	Liquid turns green.
2	Purple cabbage juice	Cream of tartar	Liquid turns pink.
3	Vinegar	Baking soda	Bubbles form.
4	Vinegar	Cream of tartar	Liquid does not change.

When baking soda is mixed with purple cabbage juice, the liquid changes color. That's because a chemical property of baking soda is that it turns purple cabbage juice green.

> **What is another chemical property of baking soda?**

When mixed with vinegar, bubbles start to form.

> **What is a chemical property of cream of tartar?**

When mixed with purple cabbage juice, the liquid turns pink.

(Activity, continued from page 93)
to 10 minutes in six cups of water and then let it cool to room temperature. Strain and keep the juice. It should be pale bluish purple in color.

- Set up a distribution station for materials. Provide boxes of baking soda and cream of tartar, as well as a bottle of vinegar and a bottle of purple cabbage juice indicator. Provide measuring spoons for measuring out powders and liquids, and toothpicks for stirring each

mixture. Provide paper towels to clean up any spills.
- Have students come to the distribution station in pairs or small groups. You may choose to have students wear safety goggles as they work with the chemical mixtures.
- Help students conclude that a compound's chemical properties determine how it will react with other compounds.

As an added challenge, give students a small amount of one of the powders in two separate cups. Have them

identify the powder by seeing how it reacts with the indicator solution and with the vinegar. (Students should be able to identify the powder experimentally: if the powder bubbles with vinegar, it is baking soda. If not, it is cream of tartar. If it turns green with indicator solution, it is baking soda. If it turns pink, it is cream of tartar.)

Secret Messages

Chapter 14

Sometimes, you need to send a message that no one else can read.

Imagine that you are away at summer camp. You want to write to your parents and tell them how homesick you are. You don't want anyone else to find out. Unfortunately, the camp counselors read all the letters you write before they go in the mail. How can you get a secret message to your parents? Why not use invisible ink?

Invisible inks are inks that cannot be seen when they are written or after they have dried. Only the person who sent the message and the person who is supposed to read the message know how to make the ink visible and uncover the message. In this chapter, you'll read about different kinds of chemicals that are used as invisible inks. Then, you'll use what you learned to create your own secret messages.

Before You Read

Spies have been using invisible ink to send secret messages for hundreds of years. Look at the picture at right. It shows a letter written by an American spy during the Revolutionary War. In between the lines of the ordinary letter is a secret message that the spy wrote using invisible ink. You can see now that the message has been uncovered and looks very dark. Whoever received the letter knew what to do to the paper to reveal the message hidden between the lines.

A letter written by Benjamin Thompson on May 6th, 1775

> **Why do you think the spy wrote the secret message between the lines of an ordinary letter?**

Students may guess that the spy wanted to

fool anyone who captured the letter into

thinking it did not contain a secret message.

 Physical and Chemical Properties ... p. 246
Chemical Changes ...... p. 266

 www.scilinks.org
Keyword: Chemical Changes
Code: GS5D075

Key Idea

Chemical changes often involve a change in color and can therefore be used to reveal secret messages.

Focus

• Change, constancy, and measurement
• Properties and changes of properties in matter

Skills and Strategies

• Compare and contrast
• Conduct investigations
• Interpret data
• Draw conclusions
• *Communicate (TG)*

Vocabulary*

Before beginning the chapter, make sure students understand this term.

• evidence

* A definition is in the Glossary on pages 166–172.

Introducing the Chapter

Materials invisible ink puzzle books

This chapter introduces students to chemical changes and how they can be used to write and reveal secret messages.

To get students familiar with the idea of invisible ink, share with them a few invisible ink puzzle books. (These books come with two marking pens—one for writing invisible messages and one for revealing them.) Encourage students to discuss what they did to reveal the invisible ink on the pages.

Point out that there is nothing "magic" about this process. It can all be explained by chemistry, as they will discover.

Before You Read

Point out that the secret message in this letter now appears dark, but when the letter was written, it was invisible. Have students speculate as to how the message was revealed. ***What do you think was done to this letter to reveal the secret message?*** (Student answers will vary. Accept all answers for now.) Explain to students that they will learn more about how secret messages are revealed in the rest of the chapter.

More Resources

The following resources are also available from Great Source and NSTA.

SCIENCESAURUS
A STUDENT HANDBOOK
BLUE BOOK

Reader's Handbook (Yellow Book)

Writers Express

www.scilinks.org
Keyword: Chemical
Changes
Code: GS5D075

Read

Jimmy and his friend The Bug are characters in a magazine column. They answer questions about science and nature. In this issue, they answer a question about invisible ink. How does invisible ink work?

"Invisible Ink"

notes:

> Why do you think the inks described in the reading look "invisible" on paper?

They are light and are written on paper, which is also light.

Secret writing is very old and there are lots of invisible ink recipes. These inks work in different ways to hide and <u>reveal</u> messages written with them.

Some invisible inks—like milk, vinegar, or lemon juice—darken when they're heated. You can read messages written with them because they burn faster than the paper they're written on.

Other secret inks are <u>solutions</u> of chemicals that are colorless when dry but become visible when <u>treated</u> with another chemical, called a <u>reagent</u>.

Messages can even be written inside eggs, using a mixture of vinegar and a chemical called alum. Messages written with this ink are <u>absorbed</u> through the shell. When the egg is boiled and peeled, the message appears [on the boiled egg].

reveal: show
solutions: liquid mixtures
treated: combined

reagent: a chemical that causes another chemical to change
absorbed: soaked up

Read

Individual Reading Explain to students that this cartoon is from a kids' science magazine. In each issue, the two characters in the cartoon— discuss a different science topic.

Draw students attention to the first sentence of the reading. ("Secret writing is very old and there are lots of invisible ink recipes.") To get students thinking about what makes a good invisible ink, ask: ***What are the most important characteristics of invisible ink?*** (Lead students to see that it must be invisible when dry and able to be revealed somehow later.)

What secret message is revealed in the second cartoon? ("Jim is bossy.") ***How is the message revealed?*** (by holding the paper over a light bulb)

Point out to students that the wavy lines above the bulb indicate heat rising up from the bulb. ***According to the reading, why does the ink turn dark when held over the hot bulb?*** (because the ink burns faster than the paper)

notes:
_____
_____
_____
_____
_____
_____
_____
_____
_____
_____
_____
_____
_____
_____

From: "Jimmy + The Bug," *ASK* magazine, Jan/Feb 2003.

97

Secret Message

Materials alum, white vinegar, cotton swabs or paint brushes, eggs, pot of boiling water

Have students write secret messages inside eggs, as described in the reading.

Safety Note

Have students use extra caution when handling the raw eggs. You may choose to hand them out in shallow containers to reduce the chances of breakage.

Instruct students not to eat the hard boiled eggs.

- Prepare the ink by dissolving 15 g (about $\frac{1}{2}$ oz) of alum in 500 mL (about 1 pint) of white vinegar. (Alum is available at most drug stores.)

- Have students use the cotton swabs or paint brushes to write a secret message or draw a secret picture on the shell of an egg.

- Let the eggs dry completely. The messages will no longer be visible.

- Boil all the eggs for 15 minutes.

- Have students peel the eggs and reveal the messages on the inside.

The definition of "solution" given for the reading is just meant to get students through the reading. The complete definition of solution is a mixture whose particles are spread out evenly. The most familiar solutions are made of a powder (solute) dissolved in water (solvent), but there are many different kinds of solutions, including gases dissolved in liquids, liquids dissolved in liquids, and solids dissolved in solids.

Science Background

Invisible inks that are revealed by reacting them with a chemical are either acids or bases. When a pH indicator solution is brushed on them, they turn the indicator a different color. As the indicator changes color, the message is revealed.

Check Understanding

Skill: Communicate

What two chemical changes were described in the reading? What caused each change? (Invisible inks darkening when heated and invisible inks darkening when treated with another chemical. The heat and the other chemical causes each change.)

Differentiating Instruction

Musical Have students compose a short rap that describes one of the two types of secret ink diagrammed on this page. The raps should make use of rhymes and be set to a rap beat. For example:

Yo, check out Mr. Vinegar
Sure is sour
But as you'll see
That chump's got power.
Paint it on a plain white sheet,
Hold it right up to the heat.
Man you won't believe your eyes,
Secret words you can't disguise.

Students may also want to use the characters of Jimmy and the Bug in their raps.

Have student volunteers perform their raps in front of the class.

 Look Back

> There were two types of secret inks described in the reading. Fill in the diagram below to compare the two types of ink and how they change.

Secret Ink: Milk, vinegar, or lemon juice	**Secret Ink:** Solutions that can be treated with a chemical
What does it look like when it is dry? colorless	**What does it look like when it is dry?** colorless
How do you change the ink to reveal it? Heat it.	**How do you change the ink to reveal it?** Add a chemical.
How does the ink change? It darkens.	**How does the ink change?** It becomes visible.

 Explore

CHANGES IN MATTER

Invisible inks go through a chemical change when they are made visible. What is a chemical change? Wood burning, an old bike rusting, bread baking in the oven—all these are examples of chemical changes. A **chemical change** happens when two or more chemicals combine to produce new chemicals. The new chemicals might have different colors, textures, or smells than the original chemicals. These differences can be clues that a chemical change has taken place.

> Look back at diagram you just completed above. What clue tells you that a chemical change has taken place when invisible ink is revealed?

A color change occurs when the ink is revealed—the ink darkens and

becomes visible.

Look Back

You may choose to fill in the diagrams as a class. Once students have completed the diagrams, have them compare the two. **What do the two inks have in common?** (They are both colorless when dry.) **How are they different?** (They are different liquids, different chemicals, and they are revealed differently. One is revealed with heat and one with another chemical.)

Explore

Changes in Matter Illustrate each example of chemical change on the board (wood burning, old bike rusting, bread baking in oven). Below each, write "Chemicals combined" and "Clue that change took place." Have the class help you fill in the information for each picture. For example:

Wood burning
Chemicals combined:
  wood, oxygen from air
Clue that change took place:
  flame, smoke, ash

After students have answered the question, do the same illustrations and labels for each of the two inks.

Activity

INVISIBLE INK #1

What's the recipe for invisible ink?

What You Need:
- lemon juice
- cotton swabs or toothpicks
- white paper
- lamp

WHITE PAPER

Lemon Juice

COTTON SWABS

Meet me at the slide.

What To Do:

1. Dip the cotton swab or toothpick in the lemon juice.
2. Use the wet cotton swab or toothpick to write a secret message on a piece of white paper.
3. Let the paper dry for 15 minutes. You should not be able to see the message.
4. Once the message is dry, exchange secret message papers with a friend.
5. Turn the lamp on.
6. Carefully hold your friend's paper near the warm light bulb for several minutes.

> **Can you read the secret message? What does it say?**

Answers will vary.

> **What evidence, or clue, tells you that a chemical change has taken place?**

The ink changed color.

> **What caused the chemical change to take place?**

heat

> **Look back at the reading. What other inks besides lemon juice could be used in this activity?**

milk or vinegar

(99)

Connections

Materials lined paper, pens, lemon juice, toothpicks

Writing Have students imagine that they are spies working for George Washington during the Revolutionary War. (Alternatively, you could choose any historical war or incident from your current curriculum.) Have them compose a letter to a friend or family member using regular ink on lined paper. They should write on every other line of the paper. Encourage them to write using the voice of a person alive during that time in history.

Then, between the written lines of their letters, have them use lemon juice to write a secret message to George Washington (or other leader from your curriculum) alerting him to some important development. Once the papers are dry, have students exchange papers, reveal the messages using heat, and read the messages aloud to the class

Activity

Time 30–40 minutes

Materials lemon juice, small paper cups, cotton swabs or toothpicks, white paper, lamp, paper towels

Safety note

Warn students not to touch the lit bulbs as they get quite hot.

- Set up one or more lamps with incandescent bulbs around the classroom. Remove any shades from the lamps so that the bulbs are exposed.

- If you do not have lamps available, have students leave their papers out in the sun. The ink should darken after a while. Cloud cover and high humidity may slow the result.

- Put a few teaspoons of lemon juice into a cup for each student or group. Distribute lemon juice and other materials to students.

- Make sure students wait until their papers are completely dry before exchanging papers with a partner.

If students are struggling with the second question, have them look back at page 98 for a list of clues that indicate a chemical change (a change in color, texture, or smell).

The color change is the result of burning—a chemical reaction between the lemon-juice-soaked paper and oxygen in the air. The lemon-juice soaked paper burns faster than the unsoaked paper and so darkens first.

(99)

Assessment

Skill: Communicate

Use the following question to assess each student's progress.

In order for an invisible ink to be revealed, what kind of change takes place? What makes this change happen? (A chemical change that produces a change in color. The addition of heat to a chemical, or a chemical reaction.)

Review "Find Out" Question

Review the question from the Unit Opener on page 86. *Why do spies need to know about chemicals?* (Invisible inks used by spies require a knowledge of chemicals for the message to be revealed.) Have students use what they learned in the chapter to suggest an answer to the question. Use their responses as the basis for a class discussion.

Activity

INVISIBLE INK #2

Can you make another kind of invisible ink?

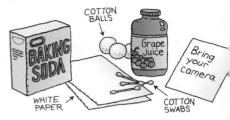

What You Need:
- baking soda mixed with water
- purple grape juice
- cotton swabs or toothpicks
- cotton balls
- white paper

What To Do:

1. Dip the cotton swab or toothpick in the baking soda solution.
2. Use the wet cotton swab or toothpick to write a secret message on a piece of white paper.
3. Let the paper dry for 15 minutes. You should not be able to see the message.
4. Once the message is dry, exchange secret message papers with a friend.
5. Dip a cotton ball in grape juice.
6. Gently rub the wet cotton ball all over the paper.

> **Can you read the secret message? What does it say?**
> Answers will vary.

> **What evidence, or clue, tells you that a chemical change has taken place?**
> The ink changed color, while the paper became the color of the juice.

> **What caused the chemical change to take place?**
> the addition of grape juice

> **Look back at the reading. Which of the two types of inks did you use in this activity?**
> a solution that becomes visible when it is treated with another chemical

Activity

Time 30–35 minutes

Materials baking soda, water, small paper cups, purple grape juice, cotton swabs or toothpicks, cotton balls, white paper, paper towels

Safety note
Grape juice can stain clothing. Warn students to handle it carefully.

- Mix a small amount of baking soda and water in a cup. Each student or group will need one cup of baking soda solution and one cup of grape

juice. (Grape juice concentrate produces an even greater color change than grape juice.)

- Distribute the materials to students or groups.

- Make sure students wait until their papers are completely dry before exchanging papers with a partner.

If students are struggling with the second question, have them look back at page 98 for a list of clues that indicate a chemical change (a change in color, texture, or smell).

The color change is the result of a pH indicator (grape juice) reacting to the base (baking soda) on the paper. The base turns the indicator a darker color.

How can a bike make electricity?

Most homes in the Unites States have electricity. This electricity is used to run all sorts of useful machines and fun toys. But not everyone around the world is so lucky. In many places—especially those that are far away from big cities—people don't even have electricity to light their homes.

Electricity is a form of energy. It is also called electrical energy. Electricity is produced from other forms of energy. For example, the heat energy given off by burning coal can be changed into electricity. So can the energy of motion from wind or moving water. In this chapter, you will read about a student in South America who came up with a very original way to produce electricity.

Before You Read

There are many ways to produce electricity. There are even more ways to use electricity. How is electricity used in your home?

> **List at least six ways that electricity is used in your home.**

Students might mention lamps, radios,

televisions, heaters, stoves, and

refrigerators.

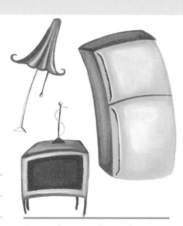

SCIENCESAURUS
A STUDENT HANDBOOK
BLUE BOOK

Forms of Energy .... p. 285
Energy Changes ..... p. 286
Electricity ... p. 296

SC/LINKS.
THE WORLD IS A CLICK AWAY

www.scilinks.org
Keyword: Energy
Code: GS5D080

(101)

Key Idea

Generators convert mechanical energy to electrical energy, which can be used to power light bulbs.

Focus

- Change, constancy, and measurement
- Light, heat, electricity, and magnetism
- Transfer of energy
- Science and technology in local challenges

Skills and Strategies

- Communicate
- Interpret scientific illustrations
- Conduct investigations
- *Concept map (TG)*

Vocabulary*

Before beginning the chapter, make sure students understand these terms.

- electricity
- energy

* Definitions are in the Glossary on pages 166–172.

Introducing the Chapter

Materials local maps, research materials on how electricity is generated in your area

This chapter describes how mechanical energy can be converted into electrical energy by a generator. It also touches on the use of alternative energy resources in Peru.

Get students thinking about how electricity is generated in your area. Is it produced by a hydroelectric dam, by coal, by wind, by nuclear energy? Do

some research to find out, then share what you learned with the class. Use local maps to show students where the power plants in your area are located.

Reinforce the idea that electricity is produced from other sources of energy, including fossil fuels (petroleum, coal), renewable energy sources (wind, water), and radioactive materials.

Before You Read

If students are having difficulty coming up with a list of things in their houses that use electricity, ask: ***What things don't work when the power to your home goes out?*** (Students will probably remember that when the lights go out, they can't watch TV, the refrigerator doesn't work, and their radio alarm clocks don't work.)

More Resources

The following resources are also available from Great Source and NSTA.

SCIENCESAURUS
A STUDENT HANDBOOK
BLUE BOOK

Reader's Handbook (Yellow Book)

Math at Hand

SCiLINKS®
THE WORLD'S A CLICK AWAY

www.scilinks.org
Keyword: Energy
Code: GS5D080

Read

Read about Renato Angulo Chu, a high school student who has come up with a new use for his bicycle.

"Electricity Bike"

notes:

> What problem does Renato see in his country? Underline your answer.

Bicycles are a great way to get around. They're fun to ride, especially down hills. And, as you whiz along the road, you might also think of ways in which you could improve your bike—make it safer, more <u>efficient</u>, more comfortable, or more <u>versatile</u>. In fact, the two-wheeled machines make for some cool science projects...

Electricity bike

Renato Angulo Chu had even <u>grander ambitions</u>. The 12th-grader from Lima, Peru, wanted to <u>address</u> some of his country's <u>economic</u> troubles.

"I see a problem in my country," Renato said. "<u>If you go to the forests in Peru, in some places you cannot find electricity</u>. If you go with my bicycle, you can turn on the lights."

Renato Angulo Chu adjusts his Multibike.

efficient: using less energy to do the same amount of work
versatile: able to do different kinds of things

grander: bigger
ambitions: dreams
address: help solve
economic: having to do with money

Read

Read Aloud Help students conclude that Renato's bike is used to produce electricity. *What is needed to turn on lights and to operate a blender?* (electricity) *How does Renato's bike operate the blender?* (Help students see that turning the pedals produces electricity that travels through the wires to operate the blender.) If students wonder how turning the pedals produces electricity in the wires, tell them that they will learn how on page 105.

Explain that most homes in the forests of Peru do not have electricity, but that many people own bicycles. They use the bikes to get around from one place to another. *Why is Renato's "contraption" the right kind of technology for the area where it is used?* (It makes use of a bicycle, which many people already have, and other inexpensive materials.)

Discuss with students the connection between a country's "economic troubles" and its inability to provide electricity to homes.

Remind students that a power grid system requires lots of money to set up and operate. Power plants are expensive to build and operate. Fuel to run generators add ongoing costs. Stringing hundreds of kilometers of wires on poles or running wires underground adds more costs.

Renato, 16, spent 3 years designing his special Multibike. The <u>contraption</u> looks like a <u>stationary</u> exercise bike. It has wires <u>strung</u> along the frame and a blender strapped to the back. Turning the pedals <u>operates</u> the <u>blender</u>....

The Multibike can work either as a stationary bike or as a bicycle able to travel city streets and country roads. It's made from inexpensive materials, and the user gets exercise while pedaling to operate a machine.

"You pedal the bike, and you can mix any drink you want," Renato said. More importantly, he added, the same <u>concept</u> could be used to (bring light to houses) in <u>remote</u> <u>regions</u> of the rainforest.

From: "Tinkering with the Basic Bike."
Science News for Kids, Aug 27, 2003.

contraption: machine
stationary: not moving
strung: attached
operates: runs

concept: idea
remote: far away from cities
regions: places

(103)

notes:

_____

_____

_____

_____

> What machine does Renato's Multibike provide energy for? <u>Underline</u> your answer.

> What would Renato like his Multibike idea to provide energy for? Circle your answer.

Enrichment

Energy Changes

Describe for students the following setup, which was used in an actual fifth grade classroom to demonstrate how various forms of energy can be transformed into other forms of energy.

A stationary bike with a generator is connected to three spotlights. As a student pedals, the spotlights shine on a solar panel which drives a small fan. The bike also provides power to another set of fans that are mounted to a big tube.

As the fans turn, a ball inside the tube rises. Challenge students to identify all the energy changes involved in this setup. (chemical energy, food; to mechanical energy, pedaling; to electric energy; to light energy; to mechanical energy, both sets of fans; to mechanical energy, moving ball)

Science Background

A generator converts magnetism into electricity. A wire loop is attached to a rod. The rod is made to spin in the magnetic field of a magnet. The spinning can be produced by a hand crank, moving water, wind, or steam. This produces an electric current in the wire. The more rapid the spin of the wire loop, the more electricity is produced.

Check Understanding

Skill: Communicate

Electricity is produced from other forms of energy. What form of energy is used to produce electricity in Renato's electricity bike? (human energy or muscle energy; energy of motion—pedaling)

Connections

Materials electric bill showing kWh

Math To give students an idea of how much energy the Multibike can produce, have them do the following exercise.

Have students look at the electric bill and determine how many kilowatt hours (kWh) of electricity are used each month. Let's say the number is 450 Kwh. That means that the house used 1000 watts, or 1 kilowatt, of power for a total of 450 hours.

Now tell students that the average person can produce 200 watts of power pedaling a generator-equipped bicycle

Challenge students to answer the following question: *If a Multibike produces 200 watts and you need 450 kWh, or 450,000 watt hours, how many hours must you pedal?* (450,000 Watt hours ÷ 200 Watts = 2250 hours)

While this number may seem impossibly great to students, remind them that the energy required to light a rural home in Peru is much less than the energy required to run an American house full of appliances. Also, the standard incandescent bulb used in most American households is far less efficient than an energy-saving bulb. A fluorescent light bulb uses one quarter of the energy used by incandescent bulbs and lasts ten times longer.

Look Back

> **Use what you learned in the reading to fill in the diagram below.**

Energy Source for Multibike

person pedaling the bike

How Energy Is Used

to operate the blender

How Energy *Could Be* Used

light houses

Explore

ENERGY CHANGES

Energy comes in many different forms. Electricity is just one of them. Other forms of energy include light energy and heat energy. When you hear a noise, you are experiencing sound energy. Any object that is moving has energy of motion. Another form of energy is chemical energy, which can be stored in the chemicals found in food.

> **What forms of energy are discussed in the reading?**

Light energy, electrical energy, and energy of motion

Energy can change from any one of these forms to another. For example, a car's engine changes the chemical energy in gasoline into the energy of motion. When you drop a book, its energy of motion changes to sound energy as the book hits the floor with a loud thud.

> **Describe two other examples of energy changing from one form to another.**

Students might mention the chemical energy of food changing to energy of motion in muscles, electricity changing to heat energy on the stove, and so on.

Look Back

After students have completed the diagram, ask a volunteer to name the energy source for the Multibike (person pedaling the bike). **What is the energy source for the person?** (the food the person eats) Lead students to see that food provides people with the energy needed to pedal the bike. **What is the energy source for a cow or a chicken?** (the plants they eat) **What is the energy source for a plant?** (the sun). Help students see that the sun is the ultimate source of energy in this chain.

Explore

Energy Changes

Materials drum, uncooked rice grains

Have students diagram the changes described in the second paragraph (car's engine, dropped book). Tell them to label their diagrams to identify how energy changes at each stage.

To help students see that sound is energy, perform this quick demonstration: Place several grains of rice on a drum. As you beat the top of the drum, the grains will jump up and down. Explain that the skin of the drum moves up and down as you beat it. This motion creates waves of compressed air that move out in all directions. When they strike the eardrums of a person, the person hears a sound.

Explore

GENERATING ELECTRICITY

Look at the following diagram. It shows the different parts of Renato's Multibike. Notice the generator on the frame next to the back wheel. A **generator** is a device that changes the energy of motion into electricity.

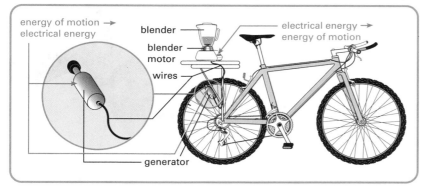

energy of motion → electrical energy

blender

blender motor

wires

electrical energy → energy of motion

generator

The generator has a small knob that presses against the wheel of the bike. As the wheel turns, the knob turns. The generator converts the **energy of motion** of magnets attached to the moving knob into electrical energy. The **electrical energy** travels along the wires to the blender. A motor on the blender uses the electrical energy to turn the blades of the blender.

> As you learned, energy can change from one form to another. Label the point on the Multibike where energy of motion is changed to electrical energy.

> The electrical energy produced by the Multibike is used to power a blender. What does a blender use electrical energy to do? What type of energy does the blender change the electrical energy into?

The electrical energy is used to turn the blades of the blender,

so the electrical energy is changed back to energy of motion.

> Label the point on the Multibike where electrical energy is changed into another form of energy.

Explore

Generating Electricity Make sure students understand the diagram. Point out where the generator is located and how its knob turns as the wheel turns. Tell students that they will learn more about how a generator changes the energy of motion into electricity on the next page.

Have students create a flow chart showing all the energy conversions in the Multibike.

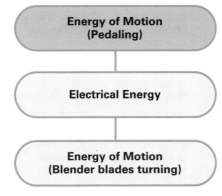

Energy of Motion (Pedaling)

Electrical Energy

Energy of Motion (Blender blades turning)

Point out to students that all the mechanical energy is not converted into electrical energy. Some of the mechanical energy is converted into heat energy, which is not useful in this device. ***Would it be possible to convert the energy of motion from the blender back into electrical energy to light a light bulb?*** (Help students conclude that, since useless heat energy is produced at each conversion, there may not be sufficient electrical energy to light the bulb.)

Assessment

Skill: Concept mapping

Use the following question and task to assess each student's progress.

What two forms of energy do generators produce? (mechanical energy and electrical energy) Have students create a concept map or flow chart to diagram all the energy conversions involved in using a hand-crank generator to light a bulb. As an alternative, have students simply list the conversions. (chemical energy, food eaten and digested; energy of motion, turning crank; electrical energy; light energy, light bulb lighting; heat energy, although it is "wasted" energy)

Review "Find Out" Question

Review the question from the Unit Opener on page 88. Ask: ***How can you use your bike to blend up a tasty smoothie?*** (You can attach a generator to the tires and string wires to the blender. When you pedal, you produce electricity to blend the milkshake.) Have students use what they learned in the chapter to suggest an answer to the question. Use their responses as the basis for a class discussion.

Activity

CRANKING OUT POWER

Can you generate electricity?

What You Need:
• hand-crank generator
• light bulb with stand

Renato Angulo Chu wanted to use his Multibike to bring light to remote villages. You can see for yourself that energy of motion can be used to light a bulb.

What to Do:
1. Attach the clips on the hand-crank generator to the clips on the light bulb stand.
2. Turn the crank slowly. What happens?
3. Now, turn the crank more quickly. What happens?

What Do You See?

> **What happens when you turn the crank of the generator slowly?**

The light bulb lights up.

> **What happens when you turn the crank of the generator more quickly?**

The light bulb lights up even brighter.

> **How is the hand-crank generator like the Multibike?**

Both use energy of motion to produce electrical energy.

106

Activity

Time 20 minutes

Material hand-crank generators, light bulbs with stands

• Hand-crank generators and light bulbs with stands are available from most science supply houses.
• Have students draw a diagram showing how the Multibike and the hand-generator are alike. Diagrams might look something like this.

Turning Object: Knob	Turning Object: Crank shaft
What Makes it Turn: Turning wheel	What Makes it Turn: Turning crank
Appliance Powered: Blender	Appliance Powered: Light bulb

After students have completed the questions on the page, ask: ***How might Renato set up the Multibike to produce light?*** (Lead students to see that he could set it up as a stationary bike and attach a light bulb where the blender was. Also explain that he may be able to store the energy he generates in a battery and then use the battery to power the light bulb later.)

Magic Machine?

Chapter 16

Can a machine run itself?

You are standing at the top of your sloped driveway. You're wearing a pair of in-line skates. You slowly inch forward and suddenly you are zooming downhill. Look out below!

What makes you start moving so fast? The answer is energy. **Energy** is the ability to cause motion or change. Your position when you are at the top of the driveway gives you stored energy. You stored that energy as you walked up the driveway. As you inch down the slope, the force of Earth's gravity sets you in motion. Your stored energy is changed into the energy of motion.

The conversion of stored energy into energy of motion powers more than just skaters on slopes. It can also be used to run machines. In this chapter, you'll read about a man who designed a very unusual machine that he could never get to work.

Before You Read

> **Where does the energy needed to run each of the following machines come from?**

Television	Electrical output
Pencil sharpener	Arm movements
Lawnmower	Gasoline
Flashlight	Batteries

> **What do you do when the energy source of a flashlight runs out?**

You replace the batteries.

SCIENCESAURUS
A STUDENT HANDBOOK
BLUE BOOK

Friction .... p. 274
Forms of
Energy .... p. 285
Energy
Changes ..... p. 286

SC LINKS.
THE WORLD'S A CLICK AWAY

www.scilinks.org
Keyword: Energy
Transfer
Code: GS5D085

Key Idea

Heat energy produced by friction makes the dream of perpetual motion machines impossible.

Focus

- Systems, order, and organization
- Change, constancy, and measurement
- Motions and forces
- Transfer of energy
- Understanding about science and technology
- Science as a human endeavor

Skills and Strategies

- Concept map
- Interpret scientific illustrations
- Communicate
- Apply knowledge

Vocabulary*

Before beginning the chapter, make sure students understand these terms.

- force
- gravity
- machine

* Definitions are in the Glossary on pages 166–172.

Introducing the Chapter

This chapter introduces the idea of a perpetual motion machine—a machine that in theory uses the energy of motion to produce stored energy and stored energy to produce the energy of motion, perpetually.

After students read the introduction, draw a diagram on the board showing their position at the top of the driveway and their position moving down the driveway. Label their top position "stored energy" and their lower position "energy of motion."

Before You Read

Help students as needed to identify the energy source for each of the machines listed. Point out that the pencil sharpener is a manual sharpener. Draw students attention to the fact that machines need energy to run. That energy can come from a person (manual labor), a fuel source (gasoline, oil, coal), electricity (from a power plant or battery), or other source. **Where does the energy needed to turn the blades of a windmill come from?** (wind, or moving air)

More Resources

The following resources are also available from Great Source and NSTA.

SCiLINKS
THE WORLD'S A CLICK AWAY

www.scilinks.org
Keyword: Energy Transfer
Code: GS5D085

Read

Read about a man who invented a machine he hoped would run itself forever.

"Something for Nothing?"

notes:

> What did people use to power the machinery that grinds grain?

a waterwheel

> What causes the waterwheel to turn?

the water flowing downstream

One of the earliest and simplest machines was the waterwheel—a wooden paddlewheel that dips into a fast-running river, so that water flowing downstream makes the wheel go round. For <u>centuries</u> people have attached waterwheels to machinery that can grind grain into flour, or lift water from a well....

Before scientists had figured out the rules about energy, it may have seemed that a waterwheel produced something for nothing. The wheel turns, <u>operating</u> some machine, but the river keeps on running. Go downstream a few hundred yards and it might be flowing just as fast as it was above the wheel.

So it's not surprising that people thought waterwheels could be turned into <u>perpetual motion machines</u>.

This waterwheel is attached to a machine that pumps water to the top of a hill.

centuries: hundreds of years
operating: running

perpetual motion machin
machines that run forever without any outside ener

Science Background

Even though the law of conservation of energy explains why perpetual motion machines can never work, patents for new perpetual motion machines are filed every year with the U.S. patent office.

Read

Paired Reading Draw students' attention to the phrase "rules about energy" at the beginning of the second paragraph. Explain that the "rule" the scientists figured out was that energy comes in many different forms, and it can change from one form to another, but it can never be created or destroyed. The waterwheel was using energy from the running river water to turn. And the river water did, in fact, run slower below the machine. But gravity pulling the water downhill

eventually made it speed up again.

Have students examine the photo of the waterwheel. Explain that as the water flows under the wheel, the wheel turns. An axle attached to the wheel also turns, running a machine that is attached to it. *Where does the energy used to run the machine come from?* (the running water)

Help students make the connection between the diagram of Fludd's machine and the text from the reading that describes how it works. (Students will have underlined this text as part

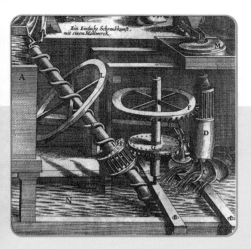

Around 1618 an Englishman named Robert Fludd came up with an idea for a waterwheel that would run without stopping. It seemed perfectly simple. Fludd arranged for water to flow out of an upper tank, drive a wheel around, and collect in a lower tank. Then he attached a pump (in the form of a big screw) to the waterwheel, to push water from the lower tank back to the upper one again. This arrangement, he thought, would run itself forever. What's more, it could also drive a mill to grind grain. But somehow, Fludd could never quite manage to make his perpetual motion engine work. Still, he couldn't see why it *shouldn't* work, so he and other inventors kept on trying. Not realizing they were up against a fundamental problem, they thought their machines would work if only they could get the designs *just right*....

From: "Something for Nothing?" *Muse* magazine, May/June 2003.

drive: move
fundamental: very important

notes:

_____

_____

_____

_____

_____

_____

_____

_____

_____

_____

_____

_____

> Underline the sentences that describe how Robert Fludd's machine was set up.

109

Differentiating Instruction

Interpersonal Have small groups of students participate in a discussion of the reading. Why do they think Fludd's machine was never able to work right? Have students propose their ideas and discuss them as a group. Then have students write up their final ideas in the form of a short report or bulleted list. You may choose to have them present their reports or lists to the class.

After students have completed the chapter, have them return to their reports and compare what they know now about why the machine wouldn't work and what they thought originally.

of the Notes questions.) As you or a volunteer reads the passage aloud, have students trace the path of the water on the diagram.

Once students have had a chance to examine the diagram, ask: *Do you see any reason why the machine wouldn't work from looking at this diagram?* (Students answers will vary. Accept and discuss all reasonable answers for now.)

Remind students of the machines listed in the Before You Read section and the energy sources they used to

run. Then have students note the title of the article from which the reading came ("Something for Nothing?"). *What do you think the author means by "something for nothing"?* (Accept all answers.) Help students see that a machine that ran itself with no added energy would be doing work for "free."

Check Understanding
Skill: Communicate
What machine did Fludd base his design for a perpetual motion machine on? (waterwheels in moving river water)

Connections

Language Arts Like many other scientific words, the word "energy" has come to be used as part of everyday language. People who are very active, talkative, or playful are described as having a lot of energy.

Have students think of a person they consider as having a lot of energy. Then have them compose a list of words or phrases that describe how that person acts and what makes them energetic (running around, jumping, laughing, singing, skipping, throwing balls, making things happen). Then ask students to compare these words and phrases with the definition of "energy" in the scientific sense. (The ability to cause motion or change.) *How does this energetic person cause motion or change?* (Help students see the connection between the colloquial and scientific senses of the word.)

Look Back

> Arrange the following three phrases to describe how water cycles through Robert Fludd's waterwheel machine. Look at the picture of Robert Fludd's machine on the previous page to help you. One has been done for you.

Screw turning and pushing water up
Water sitting in raised tank
Wheel turning due to flowing water

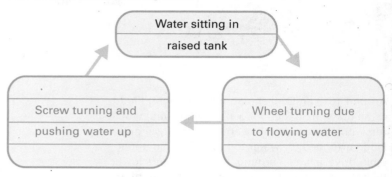

> **How is the water in Fludd's machine like a flowing river that turns a waterwheel?**
Like water flowing downstream in the river, the water in Fludd's machine turns a waterwheel when it flows from one tank to the other.

> **Why did Fludd think that his machine should be able to run without stopping?**
Because the water just kept moving through the machine; water flowing from the top tank moved the wheel, the wheel powered the pump, and the pump moved the water up to the upper tank again.

> **Could his machine *really* run without stopping?**
No, he couldn't get the machine to work.

Look Back

To help students see that Fludd meant the three diagram stages to form a never-ending cycle, ask: *Where does the cycle begin? Where does it end?* (Help students see that there is no beginning and end; the water is meant to cycle through the machine continually.)

Once students have completed the Explore exercise on page 111, have them return to the diagram here and label each of the three boxes "stored energy" or "energy of motion" to describe the energy of the water at each stage. (Top box = stored energy, bottom two = energy of motion.)

Remind students that Fludd's machine was inspired by river-driven waterwheels that were used to grind grain. Encourage students to think about how Fludd's machine was similar to and different from the river waterwheel. *What is different about the water in Fludd's machine and the water in a river?* (The river water ran past the waterwheel and kept going, but there was always more water coming down; Fludd's machine reused the same water, lifting it back up to the upper tank over and over.) Help students see that lifting the water back to the upper tank requires energy, energy not required by the river waterwheel setup.

Explore

ENERGY OF MOTION AND STORED ENERGY

Moving objects have **energy of motion**. Objects that are up high have **stored energy**. The two forms of energy can change back and forth, forming a sort of cycle. For example, when you let go of a ball, it falls and its stored energy is changed into energy of motion. When it bounces back up, some of its energy of motion is changed back into stored energy. Then it falls again, and so on.

Think about the energy in Robert Fludd's machine.

> **What type of energy does the flowing water have?**

Energy of motion

> **What type of energy does the water sitting in the upper tank of Fludd's machine have?**

Stored energy

> **How do these two kinds of energy change back and forth in Fludd's machine?**

As water moves from the upper tank to the lower tank, stored energy is

changed into the energy of motion. As water is pumped back to the

upper tank, energy of motion is changed back into stored energy. Then

the water moves to the lower tank again, and so on.

(111)

Energy Changes

Materials rubber ball, graph paper, pencil

- Have students work in pairs or small groups.
- Distribute a rubber ball to each group. Have students work on a hard surface.
- Have students toss the ball with a slight forward motion from shoulder high and watch the path it takes before settling to the ground. (The ball will bounce back to an ever decreasing height.)
- Have students draw the approximate path of the bouncing ball on a sheet of graph paper. It should look like this:

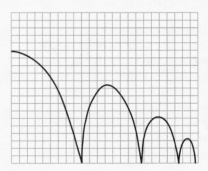

- Challenge students to label one point on their drawings where the energy of motion is decreasing (left side of each peak) and one point where it is increasing (right side of each peak). Then have them label one point where stored energy is decreasing (right side of each peak) and one point where it is increasing (left side of each peak).

Science Background

All moving objects possess the energy of motion, or kinetic energy, whether they are set into motion by the force of gravity or by other forces. Water standing still at a high elevation, say in a mountain lake, possesses stored energy, or potential energy. As the water moves down a river from the lake, some of its potential energy is converted to kinetic energy.

Explore

Energy of Motion and Stored Energy
Invite students to compare the conversions between stored energy and the energy of motion in the bouncing ball and Fludd's machine.

Stored energy
Bouncing ball: unmoving held in hand ball above the ground

Fludd's machine: water in upper tank

Energy of motion
Bouncing ball: ball moving up or down

Fludd's machine: water moving down to lower tank or up to upper tank

Then ask students to think about what eventually happens to a bouncing ball. ***Does a dropped ball bounce forever? What happens?*** (Students should know that a dropped ball bounces ever lower until it stops and rolls along the ground to a stop.) Have them look for any connection between this fact and the fact that Fludd's machine could not keep running by itself. Accept all ideas for now.

Assessment

Skill: Communicate

Use the following question to assess each student's progress.

Why can't perpetual motion machines ever work? (Because some of the energy of motion is converted to heat energy due to friction, the machines can't produce as much energy as they use. So they will eventually soon stop running.)

Review "Find Out" Question

Review the question from the Unit Opener on page 88. ***What do all machines need in order to run?*** (energy) Have students use what they learned in the chapter to suggest an answer to the question. Use their responses as the basis for a class discussion.

Explore

IT'S FRICTION'S FAULT

Here is how Robert Fludd imagined that his machine would work.

Fludd could never get his machine to work.

In an imaginary perpetual motion machine, energy flows in a cycle that never ends. To be a perpetual motion machine, Robert Fludd's machine would have had to produce all the energy it used. That means that all of the energy of motion produced by the machine would have to be "recycled" back into the machine to keep the machine running. No energy could escape from the cycle, or the machine would eventually stop running.

Unfortunately, perpetual motion machines *never* work—even when the designs are "just right." That's because some energy is always escaping from a machine as it runs. Most energy escaping from machines leaves because of friction. **Friction** is a force that makes it hard for two surfaces to slide past one another. When moving parts slide past each other, the friction produces heat energy. The heat energy does not help keep the machine moving. Instead, it is lost to the air around the machine.

> **Look at the perpetual motion machine above. Circle the places where you think there would be a loss of energy because of friction.**

> **Why couldn't Robert Fludd's machine run itself forever?**
>
> Some energy would escape because of friction as the machine ran. So, the machine could not produce as much energy as it used.

Explore

It's Friction's Fault After students look at the diagram and read the first paragraph, explain that exactly the same amount of energy was needed to pump the water back into the upper tank as had been gained from it moving to the lower tank. Have students write "+ energy of motion" next to the descending water on the diagram of Fludd's machine. Have them write "– energy of motion" next to the ascending water on the diagram.

Where else is energy being used in Fludd's machine? (Students may note that a mill is grinding grain on the side.) Have them write "– energy of motion" next to the mill on the diagram.

Have students demonstrate friction by rubbing their hands together. ***What do you feel?*** (Students should report that they feel heat.)

After students circle the places on the diagram where they think friction would occur, ask: ***Why do you think friction would occur here?*** (Students

should explain that friction would occur anywhere two surfaces are sliding past each other.)

Finally, have students write "– energy of motion" next to all places where friction would occur. Point out that energy is never "lost." But, as in the case of friction in the operation of a water wheel, in can be converted into a form of energy (heat) that is not useful. In other words, some of the useful energy of motion is converted into useless energy of heat.

Desert Refrigerator

Chapter 17

How can you keep your lunch cool without a refrigerator?

Imagine that you are hiking on a hot day. You have your lunch with you—a turkey and lettuce sandwich and a carton of milk. When you sit down for a quick lunch break, you find that your milk is warm and your lettuce is wilted. Yuck!

How could you keep your lunch cool? Remember, you're on a hike, so there's no ice and no electricity to run a refrigerator. Any ideas?

In this chapter, you'll read about a teacher in Africa who solved a similar problem. He found a way to make a cooler out of local desert materials.

Before You Read

Keeping food and drink cool while hiking may be tricky. It's much easier at home.

> **How do we keep our food and drink cool at home?**

Students will probably name refrigerators.

> **How do we keep our food and drink cool when we go places, like on a picnic?**

Students may mention coolers and ice.

> **How do we keep our bodies cool at home and in the car?**

Students may mention fans and air conditioners.

SCIENCESAURUS
A STUDENT HANDBOOK
BLUE BOOK

Heat
Energy .... p. 289
Transfer of Heat
Energy .... p. 292

SCiLINKS.
THE WORLD'S A CLICK AWAY

www.scilinks.org
Keyword: Heat Transfer
Code: GS5D090

(113)

Key Idea

People in hot, rural areas can use evaporation to keep perishable items fresh.

Focus

• Systems, order, and organization
• Change, constancy, and measurement
• Light, heat, electricity, and magnetism
• Transfer of energy
• Science and technology in local challenges

Skills and Strategies

• Make and use scientific illustrations
• Infer
• Conduct investigations
• Generate ideas
• Design an experiment
• *Compare and contrast (TG)*
• *Communicate (TG)*

Vocabulary*

Before beginning the chapter, make sure students understand these terms.

• electricity
• heat energy
• temperature

* Definitions are in the Glossary on pages 166–172.

Introducing the Chapter

Materials cotton ball, water

This chapter examines how evaporative cooling can be used to keep produce fresh in a desert environment.

To get students thinking about evaporation and cooling, have students remember a time when they got out of a swimming pool on a sunny day and felt really cold. *Why did you feel so cold? What made you warmer?* (Students should relate that they felt cold because they were wet, but drying off with a towel made them feel warmer.)

Now walk around the classroom and rub a wet cotton ball on the back of each student's right hand. Then have them blow on the back of both their left and right hands. *What difference do you notice?* (Students should report that the wet hand felt colder than the dry one when they blew on it.)

Before You Read

In order to generate the greatest variety of ideas, you may choose to have students answer this question as part of a class discussion. After the discussion, ask: *How does having wet skin or clothing affect the way you feel on a hot day?* (Students should say that wet skin or clothing makes them feel cooler.)

More Resources

The following resources are also available from Great Source and NSTA.

SCI LINKS.
THE WORLD'S A CLICK AWAY

www.scilinks.org
Keyword: Heat Transfer
Code: GS5D090

Read

Read about a man in Africa who invented a "desert refrigerator."

"Cool Pots"

notes:

In <u>hot climates</u>, fruits and vegetables begin to <u>rot in a few days.</u> Refrigeration gives you a headstart in the race against <u>spoilage</u>, but what if <u>you don't have electricity, much less a fridge?</u> A <u>Nigerian</u> teacher, Mohammed Bah Abba, won an award for a simple invention designed to keep food cool without electricity or expensive parts.

 <u>Underline</u> the two problems identified in the paragraph on this page.

114

hot climates: areas of the world where the weather is usually warm

spoilage: spoiling, or rotting
Nigerian: from the African country of Nigeria

Science Background

Earthenware pots have been used for cooking and storing water in West Africa since ancient times. Today, aluminum cooking pots have largely taken the place of clay ones, but water is still stored in clay pots as evaporative cooling keeps the water cool and fresh.

Read

Individual Reading
Materials world map

After students read the first paragraph, have them look at the world map and locate Nigeria. (Nigeria is in West Africa.) Point out that northern Nigeria is part of a region known as the Sahel—a semi-arid zone just south of the Sahara desert.

Have students look at the picture of Mohammed and his pots in the photo. ***What do you notice about the land where Mohammed lives?*** (Students should notice the desert-like conditions behind Mohammed.) Point out that rainfall is low in the Sahel, and temperatures are high. ***According to the reading, what's the connection between high temperatures and food spoilage?*** (In hot climates, fruits and vegetables rot quickly.)

If students are having trouble visualizing the description of how the clay pot refrigerator is put together, have them look at the diagram on page 116.

Here's how it works: you put fruit, veggies, or other <u>perishable</u> food into a clay pot that's nestled inside another pot. On top of the food, you lay a damp cloth, and between the two pots, there's a layer of wet sand. As hot air dries the outer pot, it draws water from the sand. Water continuously <u>evaporates</u> from the nestled pots, carrying away heat energy and thereby cooling the inside. The <u>principle</u> is similar to the way the evaporation of sweat cools the body. As long as you keep the sand and cloth damp, the evaporation and cooling continue.

The simplicity of this invention makes it <u>practical</u> for poor people in hot climates. Inside the clay pot cooler, fruits and veggies last several weeks, instead of a few days. According to inventor Abba, the cooler is already having an <u>impact</u> on people's lives. Since it was introduced in villages in <u>semi-arid</u> northern Nigeria, more girls have enrolled in school. What's the connection? Produce from family farm plots lasts much longer than before. That means that families don't need to send girls out every day to sell produce, but can send them to school instead. And that's really cool!

From: "A Cooler for the Sahara" *A Moment of Science*, Radio Station WFIU and Indiana University.

perishable: able to rot
evaporates: turns from liquid to gas
principle: idea

practical: well-designed
impact: effect
semi-arid: almost desert

notes:

> How do you make sure that the coolers continue to stay cool on the inside?

The cloth and sand must

remain damp.

> How long does food last inside the cooler compared to outside the cooler?

Food lasts several weeks

inside the cooler, but only

a few days outside the cooler.

(115)

Differentiating Instruction

Logical/Mathematical Have students write an outline covering the main points of the reading. The outline should identify the problem described in the reading, explain the solution and how it works, and finally summarize its impact. A sample outline might look like this:

1) Problem
  a) Rotting food
    i) Hot climate
    ii) No electricity for refrigerator
2) Solution
  a) Clay-pot cooler
    i) Small clay pot inside larger clay pot
    ii) Wet sand between pots
    iii) Food inside small pot
    iv) Damp cloth on top of food
  b) Cooling by evaporation
    i) Hot air dries outer pot
    ii) Water drawn from sand
    iii) Evaporating water carries away heat energy
    iv) Inside of pot cooled
3) Impact
  a) Food lasts several weeks rather than several days
  b) More girls go to school
    i) Don't need to sell produce every day

Draw students' attention to the sentence "The principle is similar to the way the evaporation of sweat cools the body." Remind students of the cotton ball experiment you did with them as part of the introduction. **How do you think that sweat cools the body?** (Students should infer that the body sweats when it is hot because heat energy is carried away when sweat evaporates from the skin.)

Why is it important to keep the sand and cloth damp in the desert cooler? (Because it is the evaporation of the water that carries heat energy away and cools the inner pot.)

Check Understanding

Skill: Compare and contrast
How is the human body's method for staying cool like the desert cooler's method for staying cool? (Both use evaporation to carry away heat energy.)

Connections

Math Have students use the following rainfall data for northern Nigeria to create a bar graph. The months should appear along the x-axis. The y-axis should show either the mm or inch increments.

Month	Rainfall (mm)	Rainfall (inches)
January	0.1	0.0
February	0.5	0.0
March	1.7	0.1
April	8.9	0.4
May	63.5	2.5
June	116.0	4.6
July	199.9	7.9
August	287.2	11.3
September	123.7	4.9
October	11.9	0.5
November	0.0	0.0
December	0.1	0.0
Year Total	826.1	32.5

(Data for Kano Nigeria, average for 993 months between 1905 and 1988. Worldclimate.com

Once students have completed their bar graphs, ask: *When is northern Nigeria's rainy season?* (June–Sept.) *When is its dry season?* (Oct–April) Have students conclude that northern Nigeria has a very long dry season when little or no rain falls.

Collect average rainfall data for your area. (Go to worldclimate.com) Have students graph that data and compare it to the northern Nigeria data.

Look Back

Tell students to look back at the reading as needed to help them label the diagram.

Explore

Movement of Heat Energy Review with students the process of evaporation. Draw the following diagram on the board:

Go over each part of the diagram with the class. Focus on the fact that heat energy is required in order for liquid to evaporate. *Where does the heat energy needed to evaporate the water from the wet sand come from?* (from the heat inside the cooler) Lead students to conclude that evaporation cools because it removes heat from its environment.

In the last question, help students see that without water, evaporation would not take place. The water moves through the clay pots and then evaporates. And without evaporation, there would be no cooling. So, without water, the cooler would not work.

Look Back

> Look at the diagram below. It shows what Mohammed Bah Abba's clay-pot cooler looks like on the inside. Use what you learned in the reading to label the diagram with the following terms:

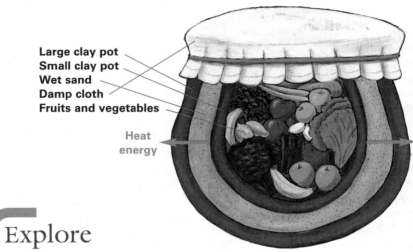

Large clay pot
Small clay pot
Wet sand
Damp cloth
Fruits and vegetables

Heat energy

Explore

MOVEMENT OF HEAT ENERGY

When water **evaporates**—turns from liquid to gas— it absorbs heat energy from its surroundings. As the evaporated water is carried away by the air moving past the pot, the heat energy is also carried away.

> Draw arrows on the diagram above to show the movement of heat energy between the cooler and the outside air.

> Would the cooler work without water (wet sand)? Explain.

No, water is needed to cool the inside of the cooler. As water evaporates from the outside pot, it draws heat energy away from the inside, cooling it. Without water, nothing would evaporate.

116

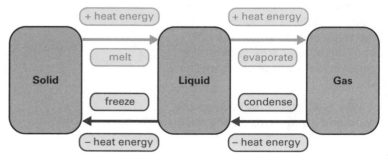

Activity

CLAY-POT COOLER

Make your own "desert refrigerator."

What You Need:

- clay pot
- smaller clay pot, same shape
- sand
- water
- dish towel
- thermometer
- lettuce leaves

What to Do:

1. Place the smaller clay pot inside the larger one.
2. Pour sand in the space between the pots until it is almost to the top.
3. Gently pour water over the sand until it is all wet.
4. Place a few lettuce leaves in the cooler. Cover the cooler with a damp dish towel.
5. Set the cooler outside in a shady spot. Place a few more lettuce leaves on the ground beside the cooler.
6. Use a thermometer to take the temperature of the air inside and outside the cooler. Record the temperatures in the chart below.
7. An hour later, remove the dish towel and take the temperature of the air inside and outside the cooler again. Record the new temperatures in the chart below.
8. Observe the lettuce leaves. Record your observations below.

What Do You See?

> **How do the leaves inside the cooler look compared to the leaves outside the cooler?**

They are not wilted. The lettuce leaves outside the cooler are wilted.

Time of Temperature Measurement	Temperature Inside Cooler (°C)	Temperature Outside Cooler (°C)
Right away	the same as outside temperature	the same as inside temperature
One Hour Later	lower than outside temperature	higher than inside temperature

117

To Heat or Not to Heat

Have students investigate the effect of insulators on heat transfer.

Time 30–40 minutes

Materials

For each student group:

- 3 beakers
- 3 thermometers
- warm water
- paper towel
- cloth rag

Procedure

Have students work in groups of three, and give them the following instructions.

1. Fill each beaker with warm water up to the 150 mL mark. Take the temperature of the water in each beaker and record it in a chart.
2. Wrap the outside of one beaker with a paper towel. Wrap another beaker with a cloth rag. Leave the third beaker unwrapped.
3. Wait for the temperature of the water in each beaker to drop by 10 degrees. For each beaker, record the time taken for the 10-degree drop in temperature.

Ask the class the following questions:

- **In which beaker did the water cool down the fastest?** (the unwrapped beaker)
- **In which beaker did the water cool down the slowest?** (the beaker wrapped in a cloth rag)

Activity

Time 20 minutes, then 20 more minutes an hour later

Materials clay pot, smaller clay pot (same shape), sand, water, dish towel, thermometer, lettuce leaves

- Do this activity on a hot, dry day for best results.
- Have students assemble their coolers outside so that clean up is easier.
- Do not use iceberg lettuce as it does not wilt easily.
- Terra cotta pots from a garden supply store are inexpensive and work well. *Do not use glazed pots.*

- Show students how to use a thermometer properly. Remind them to wait for the temperature to stabilize before taking a reading.
- Have students take the initial cooler reading right away, before evaporative cooling has a chance to start working.
- Consider having one group create a cooler with sand but no water. Compare observations and data of this cooler with that of the other coolers. (While this cooler may provide some insulation, it will not be able to reduce the inside temperature significantly.) *What can students conclude?* (That water is needed to reduce the inside temperature of the pots.)
- Challenge students to predict how many days their lettuce will stay fresh inside the clay-pot cooler. The coolers should stay outside, but not in direct sunlight.

Assessment

Skill: Communicate

Use the following question to assess each student's progress.

How does Mohammed Bah Abba's desert cooler remove heat from the area where the fruits and vegetables are stored? (It uses evaporation to draw heat energy away from the inner pot.)

Review "Find Out" Question

Review the question from the Unit Opener on page 88. ***How can you keep your food cool in the middle of the desert?*** (Using two clay pots and some wet sand. As water evaporates from the wet sand, the inner pot is cooled.) Have students use what they learned in the chapter to suggest an answer to the question. Use their responses as the basis for a class discussion.

Explore

THE RIGHT TECHNOLOGY

Technology is any tool or product that helps people solve a problem and that was created using scientific knowledge. Refrigerators are a kind of technology we use to keep our food cold. Refrigerators work well for us because most homes in the United States have electricity.

> **What problem were the people of Nigeria facing?**
>
> Fruits and vegetables were spoiling because they had no refrigeration.

> **What technology did Mohammed Bah Abba use to solve the problem?**
>
> clay-pot coolers

> **How was the technology he used a good choice for the area where it was used?**
>
> The people there are poor. Clay pots are cheap. There is no electricity in the villages, but the coolers do not need electricity.

Explore

COMPARING TECHNOLOGIES

Have you ever used a plastic cooler filled with ice to keep your food cool on a picnic? Without the ice, the cooler probably wouldn't be as useful. How is a plastic cooler different than the clay pot cooler described in the reading?

> **Design an experiment that tests how well each cooler works. Describe your experiment below.**
>
> Students might describe an experiment that involves placing lettuce in both coolers and comparing temperatures inside each cooler an hour later.

Explore

The Right Technology Remind students that clay is a type of soil. Point out that Nigeria has lots of soil with a high clay content. It also has many sandy areas. **Why are clay and sand good materials to use for the desert cooler?** (These materials are easily found in Nigeria and don't have to be purchased.)

Students may be interested to know that, in order to teach people in other villages about his cooler, Mohammed Bah Abba wrote a play and had a

drama troop perform it. He then brought a videotape of the performance around to different villages and used a generator and a projector to show the play on a wall. Many people in the villages of northern Nigeria are illiterate, but this system allowed people to learn about the cooler without having to read about it.

Explore

Comparing Technologies Have students write up a plan for their experiments. The plans should include a materials list, a hypothesis, a list of procedures to follow, and data charts for recording data collected. Have students perform the experiments and record their data. Then have them analyze their data and decide which cooler worked best.

Light Tricks

When is seeing *not* believing?

If you've ever been to a magic show, you may know that light and mirrors can be used to play tricks on the audience. Both the "saw-the-lady-in-half" and "floating head" tricks are created by fooling your eye into believing it sees something that isn't really there.

Light can play tricks in nature, too. In this chapter, you will learn about two of these tricks.

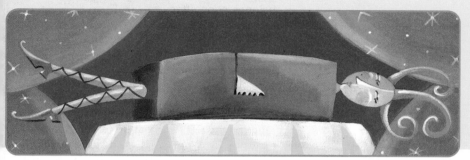

Before You Read

Some objects are dull. Others are shiny.

> **Can you name three different kinds of objects that are shiny?**

Students may name metallic objects, mirrors, objects with high gloss paint, and so on.

> **Based on your observations, what do you think makes something "shiny"?**

Students may note the fact that shiny things are smooth, made of a reflective material, or silver in color.

SCIENCESAURUS
A STUDENT HANDBOOK
BLUE BOOK

Light .... p. 309

SCLINKS
THE WORLD'S A CLICK AWAY

www.scilinks.org
Keyword:
Reflection and
Refraction
Code: GS5D095

(119)

Unit 3 Physical Science
Chapter 18

Key Idea

Reflection and refraction are two different behaviors of light.

Focus

- Systems, order, and organization
- Properties of objects and materials
- Light, heat, electricity, and magnetism
- Science and technology in local challenges

Skills and Strategies

- Infer
- Draw conclusions
- Conduct investigations
- Interpret scientific illustrations
- *Communicate (TG)*
- *Compare and contrast (TG)*

Vocabulary*

Before beginning the chapter, make sure students understand these terms.

- brain
- light

* Definitions are in the Glossary on pages 166–172.

Introducing the Chapter

This chapter covers the topics of reflection and refraction—two behaviors of light. To get students thinking about light and its role in how we see, ask: ***Why can't you see anything in a completely dark room?*** (Students will likely respond that you can't see because the light is not on.) Lead students to conclude that light bouncing off objects allows us to see them. There is no light to see by in a *completely* dark room.

Before You Read

Materials polished metal spoons

To help students answer the second question, distribute a polished metal spoon to each student or group. Encourage them to look for their reflections in the spoons. Then have them turn the spoons in the light—either artificial or sunlight—and see if they can see the light source in the spoon.

What makes the spoon shiny? (Students might suggest that the spoon is made of metal, which is smooth and shiny.) ***What makes a mirror shiny?*** (Students may say that it is smooth and made of glass.) Point out that mirrors are simply pieces of glass with a highly reflective metallic coating on one side.

More Resources

The following resources are also available from Great Source and NSTA.

SCIENCESAURUS
A STUDENT HANDBOOK
BLUE BOOK

SCLINKS.
THE WORLD'S A CLICK AWAY

www.scilinks.org
Keyword: Reflection and Refraction
Code: GS5D095

✎ Write to Learn

Journal entry Have students write a journal entry from Karana's diary that explains in the first person how she first discovered that the abalone shells reflected light and how she might use that property to scare away the gulls.

⌐Read

Karana is a Native American girl living alone on an island. Her only companion is Rontu, a wild dog. Karana lives on dried meat from shellfish called abalones.

"Catching the Sun"

notes:

> What do you think scared the gulls away?

the brightness of the shells

catching the sunlight

I gathered two more canoeloads of abalones soon after that, mostly the sweet red ones, which I cleaned and carried to the house. Along the south part of the fence where the sun shone most of the day, I built long shelves out of branches and put the meat up to dry. Abalones are larger than your hand and twice as thick when fresh, but they shrink small in the sun so you have to dry many.

In the old days on the island there were children to keep away the gulls, which would rather feast on abalones than anything else. In one morning, if the meat was left unguarded, they could fly off with a month's harvest.

At first, whenever I went to the spring or to the beach, I left Rontu behind to chase them off, but he did not like this and howled all the time I was gone. Finally I tied strings to some of the abalone shells and hung them from poles. The insides of the shells are bright and catch the sun and they turn one way and another in the wind. After that I had little trouble with the gulls.

From: *Island of the Blue Dolphins*, by Scott O'Dell.

canoeloads: canoes full
abalones: a type of shellfish
harvest: catch

120

⌐Read

Materials abalone shells

Independent Reading Point out to students that drying meat is a way of preserving it. Karana dried the large quantity of abalone meat so that she could eat it for months to come. *Where did Karana place the abalone shells to dry?* (Along the south part of the fence, where the sun shone most of the day.) Remind students that, in the northern hemisphere, the sun shines mainly from the south.

Why else was it important that the sun shone on the abalones most of the day? (The sun also reflected off the abalone shells and kept the gulls away.) Show students the abalone shells you brought in. Have them come up with individual words to describe the physical properties of the shell lining. (shiny, pearly, smooth, silky, iridescent, sparkly, and so on) Write the list of words on the board.

How do you think the light bouncing off of the shells tricked the gulls? (Students may suggest that it looked like the light was coming from the moving shells. This light probably scared the gulls into thinking the shells were moving and potentially dangerous.)

Look Back

> **What problem did Karana face?**

The gulls were trying to eat the abalone meat.

> **How did she use light to solve her problem?**

She hung the abalone shells from poles. The insides of the shells caught the sunlight and scared the gulls away.

Explore

REFLECTED LIGHT

Most of the light around us comes from the sun. We can also make light using electricity and light bulbs.

Light travels in straight lines until it hits something. Some of the light is absorbed by the object it hits, and some is **reflected**, or bounced back. You can see an object because some of the light it reflects travels to your eyes. In the diagram at right, you can see how light from a light bulb travels in a straight line until it is reflected by an object. The viewer can see the light reflected by the object.

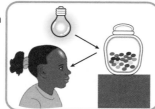

Certain objects reflect more light than others. The material on the inside of abalone shells reflects light so well that it looks like the light is actually coming from the shell itself.

> **In the diagram at right, draw the path that sunlight takes when it is reflected off the abalone shells and into the bird's eyes.**

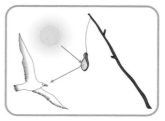

 121

Look Back

After students have answered the second question, ask: **What property of the abalone shells allowed them to scare the gulls away?** (They were shiny and light bounced off them. The light scared the gulls.) **Could Karana have hung sticks instead of abalone shells to scare away the gulls?** (Students should realize that, while they may make noises that could scare the gulls, sticks are not shiny and would not reflect light as the abalone shells did.)

Explore

Reflected Light You may choose to have students complete the *NSTA Activity* on page 87B before drawing the path of the reflected light in the lower box. This activity shows students that light rays reflect off of a surface at the same angle they strike the surface.

Check Understanding

Skill: Communicate

What behavior of light allows you to see objects? (reflection—when light reflects off of an object and into our eyes, you see that object.)

Differentiating Instruction

Visual/Spatial Have students create a sketch of the scene described in the reading. All sketches should include the following: Mafatu in his canoe, ocean water and ocean bottom, black coral reef wall, hidden octopus, and knife on sandy ocean bottom under edge of staghorn.

NSTA Activity

Bending Light

Time 15–20 minutes

Materials

For each student pair or group:
- drinking glass, empty
- drinking glass, half-full of water
- pencil

Procedure

1. Place the pencil in the empty glass. Draw what the pencil looks like from the top and the side.

2. Place the pencil in the glass of water. Draw what the pencil looks like from the top and the side.

Ask the class the following question:

- **What ideas do you have for the difference you see between the two drawings?** (Answers will vary.)

Tell students they will learn more about why the pencil appears broken in the activity on the next page.

Read

Independent Reading As students read the passage, encourage them to look for evidence of reflection. ("It spiraled rapidly, catching the sunlight as it dropped down..." and "There it lay, gleaming palely.") Tell students that Mafatu's knife was carved from an old whale bone. **What color is bone?** (white) Point out that white objects reflect light better than similar objects of different colors.

Read

Mafatu is a boy stranded on a desert island. One day, Mafatu accidentally drops his only knife into the water. He stares down at the water, trying to decide what to do.

"So Very Near, and Yet..."

notes:

> Why was Mafatu scared to get his knife?

He had never dived that deep, it was dark, and there was a giant octopus living there.

> What made it hard for Mafatu to tell how far away his knife was?

The clarity of the water confused all scale of distance.

With dismay the boy watched it descend. It spiraled rapidly, catching the sunlight as it dropped down, down to the sandy bottom. And there it lay, just under the edge of a branching staghorn. Mafatu eyed it uncertainly. His knife—the knife he had labored so hard to shape.... He knew what he ought to do: he should dive and retrieve it. To make another knife so fine would take days. Without it he was seriously handicapped. He *must* get his knife! But...

The reef-wall looked dark and forbidding in the fading light. Its black holes were the home of the giant *feké*—the octopus.... The boy drew back in sudden panic. He had never dived as deep as this. It might be even deeper than he thought, for the clarity of the water confused all scale of distance. The knife looked so very near, and yet...There it lay, gleaming palely.

From: *Call It Courage*, by Armstrong Sperry.

descend: sink
branching staghorn: part of a coral reef

confused all scale of distance: made it hard to tell how far away an object was

122

Draw students' attention to the fact that Mafatu was above water while the knife was beneath the water. **How do you think the fact that the knife was under water affected how it appeared to Mafatu above water?** (Answers will vary. Students may know from experience that objects look slightly different under water.)

Have students share any experiences they may have had with diving for objects under water. **Have you ever dived to the bottom of the pool to retrieve a sunken object? Were you surprised by how deep the object actually was?** (Allow students to recount their experiences with diving for submerged objects.)

Look Back

> **How far away did the knife *look* to Mafatu?**

"so very near"

> **How far away did Mafatu think the knife might *actually* be?**

deeper than it looked, deeper than he thought

> **Mafatu explains that the water made it hard to tell how far away the knife really was. Based on your answers above, do you think the water made the knife look closer than it really was or farther away than it really was?**

Students should conclude that the water must have made the knife look
closer than it really was.

Activity

LIGHT TRICK

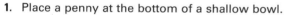

What You Need:
- shallow bowl
  (not see-through)
- penny
- water

1. Place a penny at the bottom of a shallow bowl.
2. Stand a few feet away from the bowl. The penny should be just hidden from view by the sides of the bowl.
3. Now fill the bowl with water. Stand in the same place you did before.

> **Can you see the penny now?**

yes

(123)

Connections

Materials research materials on free diving and SCUBA diving

Physical Education Have students research and report on the difference between free diving and SCUBA diving. (Free diving is done without special breathing equipment. The diver simply holds his or her breath for the duration of the dive. SCUBA diving involves the use of special breathing equipment known as SCUBA gear. SCUBA stands for "self-contained underwater-breathing apparatus."

The basic parts of SCUBA gear include tanks of pressurized gas (oxygen mixed with an inert gas), hoses, and a regulator that brings the pressurized gas to the same pressure as that of the surrounding water, which increases with depth. SCUBA gear allows divers to stay underwater for longer periods of time.)

Invite a volunteer to report on Tanya Streeter, a female free diver who holds the women's record for free diving at 160 m (524.8 ft), a dive she performed in August 2002. This was the men's *and* women's world record for two months, until Frenchman Loic Leferme dove to 162 m (531.4 ft) on October of 2002.

Look Back

Have students look back at the reading to answer the first two questions. **How do you think Mafatu knew that the knife might be deeper than he thought?** (Students should infer from the sentence "He had never dived as deep as this..." that Mafatu had dived many times before and was familiar with how the depth of underwater objects could be deceiving.)

Activity

Time 10–15 minutes

Materials shallow bowl (not see-through), penny, water, pitcher (optional), masking tape (optional)

- Set up a distribution station for materials. You may choose to fill a pitcher with water for students to pour from. To keep the penny from moving, you may want to attach it to the bottom of the bowl with a piece of clay.
- You may want to have students mark the place where they are standing

with masking tape so that they are sure to return to the same spot.

- When students have finished the activity, ask: **Why do you think you could see the penny with the water in the bowl?** (Accept all answers for now. Students may make the connection between Mafatu's knife appearing closer to the surface than it actually was and the penny appearing higher in the bowl once the water was added.) Tell students that they will learn how this trick works on the next page.

Assessment

Skill: Compare and contrast

Use the following question to assess each student's progress.

How are reflection and refraction alike? How are they different? (Both are behaviors of light rays. Reflection is the bouncing back of light rays from a surface. Refraction is the bending of light rays as they move from air to water, or vice versa.)

Review "Find Out" Question

Review the question from the Unit Opener on page 88. *How can light trick your eye?* (It can make you think it is coming from one source when in fact it's coming from another, which is caused by reflection. And it can make objects appear closer to the surface of the water than they really are, which is caused by refraction.) Have students use what they learned in the chapter to suggest an answer to the question. Use their responses as the basis for a class discussion.

Explore

REFRACTED LIGHT

Look at a diagram below. It shows how light rays reflect off of an underwater object and travel to a viewer's eye.

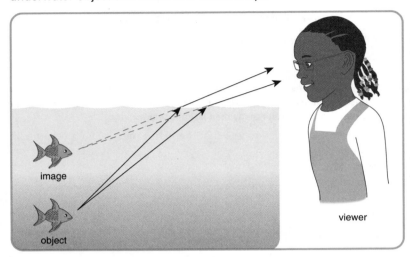

image

object

viewer

Light rays reflecting off the object are **refracted** as they leave the water. That means that they change direction slightly. When the rays enter your eye, your brain "thinks" they have traveled in a straight line from the object to your eye. Why? Because light rays always travel in straight lines. So the brain forms an **image** of where the object would be if the reflected light rays had traveled in a straight line without refracting. But that image isn't where the object actually is!

> **Was Mafatu right? Is his knife deeper than it looks? Explain.**

Yes. The light reflected from the knife is refracted as it leaves the water and enters Mafatu's eyes. Mafatu's brain forms an image of the knife higher than the knife really is. So the knife looks closer to the surface than it really is.

124

Explore

Refracted Light Draw students' attention to the fact that light reflects off of objects below water just as it reflects off of objects not below water. That's because water is transparent, and light moves through transparent materials.

Have students note the water line in the diagram. *What happens to the light rays reflecting off the fish when they reach the water line?* (They bend and move in a slightly different direction.) You may choose

to share with students the fact that as light rays move from one medium to another, they change speed. In this example, as the rays move from the water to the air, they speed up. This change in speed causes a slight change in direction.

Explain as needed that the dashed lines represent from where the light rays *appear* to be emanating. This is where our brain *thinks* the submerged object is located.

Check Understanding

Skill: Communicate

What behavior of light makes underwater objects appear closer than they really are? (refraction— when light rays move from the water to the air, they are refracted, or bent.)

UNIT 3: Physical Science

What Did We Learn?

CHAPTER 13
How does the poison dart frog make its toxic chemicals?
It takes the toxins it gets from the insects it eats and changes them into a different toxin.

CHAPTER 14
How can a spy uncover a message written in invisible ink?
Knowing which chemicals were used to write the message, the spy can heat the ink or add another chemical to cause a chemical change that uncovers the message.

CHAPTER 15
How is energy converted in the "Multibike"?
Energy of motion from pedaling is converted by a generator to electrical energy.

CHAPTER 16
Why can't perpetual motion machines ever really work?
They cannot produce as much energy as they use because they lose energy due to friction.

CHAPTER 17
How does evaporating water allow a desert refrigerator to cool food?
As water evaporates from the clay pot, heat energy is carried away.

CHAPTER 18
How can refraction change the way you see an object underwater?
Refraction can make an object seem closer than it really is.

What Did We Learn?

The questions on this page complement the questions in the Unit Opener on page 88. Discuss the questions as a class. Invite students to share their ideas about the chapters they have completed. What new questions do they have after completing these chapters?

UNIT 3 Wrap Up
Physical Science

Newspaper or Magazine Issue Have students create a newspaper or magazine issue covering what they learned in this Unit. Each article or feature should relate content information from one of the chapters, but should not be simply a collection of facts lifted from the chapters.

Articles and features should be presented in the style of a newspaper or magazine. Encourage students to look through real newspapers and magazines to get ideas for different ways to present information (breaking news, interviews, profiles, reviews, cartoon art, photos, editorials, and so on).

Assign different "stories' to different students and appoint an editorial staff to check facts and improve writing. Finally, have students use a word processing program to put the articles into a newspaper or magazine format before sharing the product with another class.

This chart describes science content and process skills and also includes the reading and writing skills used in each chapter.

Chapter Title	Science Concepts	Science Skills	Reading & Writing Skills
19. On the Dung Trail	• Energy resources • Resources and the environment	• Infer • Interpret illustrations • Compare and contrast • Understand that scientists change ideas in face of evidence that does not support hypotheses • *Sequence (TG)*	• Connect prior ideas and experiences to text • *Locate information (TG)* • *Read critically (TG)* • *Compare and contrast (TG)*
20. Early Warning System	• Pollution • Indicator species	• Infer • Generate ideas • *Observe (TG)* • *Recognize cause and effect (TG)* • *Predict (TG)*	• Read critically • Write an opinion • *Write a description (TG)*
21. Paging Dr. Nature	• Natural resources	• Interpret data • Make a concept map • Interpret illustrations • *Predict (TG)* • *Infer (TG)*	• Read for details • Evaluate information sources • *Write letters (TG)*

*Skill appears only in Teacher's Guide
Skill appears in Teacher's Guide and Student Book

NSTA Activity

Use with chapter 20, page 134.

This NSTA activity is best used with Chapter 20.

Fishing for Clean Water

Time 45 minutes

Materials
For the class:
• large glass or plastic jar (4–8 L)
• cold tap water
• colored sponge
• small metal washer
• 12–15 cm length of string
• pencil
• scissors
• 8 small plastic cups, 7–8 cm high, each containing

about 60 mL of one of the following "pollutants": soil, green or blue colored sugar, cooking oil, rock salt, punched paper dots, molasses or dark brown corn syrup, liquid dish detergent
• 2–3 drops red food coloring
• 9 "Fishing for Clean Water" Script Cards (prepare from the Copymaster on pp. 177, 178)

This activity is designed to increase students knowledge of water pollution. The objective is for students to recognize that water is a valuable resource, and to understand the living and nonliving elements of freshwater systems.

Procedure

Steps 1–6 should be done before the activity begins.

1. Cut a fish shape out of the sponge.
2. Fill the jar three-quarters full of cold tap water.
3. Tie one end of the string around a pencil. Tie the other end around the fish. Number the pencil 1.
4. Tie the small metal washer to the sponge fish.
5. Number the plastic cups 2–9. Put each material in a numbered cup, as follows. (Note that some items are actual pollutants, while others are represented by student-safe materials.)
   2—soil
   3—colored sugar ("fertilizer")
   4—cooking oil ("motor oil")
   5—rock salt
   6—punched paper dots ("trash")
   7—liquid dish detergent ("factory waste")
   8—molasses or corn syrup ("raw sewage")
   9—red food coloring ("toxic waste"; 2–3 drops only)
6. This activity works well as a whole-class discussion and demonstration. Distribute the fish and cups 2–9 to nine students; distribute the Script Cards to nine other students. Any students who do not have cups or cards are Recorders; they answer the question asked at the end of most Script Cards ("How does this affect the fish?")
7. Explain to the class that the students holding Script Cards will be telling a story about a fish's journey. The students holding the fish and the cups will be acting out what happens in the story.
8. Call on the student holding Script Card 1. Ask that student to read his or her card. At the appropriate time, the student holding the fish should put it into the "river" (jar).
9. Call on students 2–9 in order. After each Script Card is read, have the student holding that numbered cup add the material to the jar. Have Recorders write down the name of each pollutant as it is added, and describe how the fish is affected by that pollutant.
10. At the end of the story, have a student lift the fish out of the jar. Discuss how its appearance has changed.
11. Review in order the pollutants that were added to the "river."
12. As a class, discuss how the fish was affected by each pollutant. ***Do you think the fish would stay healthy through its whole journey?*** (Answers will vary. Some students should recognize that a real fish may not have survived the whole journey.)

UNIT 4: Chapter Overviews (19–21)

Chapter 19   On the Dung Trail

Key Idea: Animal dung has been used as a fuel source for thousands of years.

Students read that lack of fuel was not a problem for early humans who were crossing a land bridge, because of the large quantity of dung available.

Materials

Connection (p. 129), and Enrichment (p. 131), for the class:
• access to the Internet

Chapter 20   Early Warning System

Key Idea: Death and deformities among species sensitive to environmental changes may indicate that an area has become polluted.

Students read an article about frogs and the possible connection between water pollution and deformed frogs.

Materials

Differentiating Instruction (p. 136), for the class:
• Materials for making posters such as paper, poster board, markers, colored paper

Enrichment (p. 137), for the class:
• pH test kits for soil and water

Chapter 21   Paging Dr. Nature

Key Idea: Many plants have medicinal properties.

Students read a poem about an imaginary medicine that contains plant and animal ingredients, then read the labels of herbal supplements to identify the plant ingredients. Next they read about the historic discovery of a real medicine—quinine—that is made from a tree bark.

Materials

Project (p. 141), for the class:
• empty bottles of herbal supplements

Connection (p. 141), for interested students:
• Poetry collections by Douglas Florian

Enrichment (p. 143), for the class:
• access to the Internet

The following sources are used in this unit.

Chapter 19 On the Dung Trail
Online Magazine Article
"A Human Migration Fueled by Dung?" *Science News for Kids* web site, August 13, 2003

Chapter 20 Early Warning System
Magazine Article
"Weird World of Frogs," *National Geographic World*, March, 2002

Chapter 21 Paging Doctor Nature
Poem
"Silly Pilly" from *Laugh-Eteria* by Douglas Florian
Nonfiction
Accidents May Happen: Fifty Inventions Discovered by Mistake, by Charlotte Foltz Jones

www.scilinks.org
Keyword: Current Research
Code: GSSD04

UNIT 4: Natural Resources and the Environment

Chapter 19
On the Dung Trail
Find out: How can you build a fire if you can't find any wood?

Chapter 20
Early Warning System
Find out: What can an animal's deformed leg tell you about its environment?

Chapter 21
Paging Dr. Nature
Find out: Can tree bark save your life?

126

Introducing the Unit

To generate interest in the chapters, use the questions on the student page. Invite students to read the questions, but explain that they do not have to answer them right now. Ask students what they think they will find out in each chapter, based on the questions and images on this page. Accept all answers at this point.

On the Dung Trail

Chapter 19

Could mammoth poop keep you warm?

If you have ever gone on a long camping trip, you know that you have to carry a lot of things to keep you safe. You need a tent to protect you from the rain, a sleeping bag to keep you warm, and lots of food and water so that you do not get hungry or thirsty. Some camping areas do not allow you to collect firewood. So, if you want to cook your food, you will also need to bring along some firewood or some other source of fuel.

Tens of thousands of years ago, humans living on the continents of Africa and Asia began a long journey to North America. (Today an ocean separates Asia from North America. But 50,000 years ago, there was no ocean between the northern parts of the two continents.) The trip was a long one, and people would have needed a source of fuel for keeping warm and cooking food. Since there were almost no trees in this cold landscape, scientists have wondered what the people might have used for fuel. In this chapter, you'll read about a scientist who came up with one explanation that may surprise you.

Before You Read

Have you ever been camping? If not, maybe you've seen people camping in a movie.

> **Why do people need to burn fuel when they are camping?**

to stay warm, cook their food, and toast

marshmallows

> **People often make a fire using firewood. Can you think of any other sources of fuel people use when they are camping?**

Students may mention camp stoves, which

use canned or bottled fuels.

 Getting and Using Energy .... p. 77
Energy from Plants and Animals .... p. 328

 www.scilinks.org
Keyword: Natural Resources
Code: GS5D100

(127)

Key Idea
Animal dung has been used as a fuel source for thousands of years.

Focus
- Types of resources
- Populations, resources, and environments
- Evidence, models, and explanation

Skills and Strategies
- Infer
- Interpret illustrations
- Compare and contrast
- *Sequence (TG)*

Vocabulary*
Before beginning the chapter, make sure students understand this term.
- fuel

* A definition is in the Glossary on pages 166–172.

Introducing the Chapter
This chapter introduces a fuel source that may be unfamiliar to most students, dried animal dung. Students read about a scientist's hypothesis concerning ancient fuel sources during the human migration across the land bridge connecting Asia to North America, thousands of years ago. Students consider modern evidence that supports the hypothesis, then trace the source of the energy in dung. The chapter ends with a consideration of places in the world where dung would be readily available as a source of fuel.

Introduce the chapter by asking, **What is a fuel?** (something that contains energy that can be used by people) **What are some kinds of fuels people use today?** (oil, gasoline, natural gas, coal, wood, propane) If students suggest electricity as a fuel, use the opportunity to explain that electricity is a kind of energy, but it is not a natural resource, nor is it a fuel. It must be generated from other energy sources, including fuels.

Before You Read
If only a few students have camping experience, you may wish to do this exercise as a class discussion.

Hiking often is associated with camping. Use this connection to reinforce the relationship between energy and fuel. **Where does the energy that a person uses for hiking come from?** (it is stored in food) **So, what is the fuel a person uses for hiking?** (food) Point out that an animal's food is also its fuel.

More Resources

The following resources are also available from Great Source and NSTA.

SCIENCESAURUS
A STUDENT HANDBOOK
BLUE BOOK

Writers Express

SCiLINKS
THE WORLD'S A CLICK AWAY

www.scilinks.org
Keyword: Natural Resources
Code: GS5D100

Read

Read about a scientist who thinks he might know how people stayed warm during their long journey from Asia to North America.

"A Different Kind of Fuel"

notes:

> **Circle** the kind of fuel scientists first thought people migrating to North America would have needed for heating and cooking.

If you think traveling to Alaska in the winter sounds cold today, imagine what it was like thousands of years ago.

Before the invention of central heating and hot cocoa, it would have been too cold for people to <u>migrate</u> to North America through the <u>frigid tundra</u>—without trees or (firewood). Or so scientists thought.

Now, researchers suggest that our <u>ancestors</u> could have survived cold-weather travel if they had taken advantage of all the <u>dung</u> lying around.

More than 50,000 years ago, Alaska was connected to northern Russia by a land bridge that is now largely underwater. Yet [evidence shows that] people didn't make the crossing until about 14,000 years ago…. Scientists have long blamed the delay on cold weather and a lack of fuel for heating and cooking.

migrate: move
frigid: very cold

tundra: regions where it is very cold and there are almost no trees

ancestors: people who came before us
dung: animal poop

Read

Independent Reading Unless you live in a rural area, most of your students will not have direct, daily experience with large, plant-eating animals, even if they depend on such animals for milk, meat, or leather. To help them understand the quantity of animal waste that is available, ask, **Who has a pet at home?** (Some students may have a cat, dog, or small mammal.) **What is done with your pet's waste?** (It may be picked up, thrown in the trash, flushed down the toilet, left in the woods, etc.) **If your pet was as large as a horse, could you handle its waste the same way?** (probably not) Help students to understand that keeping large animals means having a lot of waste (dung) to deal with, whether or not the waste can be put to good use.

Students may have difficulty imagining the amount of dung a Tibetan family burns in a day. Tell them that 40 kilograms is equal to about 88 pounds, and suggest that they compare that value to their own weight.

In a typical upper-elementary classroom, some students weigh less than 88 pounds, while others may weigh more. However, the weight of most students will be close enough to 88 pounds to make the comparison meaningful. (Because weight can be a sensitive subject, avoid calling attention to any individual child's weight.) Eighty-eight pounds is also equivalent to about 11 gallons of water.

The yellow areas used to be land 50,000 years ago. Today, these areas are underwater except for a few small islands.

That might not be the best explanation, says [scientist] David Rhode..., who has studied the dung-burning habits of modern <u>Tibetans</u>. <u>To heat their tents and cook their food</u>, Rhode has observed, a single family...burns between 25 and 40 kilograms of dried <u>yak</u> (dung) in the summer and twice that in the winter. That's a lot of dung....

Thousands of years ago, Rhode says, the route from Russia to Alaska would have been bursting with big plant-eating animals, like bison, mammoths, horses, and wooly rhinoceroses. With animals comes <u>waste</u>. There should have been plenty of dried dung to fuel the trip.

So, why the delay? Maybe our ancestors took a while to realize the value of the poop along their path!

From: "A Human Migration Fueled by Dung?"
Science News for Kids, Aug 13, 2003.

notes:

> What activities do modern Tibetans burn dung for? <u>Underline</u> your answer.

> (Circle) the kind of fuel David Rhode thinks would have been available to people migrating to North America.

> What did big animals on the route eat?

plants

Tibetans: people from the Asian country of Tibet

yak: a large plant-eating animal kept by people for milk, meat, and work

waste: poop

(129)

Connections

Materials   Access to Internet

Social Studies   Encourage interested students to explore further the migration of early humans across the land bridge that connected what is now Russia to what is now Alaska. The Bering Land Bridge, also called Beringia, existed during the last Ice Age. It was submerged by the sea when ocean levels rose dramatically as a result of the melting ice sheets.

A children's search engine will turn up a number of student-friendly web sites on the topic, including one for the National Park Service's Bering Land Bridge National Preserve (www.nps.gov/bela). The site contains a page with a good summary of the historical and cultural significance of the area.

 Write to Learn

Write a paragraph   Have students write a paragraph comparing and contrasting a modern camping trip with the traditional Tibetan lifestyle described in the reading.

Science Background

In the past, humans used animal products as fuel. When buffalo were still plentiful, Plains Indians collected buffalo dung for use as a fuel. The Inuit (Eskimo) used seal oil to heat their tents and igloos. Whale oil was a popular fuel for lighting homes in many parts of the world including the northeastern United States until the late 1800s, when it was replaced by kerosene. Even today, people in many countries use dung as a fuel.

Exactly how and when humans made the first journey from Asia to the Americas is a lively topic in science. During the last Ice Age, Arctic ice extended over much more land than it does now. However, there is evidence of an ice-free corridor through which both large mammals and humans could have traveled to reach the Americas. An alternate hypothesis states that humans followed the coast in boats, hunting sea life along the way. David Rhode's argument about fuel for the journey, described in the article on

these pages, is just one of many interesting ideas being discussed and debated in connection with this important chapter in human prehistory.

Differentiating Instruction

Bodily / Kinesthetic Ask students to imagine themselves as a group of people in Asia tens of thousands of years ago, before people made the trip across the Bering Land Bridge. Humans are doing well, and more and more babies have survived into adulthood. Unfortunately more people means more stress on the environment. It is getting more and more difficult to find wood to make fires.

One person in your group recently discovered that some kinds of animal dung burn after they are dried out. Others are skeptical—why would we want to burn dung?

Write and perform a skit in which one person tries to convince the rest of the group that burning dung instead of wood is a good idea. The skit should include at least two points in favor of burning dried dung (easy to get, takes less time to gather enough of it, helps keep the area clean), and at least two points against (dirty, unfamiliar, "we've never done it before").

Look Back

Use what you learned in the reading to answer the following questions:

> **What explanation did scientists used to give for the fact that people waited thousands of years to migrate from Russia to North America?**

It was very cold and they didn't have fuel (firewood) for heating and cooking.

> **Why does scientist David Rhode think that this explanation is not correct?**

He thinks the people would have had plenty of dung to use as fuel.

> **What evidence did David Rhode base his conclusion on?**

People living in Tibet today use animal dung for heating and cooking. The area where the people would have migrated was full of large animals that would have produced lots of dung.

Explore

ENERGY FROM DUNG

You probably never thought of animal dung—or poop—as a source of fuel. But people have been using it ever since they started raising plant-eating animals, such as sheep, goats, and cows. Like firewood, dung is a source of fuel because it contains energy.

> **Look back at the reading. What kinds of animals lived along the route from Russia to Alaska?**

big plant-eating animals, such as bison, mammoths, horses, and wooly rhinoceroses

(continued on next page)

Look Back

Has David Rhode shown that people used animal dung as a fuel thousands of years ago? (no) **What has he shown?** (that dung used as fuel could have helped people travel across a land bridge from Asia to North America 14,000 years ago) **Why is Rhode's work important?** (It challenges a popular scientific hypothesis, that is, that cold weather *and* a lack of fuel delayed the crossing of the Arctic land bridge until 14,000 years ago. People apparently did have portable fuel–dung prior to 14,000 years ago.)

Explore

Energy from Dung All animals take in food as a source of energy, but not all animal waste makes a good fuel. Have student reread the paragraphs at the top of page 131, then ask, **Why do you suppose big plant-eating animals make the best dung for fuel?** (They eat lots of plants, but not all of the plant material is digested. Undigested plant material in dung stores energy that is converted to heat energy when dung is burned.) After students have completed the

(continued from previous page)

Why does dung contain energy? Plants are made up of materials that contain energy. When an animal eats plants, it gets energy from the plant material that it digests. But it doesn't digest all parts of the plant. Some of the plant material passes out of the animal without being digested. That means that the dung of plant-eating animals contains energy still stored in the undigested plant material.

Plants use energy from sunlight to grow and make all of their plant parts. Animals that eat plants get their energy from the plant parts that they eat.

This preserved mammoth dung contains lots of undigested plant material.

Some people use dung as a source of fuel.

> **Fill in the diagram below with the terms provided to show the path that energy takes from the sun all the way to a person's cooking stove.**

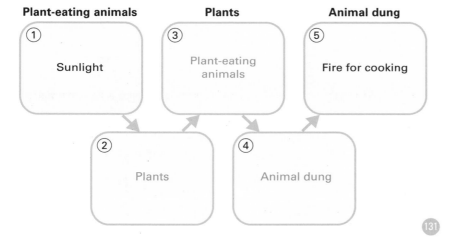

Plant-eating animals   **Plants**   **Animal dung**

① Sunlight

③ Plant-eating animals

⑤ Fire for cooking

② Plants

④ Animal dung

(131)

Electricity from Dung

Materials Access to Internet

Today, dung, or manure, is converted into two useful products: a rich organic compost (fertilizer) and methane, a clean-burning gas that can be used to generate electricity. The technology for manure-to-electricity power plants has been available for decades. However, such power plants cost more to build than ones that run on petroleum or natural gas. Until recently there has been little incentive to use this technology in the United States.

The California energy crisis in 2001 sparked renewed interest in converting the waste from dairy cattle into a useful energy source.

Have interested students use the Internet to research recent "manure-to-electricity" projects. They should answer the following questions:

- About how many power plants run on manure?
- How many more manure-burning power plants are planned?
- Where are most of these power plants, and why?
- What are the benefits of building this kind of power plant, rather than one that runs on natural gas?

diagram at the bottom of the page, have them draw a similar diagram for firewood. Diagrams will have just three components: sunlight, trees, fire for cooking. ***How are the two diagrams alike?*** (The original source of energy for both is sunlight. This energy becomes stored in plant tissues. The end product is fire, or heat energy.) ***How are they different?*** (In one, the plant materials pass through animals, becoming dung, before they are burned. In the other, the plant materials, wood, are burned directly.)

Check Understanding

Skill: Sequence

Where does the energy that is stored in dung come from? (From the plants that the animals ate; the energy in the plants came from the sun.)

Assessment

Skill: Compare and contrast

Use the following questions to assess each student's progress.

What makes dung a fuel? (it can be burned, which releases heat energy)

How long has dung been used as a fuel? (thousands of years)

Where does the energy in animal dung originally come from? (sunlight)

Review "Find Out" Question

Review the question for Chapter 19 in the Unit Opener on page 126: *How can you build a fire if you can't find any wood?* Have students use what they learned in the chapter to answer the question. (In some places dung, which burns, is more plentiful than trees.) Use student responses to lead a class discussion on fuel sources.

Explore

A GOOD CHOICE

There is often more than one source of fuel available for use in an area. People will often use the type of fuel that is the cheapest or most readily available. Dung has been used as a source of fuel for thousands of years. It may not sound very clean, but it is not any messier than other kinds of fuel. In fact, when it is dried, dung does not smell and it looks very much like dried dirt. Many people around the world still use dried dung as a fuel source today. Look at the two pictures below.

> Draw a circle around the person you think would use dung to build a fire.

> Why would dung be a good choice for this person?

There are no trees, so there is no firewood to use as fuel for the fire.

But the person has plenty of large animals who produce a lot of dung.

> Why might it be better for the environment to use dung instead of wood?

Students may suggest that dung is produced by animals every day, while trees take many years to grow. Also, trees have many other uses, such as reducing erosion and providing building materials and shade. Animal dung doesn't have many other uses.

Explore

A Good Choice Have students identify the kind of fuel used in their homes for heating, cooking, and hot water. Point out that five kinds of fuel are generally used for these purposes in the United States. These are oil, natural gas, propane gas, coal, and wood. Have students compare and contrast the pros and cons of using these fuels. They should address topics such as cost, availability, pollution, and efficiency, that is, how much heat per kilogram each fuel produces. Note:

Some homes use electricity for heating and/or cooking and hot water. Tell students that fuels are used to produce electricity in some power plants.

Science Background

As pointed out on the student page, dung is no messier than some other kinds of fuel. However, dung, wood, and other fuels that come directly from living things (biomass fuels) generally cause more pollution than natural gas and refined petroleum products. Burning dung produces more pollutants per energy unit than almost all other fuels that are commonly available in developing countries. One way to use dung and avoid the mess is to convert dung into methane gas, called biogas. Many thousands of households in India and in other countries have installed biogas plants. Cow dung ferments in the biogas plant, releasing methane, which is burned as a cooking fuel. Biogas burns even cleaner than natural gas, and as long as it has cows, a family has a source of fuel.

Early Warning System

Chapter 20

What can a deformed frog tell you about its environment?

What would you think if one day, while swimming in a lake, you found a frog with three legs instead of four? You'd probably think, "That poor frog lost a leg." But what if you found a frog that had five legs? You might be a little concerned! Having five legs instead of four is a deformity. An animal can be born with a **deformity** that it inherited from its parents. Or, a deformity at birth may be caused by something in the animal's environment.

In this chapter, you'll read about an animal whose deformities might tell scientists a lot about the environment.

Before You Read

> If you wanted to find out whether an environment was polluted or not, what signs would you look for? Name at least three signs that tell you that an environment is polluted.

Students might describe looking for litter,

smog, a bad smell, dead plants, dead

animals, deformed animals, and so on.

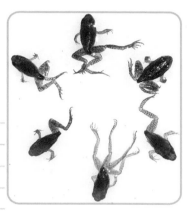

SCIENCESAURUS
A STUDENT HANDBOOK
BLUE BOOK

Amphibians
.... p. 154
Material
Resources ... p. 329
Water
Pollution ..... p. 342

SCiLINKS.
THE WORLD'S A CLICK AWAY

www.scilinks.org
Keyword: Pollution
Code: GS5D105

133

Key Idea

Death and deformities among species sensitive to environmental changes may indicate that an area has become polluted.

Focus

- Changes in environments
- Life cycles of organisms
- Organisms and environments
- Populations, resources, and environments

Skills and Strategies

- Infer
- Generate ideas
- Communicate
- *Recognize cause and effect (TG)*
- *Predict (TG)*

Vocabulary*

Before beginning the chapter, make sure students understand these terms.

- environment
- polluted
- fertilizer

* Definitions are in the Glossary on pages 166–172.

Introducing the Chapter

In this chapter, students explore the concept that some species, called indicator species, help us identify problems in the environment that might otherwise escape notice. Paying attention to indicator species can help scientists recognize problems and suggest remedies in time to reduce the damage to other species in the environment and to people.

Introduce the chapter by having students read the opening paragraphs, then ask: *How would having the* *wrong number of legs be harmful to a frog?* (A frog with too few legs might not be able to get away from predators. A frog with too many legs might trip over itself while it was trying to get away.) *What might happen if lots of frogs had the wrong number of legs?* (They might all be eaten, and there might not be many frogs left.)

Before You Read

Most students (and many adults) will think of obvious changes in appearance and smell as indicators of a polluted environment. A point made in this chapter is that a body of water can look and smell perfectly clean, even if it is polluted. For now, accept all preconceived ideas students have about detecting water pollution. They will revisit their ideas later in the chapter to see how their ideas have changed.

More Resources

The following resources are also available from Great Source and NSTA.

SCIENCESAURUS
A STUDENT HANDBOOK
BLUE BOOK

Reader's Handbook (Yellow Book)

Writers Express

SCI LINKS
THE WORLD'S A CLICK AWAY

www.scilinks.org
Keyword: Pollution
Code: GS5D105

Read

Read about how deformities in frogs help warn scientists that an environment could be polluted.

"Sounding an Alarm"

notes:

Frogs survived the <u>catastrophic</u> <u>extinction</u> of the dinosaurs. But strangely, <u>the world's frogs and toads have suddenly begun to disappear. Some <u>species</u> that were common 20 years ago are now rare or extinct. And individual frogs are showing up with <u>deformities</u> such as too many legs....</u> Scientists are not exactly sure what is going on.

Pollution may have caused this northern leopard frog to grow a fifth leg.

But scientists do agree that because frogs drink and breathe through their thin skin they are especially <u>vulnerable to</u> <u>pesticides</u> and pollution. A deformed frog often <u>indicates</u> that all is not well with the environment. And frogs live just about everywhere on Earth.

>What two problems have scientists found with frogs? <u>Underline</u> your answer.

catastrophic: big and sudden
extinction: dying out
species: kinds

deformities: body parts that are not "normal"
vulnerable to: easily affected by

pesticides: chemicals used to kill insects and other small animals
indicates: points out

(134)

Read

Paired Reading Before students read the article, check their knowledge of a frog's life cycle. *How many legs does a normal frog have when it hatches?* (Trick question! None.) Explain that a young frog has no legs. Frogs, like all amphibians, start out as eggs that hatch into tadpoles. Tadpoles live completely in the water: they breathe through gills, swim with tails, and have no legs. As tadpoles grow up into frogs, they develop lungs for breathing air. Tadpoles also grow legs, but

usually the right number of legs (four). *Can a tadpole get out of the water while it is still a tadpole?* (no) *Can a tadpole get away from any pollution that is in the water?* (no)

Science Background

Deformed frogs have been described as far back as the 1700s. The current concern over frog deformities dates to 1994, when half the frogs caught by school children in Minnesota had some deformity. Research since that year has shown that there is no single cause. In some regions, a parasite causes deformities. However, such deformities are far more common in infested ponds that also harbor pollutants, or that are exposed to excessive ultraviolet

---

Frogs are <u>amphibians</u>, which means "double life." They generally hatch in water as tadpoles and end up living on land as fully formed frogs. Frogs' skin must stay moist, so they're usually found in wet places.

Because frogs are so sensitive to environmental changes, they act as an early warning system. Their <u>dwindling</u> numbers may be a sign that our planet is not as clean and healthy as it once was. By studying how frogs are affected by the environment around them, scientists may be able to predict—and sound an alarm—that a neighborhood needs to cut back on lawn <u>fertilizers</u> or that a chemical-dumping factory should clean up its act. The hidden message in frogs' familiar peeps and croaks? "I'm jumpy for a reason!"

From: "Weird World of Frogs,"
National Geographic World, March 2002.

amphibians: animals that start life in water but live on land as adults

dwindling: decreasing
fertilizers: chemicals used to help grass grow

notes:

> How do frogs act as an "early warning system"?

They are very sensitive to environmental changes.

> How can you tell that the last sentence is a joke and not a scientific fact?

because there is no way to know what a frog is thinking or that it is aware of pollution in its environment

135

 Activity

Fishing for Clean Water
See pages 125A-125B for an NSTA activity on sources of water pollution and the effects of water pollution on living things.

 Write to Learn

Writing a story The words used to describe something depend on the purpose of the written piece. For example, the language of a horror story differs from the language of a science report. Have each student write a description of the deformed frog shown on page 134. Before they begin, assign or have each student choose one of the types of writing described below.

- **Horror story:** Purpose is to make the reader feel that the frog is creepy and weird.
- **Story for young children:** Purpose is to make the reader feel sorry for the frog.
- **Science report:** Purpose is to describe the frog in detail, so the reader knows what it looks like.

Frog descriptions should be appropriate to the type of writing each student is doing.

(UV) radiation (which is increasing as the protective ozone layer in the atmosphere thins). One hypothesis is that pollutants and excess UV weaken the tadpoles' immune systems, making them more vulnerable to the parasites.

Even in water without parasites, UV radiation, combined with pollutants derived from detergents, seems to cause other health problems for frogs. Experiments show that both of these factors work together to prevent some tadpoles from maturing into adult frogs. Other experiments show that a common weed killer affects male frogs in such a way that they cannot reproduce. Fewer healthy adult frogs translates into fewer new tadpoles. Indeed, there is evidence that frog populations worldwide have been declining for decades.

Check Understanding
Skill: Recognize cause and effect
Where do frogs grow up, and how does this make them especially sensitive to pollution? (They grow up in the water; they cannot avoid any pollutant that is in the water.)

Differentiating Instruction

Materials paper, poster board, markers, colored paper, and other materials for making posters

Visual/Spatial One way that everyone can help to prevent water pollution is by keeping pollutants out of catch basins and storm sewers. These street drains, which are installed to prevent flooding during a rainstorm, flow directly into local waterways. Anything poured into a drain or spilled on a paved surface goes directly into local bodies of water, through the catch basins. Have students create posters alerting people to the importance of preventing pollution through catch basins. Posters should describe the activity that people should avoid, show what can happen to living things as a result of the activity, and explain what to do instead. Common practices to avoid include:

- Pouring used motor oil or other car fluids down a street drain (Take the used oil back to the store or to a recycling center.)
- Washing a car in a driveway, where suds flow into a drain (Wash car over grass or gravel, which filter out suds, or go to a commercial car wash.)
- Letting car fluids drip onto a driveway, where rain washes them away (Get leaks fixed promptly.)
- Using too much fertilizer or weed killer on the lawn (Use lawn chemicals sparingly or not at all.)

Look Back

Scientists who want to know how an environment is changing will often study an indicator species in that environment. An **indicator species** is a kind of plant or animal that reacts quickly to changes in the environment. By looking for changes to the indicator species, scientists can find out how the environment as a whole might be changing.

> **What indicator species were described in the reading?**

different species of frogs.

> **What changes did scientists notice in the indicator species?**

Some species common 20 years ago are now rare or extinct.

Individuals are showing up with deformities.

> **What did the changes in the indicator species tell scientists about the environment as a whole?**

All may not be well with the environment. It's not as clean and

healthy as it once was.

> **According to the reading, what might have caused the changes to the environment? Name at least three things.**

pesticides, pollution, neighborhood using a lot of fertilizer on lawns,

factories dumping chemicals

136

Look Back

Introduce the vocabulary term *indicator species*, which is boldfaced on the page. **What does it mean to indicate something?** (It means to point it out or to show it.) **What is a species?** (a kind of living thing) **What do you think an indicator species is?** (It is a kind of living thing that reacts quickly to changes in the environment.) Changes in an indicator species show that there have been changes in the environment. **What changes in an indicator**

species might show that all is not well in an environment? (The population of an indicator species may fall, or offspring may be born with body parts different from those of their parents, as was the case with the deformed frogs.)

Science Background

Other terms for indicator species are *bioindicator* and *biological indicator species.*

Explore

FROGS AS INDICATOR SPECIES

Polluting chemicals from lawns and factories usually end up in rivers, streams, and lakes. Sometimes the water in these rivers, streams, and lakes looks clear and tastes fine but still contains pollution.

> **Why are frogs more easily affected by polluting chemicals than some other animals?**

Frogs live in wet places and "drink" (absorb moisture) through their skin, so they would get more water-polluting chemicals in their bodies than animals that didn't live in or near water.

> **Why do you think frogs are useful as indicator species?**

They are easily affected by environmental changes and would react quickly to environmental changes. So, scientists would know quickly if there was a change to the environment.

> **Why do you think it's important that scientists look at indicator species to see if an environment is polluted? Why don't they just rely on the water's taste or appearance?**

Sometimes pollution that would harm other organisms or people cannot be seen or tasted in the water. An indicator species might tell scientists that the pollution was there.

(137)

Explore

Frogs as Indicator Species Have students re-read their answers to Before You Read on page 133. *What did you think polluted water would be like?* (Answers will vary.) *What do you think about polluted water now? Would you be able to recognize it if you see it?* (Answers will vary. Students should recognize that water may or may not look or smell bad if it is polluted.) *How do indicator species, such as frogs, help scientists know what is going on in a body of water?* (An indicator species can be affected by pollution in the water, which tells scientists to look for something wrong with the water.)

Remind students that an animal may inherit a deformity, or it may be deformed because of something in the environment while it was growing.

Assessment

UNIT 4: CHAPTER 20

Skill: Predict

Use the following questions to assess each student's progress.

What makes frogs so sensitive to changes in water quality? (They develop in water, and take in water through their skins.) *What other animals do you think might be sensitive to changes in water quality?* (Students may suggest other amphibians, such as salamanders, newts, and toads, as well as fish, which live their entire lives in water.)

Review "Find Out" Question

Review the question for Chapter 20 in the Unit Opener on page 126: *What can an animal's deformed leg tell you about its environment?* Have students use what they learned in the chapter. (A deformed frog leg can tell you that something might have polluted the environment.) Use student responses to lead a class discussion on indicator species.

Science Journal

Imagine that there is a large fertilizer company located in your town. The company just opened up a new factory near a river. Lately, frogs with deformities have been found in the river.

Some people believe that the deformities must be due to chemicals that are washed from the factory grounds to the river by rainwater. Others believe that the deformities are due to parasites, tiny organisms that live on the frogs' bodies and make them sick. Still others believe that the deformities are caused by harmful radiation from the sun.

> In the space below, write a letter to the president of the fertilizer company. In your letter, explain what evidence you have that the environment is changing. Use what you have learned about indicator species to support your argument. Finally, explain why it's important that the company stop making fertilizers at the new factory until scientists can figure out what is going on.

Science Journal

Encourage students to outline letters before beginning to write. Here is a sample outline, based on the instructions on the student page:

1. Greeting (Dear company) and purpose of letter

2. Explain evidence that river environment is changing
   • frogs are an indicator species (define)
   • fewer frogs
   • many deformed frogs

3. We do not yet know the reason for deformed frogs. Possibilities:
   • chemicals from your factory
   • parasites in the water
   • radiation from the sun

4. Explain why it's important to stop making fertilizer until we know what's causing the deformed frogs.

5. Discuss the trade-offs involved in shutting down a fertilizer factory. (People will lose jobs, which would adversely affect the economy of the area.)

If students cannot fit letters on the lines provided, suggest they use a separate sheet of paper.

Don't feel good, have a fever? Try some wood, says the beaver.

It's Monday morning and your alarm is going off. HONK HONK HONK. Time for school! But you don't feel much like getting out of bed. You feel hot and your throat hurts. Uh oh, it looks like you're sick.

Where do you go when you get really sick? You probably go to the doctor or to a hospital. But long before there were doctors and hospitals, people had to find other ways to cure their sicknesses. Often, they found those cures in nature.

In this chapter, you'll read about different kinds of "natural" medicine used today and long ago.

Before You Read

If you get very sick, you can get medicine from a doctor. But before you get very sick, you might try a natural cure to help you feel better. Some plants and foods are thought to heal people and keep them from getting very sick.

> **Name at least three plants or foods that are sometimes used to help people get over an illness.**

Students might suggest foods, such as orange juice and chicken soup, or plants (herbs) such as echinacea, aloe vera, chamomile, peppermint, ginseng, garlic, ginger, etc.

Material Resources p. 329
Many Different People Contribute to Science p. 367

www.scilinks.org
Keyword: Medicine from Plants
Code: GS5D110

> **Think of a time when you felt sick but did not take any medicine or go to the doctor. What did you do or take to make yourself feel better?**

Answers will vary.

Key Idea

Many plants have medicinal properties.

Focus

- Populations, resources, and environments
- Types of resources
- Science as a human endeavor

Skills and Strategies

- Interpret data
- Make a concept map
- Interpret illustrations
- Communicate
- *Predict (TG)*
- *Infer (TG)*

Vocabulary*

Before beginning the chapter, make sure students understand this term.

- herbal supplement

* The definition is in the Glossary on pages 166–172.

Introducing the Chapter

This chapter focuses on medicines that originated in the natural environment, rather than in a laboratory, and concludes by emphasizing the importance of preserving natural habitats as a potential source of new medicines.

Introduce the chapter by asking, **Where do medicines come from?** (Students will probably say from the doctor or from the drugstore.) **What did people do before there were drugstores?** (Students may not know, or they may suggest that people used plants, herbs, or practiced bloodletting.) Tell students that, in this chapter, they will learn about some traditional plant-based medicines, and about how one medicine was first discovered.

Before You Read

Student experiences with home-based remedies may vary, depending on the family's cultural background. Be prepared to accept a wide range of responses. Encourage students to share their knowledge of home remedies in a class discussion.

More Resources

The following resources are also available from Great Source and NSTA.

SCIENCESAURUS
A STUDENT HANDBOOK
BLUE BOOK

Writers Express

SCiLINKS®
THE WORLD'S A CLICK AWAY

www.scilinks.org
Keyword: Medicine
from Plants
Code: GS5D110

Read

Read about an imaginary pill that contains some strange ingredients.

Silly Pilly

notes:

_____

> Circle all the Silly Pilly ingredients that come from plants or animals.

> Underline all the ways that the poem claims Silly Pilly helps you.

If you feel sick,
If you feel ill,
Try swallowing
This ten-pound pill.
It's fortified with lizard knee,
The eye of newt,
Extract of bee.
It satisfies your daily need
For rhubarb root
And maple seed.
With wild weeds and five raw eggs,
It helps you grow
Grass on your legs.
It clears your head,
It clears your skin,
And if you're fat,
It makes you thin.
So open wide and bottoms up!
Just gulp it down—
And don't throw up.

From: *Laugh-Eteria*, by Douglas Florian.

fortified: made stronger
newt: a kind of salamander, an amphibian

extract of: part of
rhubarb: a kind of vegetable plant

Read

Read Aloud Help students to recognize that the poem describes a fictional pill. *What does the author say that suggests this pill is imaginary?* (The pill is called "silly" and weighs ten pounds; it satisfies needs nobody has ever heard of; it does things that just can't happen, like grow grass on your legs.) *What do real medicines do?* (Answers will vary. Most students will say that real medicines cure illness, or treat real symptoms such as a sore throat or fever.)

Science Background

Although herbal supplements are sold for their purported health benefits, in the United States they are classified as "dietary supplements" and as such are not regulated by the Food and Drug Administration (FDA). Some supplements may be beneficial, but they have not been subjected to the rigorous testing that a product must go through to be sold as a drug. Others can be harmful or even fatal, especially if taken at the wrong dosage. Nevertheless, herbal supplements are popular throughout the United States. Caution students against using any supplement without their parents' knowledge and permission, and encourage them to tell their doctors about any supplements they are using.

Look Back

The Silly Pilly doesn't really exist—except in the author's imagination. But it is true that many medicines are made using plant and animal materials.

> **In the left-hand column, list all the Silly Pilly ingredients that come from plants. In the right-hand column, list all the ingredients that come from animals.**

Ingredients from Plants	Ingredients from Animals
rhubarb root	lizard knee
maple seed	eye of newt
wild weeds	extract of bee
	raw eggs

> **Not all plant and animal parts help heal people, and not all pills do what their labels say they will. Why do you think that this pill won't do what the poem claims it will?**

Swallowing one pill cannot make you thin. You have to eat a healthy diet and exercise to be thin. Grass grows from seeds or cuttings and cannot grow on your legs

Project

HERBAL SUPPLEMENTS

Look at the bottle of herbal supplement your teacher has given you. An **herbal supplement** is a product made from a type of leafy plant called an herb. Many people take herbal supplements to improve their health, although not everyone believes they really work.

Study the label on the bottle. Then answer the following questions.

> **What plant do these pills contain?**

Answers will vary.

> **How is the plant supposed to improve health?**

Answers will vary.

Connections

Materials Books of poetry by Douglas Florian (see below)

Literature Douglas Florian's poetry is clever, accessible, and humorous. The language is simple enough for below-grade readers to handle independently, yet the word play is sophisticated enough to satisfy those who are reading above grade level.

Florian's work is not primarily science-related. However, many of his poetry collections focus on topics that are easily connected to science. Frequently, he imparts interesting and accurate science trivia via his rhymes.

Have students read one of the collections listed below, then choose one or more favorite poems to share with the class. You may wish to have students comment on whether they think a poem describes something that might be true, and to do research to find out if it is.

- *Beast Feast: poems*
- *Insectlopedia*
- *In the Swim*
- *Lizards, Frogs, and Polliwogs*
- *Mammalabilia*
- *On the Wing: Bird Poems and Paintings*
- other titles are available

Look Back

The poem mentions grass, but grass is not an ingredient in the imaginary pill, and should not be listed in the chart.

Project

Time 15 minutes
Materials labels or *empty* bottles of herbal supplements, such as comfrey, Echinacea, St. John's wort, gingko biloba, goldenseal, and feverfew.

- Use *only* empty bottles. *Do not* put actual herbal supplements in the hands of students.
- If too few empty bottles are available, substitute copies of bottle labels.
- Some supplements are intended to treat adult conditions such as impotence. Read all labels ahead of time and decide whether the labeling is appropriate for your class.
- Point out to students that they should never take any medicine or supplement unless their parents give it to them.

Differentiating Instruction

Interpersonal Knowledge about most home remedies have been passed by word of mouth from generation to generation, and most use ingredients that are commonly available in households. Have students interview adult family members about home remedies they may have used to treat common symptoms. In their interviews, students may suggest common symptoms and ingredients listed below. (Adults do not have to "answer" each item; the lists are simply meant to prompt discussion.) Have students share the results of their interviews in a class discussion.

Symptoms

- cold sores
- cough / sore throat
- nasal congestion
- skin irritations / insect bites
- upset stomach / nausea

Home Remedy Ingredients

- aloe vera
- bay leaf
- cinnamon
- elderberry tea
- fennel seed
- garlic
- ginger
- honey
- lemon
- oatmeal
- onion
- sage
- vinegar

Read

The Silly Pilly is not real. But here's a plant medicine that is. Read a story about a Spanish soldier who was saved by the bark of a tree.

"Bitter Water"

notes:

> Underline the sentence that tells you that this story might not be true.

> Why did the water taste bitter?
The bark of the cinchona tree made it taste bitter.

Quinine isn't something most Americans keep in their medicine cabinets. But quinine has had a major <u>influence</u> on the world of medicine.

Quinine is the drug used to treat patients with <u>malaria</u>, a disease spread by certain kinds of mosquitoes. <u>Legend says quinine was discovered by accident in the early 1600s.</u>

A Spanish soldier in Peru had an extremely high fever and chills caused by malaria. His <u>comrades</u> left him behind to die. The high fever made him so thirsty that he crawled to a nearby shallow pond to drink. Although the pond water tasted bitter, he drank it anyway, then fell asleep.

When he awoke, his fever had gone down. He rejoined his military company and told them of the <u>miraculous</u> pond water. They examined the water and discovered that its bitter taste came from the bark of a log lying in the pool. The soldier had accidentally discovered that the bark of the cinchona tree could cure malaria.

For almost two hundred years, the bark of the cinchona tree was made into a powder and used to cure malaria. Today <u>synthetic</u> drugs are more often used to treat the disease.

From: *Accidents May Happen: Fifty Inventions Discovered by Mistake,* by Charlotte Foltz Jones.

influence: effect
malaria: a disease that gives people a high fever
comrades: friends

miraculous: amazing
synthetic: made by people in the laboratory

142

Read

Paired Reading It can be difficult to separate fact from fiction in quinine's history. As noted on the student page, the legend of the Spanish soldier may or may not be true. ***Why would people want to tell stories about quinine?*** (It has saved millions of lives.) ***Why would different stories give credit for the discovery of quinine to so many different people?*** (Quinine was so important that everybody wants credit for discovering it. Also, different people might have discovered it independently.)

Science Background

Today, malaria is associated with the tropics, but until recently it was widespread throughout northern temperate regions during the summer months. Malaria is caused by a parasite and carried by *Anopheles* mosquitoes. A mosquito that has bitten an infected animal transmits the parasites to the bloodstream of the next animal it bites. Quinine interferes with the growth and reproduction of the parasites while they are in human red blood cells. It is not a cure for malaria since the parasites can survive outside of red blood cells. It is effective in fighting the extreme fever associated with malaria, which can otherwise kill the infected person. However, if quinine therapy is interrupted, surviving parasites can reenter red blood cells and cause the symptoms of malaria.

Look Back

> Use what you learned in the reading to fill in the concept map below.

Soldier's Disease		Cure for Disease		Source of Cure
malaria	→	bitter water (containing quinine)	→	bark of cinchona tree

Explore

WHAT ABOUT THE TREE?

Cinchona trees grow in the rainforests of South America. Look at the picture at right. It shows a person taking the bark off a cinchona tree.

> How do you think taking the bark off the tree might affect the tree?

Students will probably realize that

stripping the bark off the tree is not

good for the tree and may kill it.

Once people found out about how cinchona bark cured malaria, they started stripping it off of all the cinchona trees. Without their bark, the trees died. A few hundred years later, it was hard to find a cinchona tree growing wild in Peru. Later, people started planting the trees again and taking care to protect them.

143

Look Back

Some students may better understand the exercise if the categories in the chart are rephrased as questions.

- **What disease did the soldier have?** (malaria)
- **What did he drink that helped to cure his disease?** (bitter water)
- **What was the source of the ingredient that cured him?** (bark of the cinchona tree)

Explore

What About the Tree? Students may or may not understand the importance of bark to a tree. Briefly explain that the outermost layer of bark is dead tissue. It protects a thin layer of living tissue that carries water and nutrients up from the roots to the leaves, and food from the leaves down to the roots. Stripping the bark from a tree usually kills the living layer beneath the bark. The tree cannot move water and food between leaves and roots, so it dies.

Enrichment

Malaria and West Nile Disease

Materials Access to Internet

Malaria has not been a major health concern in the United States since about 1950, thanks to efforts to bring it under control. West Nile disease, however, spread across the country in the early 2000s. Have interested students research malaria and West Nile disease and report on similarities and differences between the two diseases. As a place to begin, students can search for answers to the following questions.

- **What do West Nile disease and malaria have in common?** (Both can be fatal, both are transmitted by mosquito bites.)
- **What causes each disease?** (West Nile is caused by a virus; malaria is caused by a one-celled parasite.)
- **Which disease occurs throughout North America now?** (West Nile)
- **What is the most common way to control the spread of both diseases?** (reduce the number of mosquitoes in an area)

One place for students to start their research is the general web site of the Centers for Disease Control (www.cdc.gov). The CDC also has a children's web site, BAM! (www.bam.gov), but the relevant information on that site is limited to the transmission of the West Nile virus.

Check Understanding

Skill: Predict

What could have happened to cinchona trees if people had not started to replant them? (They could have become extinct.)

Assessment

Skill: Infer

Use the following question to assess each student's progress.

Which would have more undiscovered plants: an uncut tropical rainforest, or grazing land that has been abandoned and allowed to grow over with wild plants? (Students should recognize that the uncut forest would have more variety. The grazing land can only contain plants like the ones that were left behind when the land was cleared, or plants that move in from other areas. Those are the only ones that can reseed the land that was cleared.)

Review "Find Out" Question

Review the question for Chapter 21 in the Unit Opener on page 126. *Can tree bark save your life?* (Yes, if it contains a medicine that fights a disease you have.)

Science Journal

Biodiversity is the term scientists use to refer to the variety of plants and animals in a given place. Some places, like the Amazonian rainforest in South America, have many different kinds of plants and animals. Biodiversity in the rainforest is very high.

Many natural medicines, including quinine, have been discovered in the rainforest. For thousands of years, people in the rainforest have eaten plant leaves and roots as food. Often, they discovered that one of these plants helped a sick person get better.

Imagine that a logging company wants to clear large areas of a rainforest in order to use the wood from the rainforest trees and provide grazing land for local cattle farmers.

> **Write a letter to the logging company explaining why you think it is important to protect biodiversity in the rainforest. Use examples from the chapter to help you.**

Students should explain that if there is a great variety of plants, then there is a greater chance of people finding new medicines. Important medicines such as quinine, one cure for malaria, have been discovered in the rainforests of South America. Destroying the rainforest could reduce the biodiversity of the region and the chances for finding new medicines there.

Many medicines come from natural sources.

144

Science Journal

Tell students to assume that the people at the logging company know nothing about biodiversity, quinine, or the history of medicines that come from plants. As a class, discuss the important points to include in letters to the logging company. *Is it enough to simply ask the company to stop logging? Why or why not?* (No, because they will want to know why.) *What can you say that might convince the company to stop cutting down entire forests?* (Point out the benefits of biodiversity, which can be maintained by limiting the cutting down of trees in a particular forest.)

Science Background

Synthetic drugs are most often used to cure diseases today. Most synthetics are cheaper to produce, less destructive to the environment to manufacture, and frequently more effective. However, some common synthetic drugs are based on compounds that were originally extracted from plant sources. Thus, new plants are an important source of new compounds that may have medicinal uses.

Ethnobotany is the science of investigating traditional medicinal plants for possible use in modern medicine. Ethnobotanists are usually trained in botany, the science of plants, and anthropology, the science of human cultures and groups.

UNIT 4: Natural Resources and the Environment

What Did We Learn?

19 **What makes dung a good choice as a source of fuel?**
Using dung does not harm the environment like cutting down trees can.

20 **Why do frogs make good "indicator species"?**
They are very sensitive to environmental changes. So scientists know quickly when there is a problem with the environment.

21 **Why is biodiversity important?**
Some species of plants and animals can provide us with medicines. By protecting biodiversity, we make sure that these species will always be around.

145

Concept map Help students to look for common threads among the chapters in the unit. For example, ask: Which two of the three chapters in this unit were about natural resources that come from living things? (Chapter 19, about dung as an energy source; Chapter 21, about plants as a resource for medicines) Which two of the chapters describe scientists making observations? What were those observations? (Chapter 19, observation that people burn dung; Chapter 20, observation that frogs are dwindling and turning up deformed.) What ideas did scientists have, that are based on those observations? (Chapter 19—that people could have used dung as a fuel on a migration; Chapter 20—that frogs may have been affected by pollutants in the water.)

Invite interested students to create a concept map showing ways in which the topics in the unit are related.

What Did We Learn?

The questions on this page complement the ones in the Unit Opener on page 126. Discuss the questions as a class. Invite students to share their ideas about the chapters they have completed. What new questions do they have after completing these chapters?

This chart describes science content and process skills and also includes the reading and writing skills used in each chapter.

Chapter Title	Science Concepts	Science Skills	Reading & Writing Skills
22. **The Invention of Paper**	• History and nature of science • Invention • Technology	• Compare and contrast • Conduct investigations • Infer • *Communicate* • *Sequence*	• Connect prior ideas and experiences to text • Extract appropriate information • *Write a journal entry*
23. **A New Beak**	• Science as a human endeavor • Technology design	• Communicate • Concept map • Generate ideas • *Sequence*	• Locate informatin • Explain • *Write a slogan*
24. **Animated Movies**	• Computer animation • Technology careers	• Sequence • Concept map • Interpret scientific illustrations • Apply knowledge • *Communicate*	• Make connections • Read for details • Organize information • *Share information*

Skill appears only in Teacher's Guide
Skill appears in Teacher's Guide and Student Book

NSTA Activity

Use with Chapter 24, page 164.

This NSTA activity is best used with Chapter 24, page 164.

Seeing in 3-D

Time 20–30 minutes

Materials
For each student:
• Images for Tube-Viewing Copymaster page 179
• 2 sheets of plain paper
• transparent tape

Procedure
1. Distribute a copy of the Copymaster to each student.
2. Instruct students to follow the directions on the sheet to view the images in 3-D.

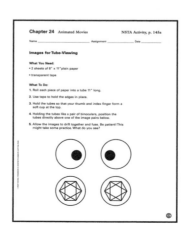

Chapter 22   The Invention of Paper

Key Idea Paper is a technology that may have been inspired by nature.

An article on paper-making considers the idea that observations of a wasps' nest may have inspired a French scientist to invent wood-pulp paper.

Materials

Before You Read (p. 147), for the class:
- cardboard box for collecting recyclable paper
- protective gloves

Connections (p. 149), for the class:
- research materials on historical figures

Differentiating Instruction (p. 149), for the class:
- metric rulers
- paper

Enrichment (p. 150), for the class:
- samples of various kinds of paper, such as copy paper, toilet tissue, paper towels, paper napkins, waxed paper

Connections (p. 151), for the class:
- research materials on the manufacture and use of papyrus in ancient Egypt

Activity (pp. 151 and 152), for the class:
- newspaper
- large plastic tub
- stirring spoon
- clothes iron
- water
- white glue
- stiff screen
- blender or food processor

Chapter 23   A New Beak

Key Idea New technologies are tested and improved until a successful design is found.

Students read about a bald eagle who lost most of its beak to a hunter's bullet. A team of dentists came up with an initial design for a prosthetic beak and then tested and improved the beak over time.

Materials

Before You Read (p. 153), for the class:
- photographs of prosthetic devices

Read (p. 154), for the class:
- samples of prosthetic devices

Enrichment (p. 157), for the class:
- raw eggs
- cardboard boxes
- foam peanuts
- old nylon stockings
- other materials suggested by students

Chapter 24   Animated Movies

Key Idea Creating an animated movie character requires many types of technology and the participation of a team of people with different skills.

An article explaining how an animated movie character was created introduces students to a very familiar application of technology.

Materials

Differentiating Instruction (p. 161), for the class:
- turntable or rotating cake plate
- laser pointer or narrow-beam flashlight
- 3-D action figure

Enrichment (p. 162), for each student or pair:
- pad of stiff paper, unlined
- pencil or pen

Look Back (p. 162), for each group:
- index cards

NSTA Activity (pp. 145A and 163), for the class:
- see page 145A

UNIT 5: SCIENCE, TECHNOLOGY, AND SOCIETY

The following sources are used in this unit.

Chapter 22 The Invention of Paper

Nonfiction

Accidents May Happen: Fifty Inventions Discovered by Mistake by Charlotte Foltz Jones

Chapter 23 A New Beak

Online News Article

"Canadian dentist gives eagle new beak, waives bill" from *Planet Ark*, August 19, 2002

Chapter 24 Making Animated Movies

Magazine Article

"The Hulk Comes Alive!" *National Geographic Kids*, July/August 2003

SCI LINKS
THE WORLD'S A CLICK AWAY

www.scilinks.org
Keyword: Science Fair
Code: GSSD03

DID YOU KNOW? The idea for the recipe for modern paper came from the way that was make paper nests by chewing wood

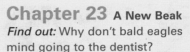

Chapter 22
The Invention of Paper
Find out: What can wasps teach us about making paper?

Chapter 23 A New Beak
Find out: Why don't bald eagles mind going to the dentist?

Chapter 24
Animated Movies
Find out: How many people did it take to create *The Hulk*?

146

Introducing The Unit

To generate interest in the chapters, use the questions on the student page. Invite students to read the questions, but explain that they do not have to answer them right now. Ask students what they think they will find out in each chapter, based on the questions and images on this page. Accept all answers at this point.

The Invention of Paper | Chapter 22

Sometimes inventors steal ideas from nature.

Each person in the United States uses an average of 580 pounds of paper every year. That's over a pound and a half per day!

Do you know where paper comes from? The paper we use today is made from wood that comes from trees. But thousands of years ago, people didn't have paper. Instead, they used to write on thin strips of bamboo, sheets of silk, or even the dried skin of animals.

In this chapter, you'll read about a person who used an idea from nature to invent the paper we use today.

Before You Read

We all use a lot of paper every day. When you think of paper, you probably think of notebook paper. But not all paper is made for writing on. For example, napkins are a kind of paper that is used to wipe your mouth and hands after eating.

> **List five different paper products you use every day.**

notebook paper, envelopes, index cards,

lunch sacks, toilet paper, facial tissue,

napkins, paper towels, newspaper,

magazines, books, and so on.

> **What is one way you could use less paper?**

Students might say they could save paper

by using cloth napkins.

SCIENCESAURUS
A STUDENT HANDBOOK
BLUE BOOK

Material Resources ... p. 328

 SC/LINKS
THE WORLD'S A CLICK AWAY

www.scilinks.org
Keyword: Paper
Code: GS5D115

(147)

Key Idea

Paper is the product of a technology that may have been inspired by nature.

Focus

- Form and function
- Understandings about science and technology
- Abilities to distinguish between natural objects and objects made by humans
- Science as a human endeavor
- Nature of science
- History of science

Skills and Strategies

- Compare and contrast
- Conduct investigations
- Infer
- *Communicate (TG)*
- *Sequence (TG)*

Vocabulary*

Before beginning the chapter, make sure students understand these terms.

- invention
- recycle

* Definitions are in the Glossary on pages 166-172

Introducing the Chapter

This chapter looks at how the invention of wood pulp paper may have been inspired by one man's careful observation of a paper wasps' nest.

Draw students' attention to the statistics cited in the introduction. Explain that 580 pounds of paper translates into two mature trees per person per year! Tell students that 440 million trees are cut down annually in U.S. to make paper.

Science Background

About 30% by weight of U.S. household garbage is paper. Most paper can be recycled. Recycling one ton of paper saves between 13 and 20 harvestable trees. Also, making paper from recycled paper uses 30-55% less energy than making paper directly from trees.

Before You Read

Materials cardboard box for collecting recyclable paper, protective gloves

Place a cardboard box in your classroom and instruct students to put all their paper trash in it for a week. Have students go through the box as you begin this chapter and identify the different categories of paper in it. List each category on the board.

Add to the list using categories students wrote on page 147. Once the class list is complete, circle any paper products that are recyclable.

More Resources

The following resources are also available from Great Source and NSTA.

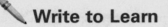
www.scilinks.org
Keyword: Paper
Code: GS5D115

✎ Write to Learn

Fictional Journal Entry Invite students to create an imaginary page out of René-Antoine Ferchault de Réaumur's journal. The page should describe Réaumur's encounter with the wasps' nest and the ideas it sparked.

⌐Read

Read about early kinds of paper, and how modern paper was invented.

"Paper Home"

notes:

> Circle all the ingredients Ts'ai Lun used to make paper.

Why do you think that paper allowed the Chinese to become "the most advanced culture in the world"? Jot down any ideas you have.

Students might suggest that information could be written on paper and shared with others so that they could also learn.

Make a list of the most <u>influential</u> people in the world's history. You might include Julius Caesar, Cleopatra, Confucius, Queen Victoria, Gandhi, Thomas Edison, Marie Curie, Albert Einstein, Ts'ai Lun.

Wait! Who is Ts'ai Lun?

Believe it or not, your life is influenced enormously by Ts'ai Lun!

Ts'ai Lun was a Chinese <u>court official</u> almost two thousand years ago. In 105 A.D. he invented paper as we know it today. He mashed Mulberry bark, hemp, rags, and water into a pulp, pressed out the liquid, and hung the thin mat in the sun to dry.

People had writing materials as early as 3500 B.C., but paper allowed the Chinese to become the most advanced culture in the world. Surprisingly, Ts'ai Lun's method of papermaking was not introduced in Europe for another thousand years. In 1151 the first <u>paper mill</u> was built in Spain.

Over the centuries the demand for paper grew—especially with the invention of the <u>printing press</u>. While the need for paper grew, the supply of rags shrank. Besides, paper-making was very time-consuming.

influential: causing important change
court official: person who worked for the Emperor

hemp: plant with tough fibers
rags: old bits of clothing, often made of cotton

paper mill: machine that makes paper
printing press: machine that uses ink to print words on paper

(148)

⌐Read

Paired Reading With the class, brainstorm a list of properties that make paper a good material for writing. (flat, smooth, light-colored, absorbs ink) Have students keep these properties in mind as they read about how paper has changed through history.

Help students to pronounce Ts'ai Lun's name (Sigh Lun). Tell students that Ts'ai Lun served as a member of the royal court during the Han Dynasty (202 B.C.–220 A.D.).

Explain that the Chinese were able to keep their papermaking knowledge secret for 500 years. But in 751, some Chinese papermakers were captured by Arabs. Soon, paper was being produced in the Middle East. The Europeans later learned the art of papermaking from the Arabs.

Why do you suppose the Chinese wanted to keep their knowledge of paper making secret? (Students may suggest that having paper was a great advantage to a civilization, as the reading emphasizes. By keeping

paper-making knowledge to themselves, the Chinese were able to maintain an advantage over other cultures.)

Tell students that the printing press was invented around 1450 by German printing pioneer Johannes Gutenberg. Have students add this date to their time lines. (See *Differentiating Instruction* in the side column, right.)

How many years passed between the invention of the printing press and the first commercially available

The world needed a solution.

One day in the early 1700s (no one is sure of the date), René-Antoine Ferchault de Réaumur, a French scientist, was walking in the woods. As he walked he spotted a wasp's nest and, since the wasps weren't home, stopped to investigate.

Suddenly Réaumur realized that the wasp's nest was made of paper. How did the wasps make paper without using rags? How did they make paper without using chemicals, fire, and mixing tanks? What did the wasps know that humans couldn't figure out?

It was quite simple. The wasps made paper by chewing <u>small twigs or tiny bits of rotting logs</u> and mixing them with <u>saliva and stomach juices.</u> Réaumur studied the digestive system of the wasp and presented his findings to the <u>French Royal Academy</u> in 1719.

It took more than 150 years before a machine was invented that could chew wood <u>efficiently</u> enough to make <u>wood pulp</u> paper <u>commercially</u>. But thanks to Réaumur and the wasps' <u>vacant</u> house, paper is widely used in today's society.

From: *Accidents May Happen: Fifty Inventions Discovered by Mistake,* by Charlotte Foltz Jones.

French Royal Academy: organization that encourages and supports scientific study
efficiently: well

wood pulp: wood that has been ground up and mixed with water

commercially: as a business to make money
vacant: empty

notes:

> <u>Underline</u> all the ingredients the wasps use to make their paper nests.

> What is most paper made out of today?
wood (pulp)

 149

Connections

Materials research materials on historical figures

Social Studies Have students research one of the names listed in the reading as "the most influential people in the world's history"—Julius Caesar, Cleopatra, Confucius, Queen Victoria, Gandhi, Thomas Edison, Marie Curie, and Albert Einstein. Instruct them to write a paragraph describing that person's influence on world history. How did their actions touch people outside of their own country? How did they change the world?

Differentiating Instruction

Logical/Mathematical

Materials metric rulers, paper

Have students create a timeline of events mentioned in the reading. (They will have to determine the year when wood pulp paper started being made commercially.) Encourage them to use a ruler and make their timeline to scale.

3500 B.C.—People had writing materials other than paper

105 A.D.—Ts'ai Lun invents paper

1151—First paper mill built in Spain using rags

1719—Réaumur presents his findings on paper making in wasps to the French Royal Academy

1872—Wood pulp paper made commercially

wood pulp paper? (1872 – 1450 = 422 years) Point out that printing presses were using hand-made paper during that period.

Draw students' attention to the phrase, "…and since the wasps weren't home…." Point out that the nest Réaumur investigated was probably abandoned. An active nest is never completely empty at any time. Warn students not to touch or try to remove any wasps' nests they may come across. While nests may appear empty, wasps may emerge and attack at any time.

Explain that while most of today's paper is made from wood pulp, rags are still often used to make specialty paper, including fine linen paper.

Have you ever accidentally left a piece of notepaper in your pocket when you did the wash? How about a dollar bill? What happened to each in the washing machine? (The notebook paper broke down but not the paper money.) Point out that dollar bills do not disintegrate in the washing machine because they are made from cotton rag fibers.

Check Understanding

Skill: Communicate

What ingredient do wasps' nests and modern paper have in common? (they are both made from wood pulp)

Enrichment

Testing Paper

Materials various kinds of paper; for example, copy paper, toilet tissue, paper towels, paper napkins, waxed paper, photocopying paper, tissue paper, notebook paper, wrapping paper

Have students work in pairs or small groups to research one kind of paper. Each group should research a different kind of insect.

Students should investigate and report on the following properties of their samples:

- texture
- resistance to tearing
- resistance to shredding
- water absorption
- ease of writing on (with ink and with pencil)
- general design

Students should identify how the paper is intended to be used and how its properties support, or do not support, that use. Have each group report its findings in a written report. Then have each group give an oral report to the class, sharing the information in their reports.

Look Back

> **What was Ts'ai Lun's paper made out of?**

Mulberry bark, hemp, rags, water

> **What was the wasp's nest paper made out of?**

twigs and logs (wood), saliva, stomach juices

> **What is most paper made out of today?**

wood (pulp)

All kinds of paper have one thing in common: they are all made from plant fibers. For example, the rags used to make Ts'ai Lun's paper are often made of fibers from the cotton plant. **Plant fibers** are the tough strands of material found in all plants. Plant fibers are what make plants strong enough to support their own weight. Plant fiber is also what makes paper strong.

> **What is the source of plant fibers in each kind of paper listed above?**

Mulberry bark, hemp, rags, wood (twigs and logs), wood (pulp)

Explore

AN IDEA FROM NATURE

Paper is an example of a technology. **Technology** is any tool or product that improves people's lives or helps them do a job. Paper allows people to write down their ideas and share them with others.

Engineers—people who design technology—often look to nature when coming up with new ideas for technology.

> **What idea from nature did Réaumur use when designing a new way to make paper?**

He used the wasps' idea of using ground-up wood to make paper.

Look Back

After students have completed the questions, ask: ***What else do these three kinds of paper have in common?*** (They all are made with water or a watery liquid.) Point out that the fibers need to be ground up and separated before being laid out to make paper. Blending them with water allows the fibers to separate and float freely. The mixture can then be drained, leaving the fibers in a thin sheet.

Explore

An Idea From Nature Draw students' attention to the picture on page 150. ***What do the wasps do with the paper they make?*** (They use it to build their homes. Specifically, students may be able to tell that the paper is used to make small chambers that house growing wasp larvae.)

After students answer the question, ask: ***What if Réaumur hadn't taken the time to explore the paper wasps' empty nest?*** (He may never

have discovered their secret for making paper from wood.) Emphasize the role of careful observation in the history of scientific discovery and invention.

Activity

MAKE YOUR OWN RECYCLED PAPER

Today, most paper is made from wood that comes directly from trees. But cutting down too many trees to make paper can lead to many problems in the environment. In this activity, you will make recycled paper—paper made from old paper that has already been used. The wood fibers that made up the old paper are still good. They just need to be separated and made into new paper. Recycling paper in this way can help save trees.

What You Need:

- 2 sheets of newspaper
- blender or food processor
- water
- large plastic tub
- 2 tablespoons white glue
- stirring spoon
- screen
- clothes iron

LARGE PLASTIC TUB

BLENDER

2 SHEETS OF NEWSPAPER

CLOTHES IRON

STIRRING SPOON

2 TABLESPOONS OF WHITE GLUE

SCREEN

What to Do:

1. Tear the paper into small pieces. Put the pieces in the blender with enough water to make the mixture watery (about 2 or 3 cups). Blend on medium to high until you can't see any bits of paper. Then blend for another 2 minutes.

2. Place the screen at the bottom of the large plastic tub.

3. Pour enough water into the tub until it is about 4 inches deep. Stir in the 2 tablespoons of glue and the paper mixture from the blender. Stir together until well mixed.

(continued on next page) **151**

Connections

Materials research materials on the manufacture and use of papyrus in ancient Egypt

Social Studies Have students research the production of papyrus, the "paper" of ancient Egypt. Paper made from papyrus is believed to be the first ever used. Have students research how paper was made from the papyrus plant, and the role papyrus played in Egyptian culture.

1. The outer fibers of the harvested plant were peeled away to expose the core or pith. The pith was sliced into very thin strips.

2. The strips were soaked in water to remove most of the plant's sugar. Then they were pounded until pliable.

3. The strips were laid side-by-side horizontally, barely overlapping. Other strips were laid vertically over those strips.

4. The strips were pounded and left to dry under a heavy weight for 6 days. The remaining sugar in the strips acted to bind them together.

5. The finished paper was polished by rubbing with a smooth shell.

6. Ancient Egyptians recorded official business on papyrus and produced literature on papyrus. These documents reveal much about the culture of ancient Egypt.

Activity

Time 40 minutes, plus 20 minutes the next day

Materials newspaper, blender or food processor, water, large plastic tub, white glue, stirring spoon, stiff screen, clothes iron

Follow the directions on the student page to prepare batches of paper pulp. You may choose to have each group of students prepare its own batch of paper, or you may choose to have the class prepare one batch together.

As you are loading the blender with ingredients, ask: **What is the source of plant fibers in this mixture?** (wood fibers in the newspaper) In addition to newspaper, you can also use old brown paper bags and old construction paper in your pulp mixture. You can also add small amounts of glitter, small leaves, or flowers for decorative effects. Mix these items up with the other materials in the blender.

As you are running the blender, ask: **What is happening to the wood fibers in the newspaper?** (They are being separated into individual fibers.) Make sure students understand that the slurry you created is made up of wood fibers suspended in water.

As you add the glue to the tub, point out that it acts to bind the fibers together to form a sheet of paper.

(continued on p. 152)

Assessment

Skill: Sequence

Use the following task to assess each student's progress.

Have students write out the sequence of steps they followed to make their own paper. Tell them to annotate the list to show the condition of the wood fibers at each stage. 1. Shred old newspapers (wood fibers held together in newspaper). 2. Mix with water (wood fibers separated and suspended in water). 3. Add glue, strain on flat surface (individual wood fibers overlapping each other). 4. Allow to dry (wood fibers binding together to form paper). 5. Iron and trim. After students have completed their lists, ask students: ***How is this process different from that used by wasps to make paper?*** (Wasps make paper by chewing small twigs or tiny bits of rotting logs, not by using shredded newspaper. They mix the chewed material with saliva and stomach juices, not with water and glue.)

Review "Find Out" Question

Review the question from the Unit Opener on page 146. ***What can wasps teach us about paper making?*** (Wasps taught inventors that "chewing" wood was an important step in making paper. This led to the invention of a wood-chewing machine.)

(continued from previous page)

4. Lift the screen up very slowly. It should take you 20–30 seconds to lift the screen to the top of the tub. Let the water drip into the tub for about a minute. Then place your screen somewhere where it can dry.

5. Once the paper is dry, you can gently peel it off the screen.
6. Have your teacher iron your paper flat. Trim the edges with scissors.
7. Write a letter to a friend on your piece of paper.

Think About It:

> **Compare the paper you made to the paper made by the wasps. What very important basic ingredient do they have in common?**

They both contain wood fibers—twigs and logs, old newspaper.

Remember that the wasps mixed the wood they chewed up with saliva and stomach juices. Saliva and stomach juices contain chemicals that break down food into smaller parts so that it can be digested.

> **How do you think saliva and stomach juices help the wasps make paper for their nests? (Hint: Compare the wasps' way of making paper with the steps you followed to make your own paper.)**

Students should realize that if saliva and stomach juices contain chemicals that break down food (plant material), they could also break down wood into separate fibers. The blender broke down the newspaper into separate fibers in the activity. Also, saliva and stomach juices are liquids, so they help in the mixing process, just as water did in the activity.

(continued from page 151)

As students are lifting the screen slowly out of the water, ask: **Why do you need to lift the screen so slowly?** (Students should be able to see that lifting slowly allows the water to drain away while leaving the fibers in place on top of the screen.)

Have students place their dripping screens in a place where they will not be disturbed. Remind students not to poke or pull at their paper while it is drying as it will tear easily.

Once the paper is dry, have students note how strong it is. Challenge them to set different objects on it and see how much weight it can hold. (The paper should be able to easily support the weight of a stapler or calculator.) **Where does the paper's strength come from?** (from the tough plant fibers that make it up)

Invite the class to help you complete a concept map showing the connections between the wasps' paper-making method and the one they used here.

A New Beak

Chapter 23

What's a bird without a beak to do?

Imagine an eagle eating a fish that it pulled out of a river. The eagle does not have sharp teeth, like a wolf, that can tear up the food. What it does have is a strong, pointed beak. It uses its beak to rip the fish into bite-sized pieces it can eat. Can you imagine, then, what would happen to an eagle that lost its beak? How would it feed itself?

Technology to the rescue! Technology is any tool or product that improves the lives of people—or sometimes—animals. In this chapter, you'll read about an eagle that was saved by technology and a team of thoughtful dentists.

Before You Read

A **prosthesis** is an artificial body part used to replace a natural part that is damaged or missing. Sometimes people injured in accidents or war need to have a prosthesis made. The prosthesis cannot do everything the original body part did. But it helps the person do many of the same activities he or she did before the injury.

> **Do you have any friends or relatives who wear a prosthesis? List any prosthesis you might have seen in real life or on TV. What body part does each prosthesis replace? How does the prosthesis help the person who wears it?**

Answers will vary, but students will probably

name arms and legs.

 SCIENCESAURUS
A STUDENT HANDBOOK
BLUE BOOK
Designing Technology p. 358

 SCILINKS
THE WORLD'S A CLICK AWAY
www.scilinks.org
Keyword: Engineer
Code: GS5D120

(153)

Key Idea

New technologies are tested and improved until a successful design is found.

Focus

- Form and function
- Properties of objects and materials
- Structure and function in living systems
- Science and technology in local challenges
- Science as a human endeavor
- Nature of science

Skills and Strategies

- Communicate
- Concept map
- Generate ideas
- *Sequence (TG)*

Introducing the Chapter

This chapter discusses how technology was used to save an injured eagle.

Have the class brainstorm a list of ways that an eagle uses its beak. (to preen, to collect twigs, to build a nest) **What would happen to an eagle that lost its beak?** (It would not be able to eat, it would not be able to keep clean, and it would not be able to build a nest and raise young.) Help students to conclude that a wild eagle without a beak could not survive.

Before You Read

Materials photographs of prosthetic devices

Use the Internet to locate some appropriate images of prosthetic limbs (arms, legs, hands, feet, joints). Share the photographs with students. Point out that while many prosthetic devices do not look like real limbs, they are designed to perform some of the same functions. For example, a prosthetic hand may feature a metal hook instead of flesh, but the hook can be used to grasp objects much like a real hand.

Invite students to share their experiences with prosthetic devices with the class. Caution students not to make light of the subject in their discussion.

More Resources

The following resources are also available from Great Source and NSTA.

www.scilinks.org
Keyword: Engineer
Code: GS5D120

Read

In 2002, an injured bald eagle was found in Canada. Most of its beak had been shot off by a hunter. A team of helpful dentists came to its rescue.

"Making a Beak"

notes:

> How many beaks does Dr. Andrews think the team will make before they get one that's just right?

3, 4, 5, or even 12

> Why does Dr. Andrews think they have to make so many beaks before they get it right?

Because this is something that has never been done before and they are new at this

> Underline what Dr. Andrews based his beak design on.

Canada: August 19, 2002

A bald eagle that was left for dead after its beak was shot off is alive and tearing its prey to shreds again thanks to a Canadian dentist who fashioned an artificial bill out of [plastic].

Now Dr. Brian Andrews is working to improve on the prototype, which is pinned to the tiny bit of beak left after the gunshot, so the 4½-year-old bird of prey can one day return to the wild.

"Because this is new ground for us, and I'm new at this, we expect to make three or four or five or even a dozen until we get it right," Andrews said last week from his dental [office] in Nanaimo, British Columbia. ...

He based the design, complete with breathing holes, on a picture of an eagle on a recent cover of National Geographic magazine as well as [on] a dried beak specimen. ...

The [people who rescued the eagle] nursed the 18-pound (8-kilogram) bird back to health, but the soft, remaining nub of its bill prevented it from eating anything but small morsels.

fashioned: made
artificial: made by people
bill: beak
prototype: early design model

new ground: something that has never been done before
specimen: sample
nub: base
morsels: bits of food

Read

Paired Reading

Materials if possible, samples of prosthetic devices, which can be borrowed from a surgical supply store or hospital

Focus the attention of students on the design and materials used in making prosthetic devices whether they are for animals, such as eagles, or for human beings.

Name or show a prosthetic device. Describe its purpose. Have students discuss the properties the device should have in order to function efficiently. Note that some prosthetic devices, such as those used to replace lost limbs, have moving parts and may have to bear weight. Other prosthetic devices, such as a false tooth, do not have moving parts but must resist wear.

You might want to lead off this discussion by reviewing the properties of the prosthetic eagle beak and how they contributed to the efficient functioning of the beak.

Fred Leak, the dental technician who made the first beak, takes care of the eagle and continues to improve its plastic beak.

Andrews [created a model of the] beak and took it to a <u>dental technician</u>, [Fred Leak,] who made a <u>replica</u> out of [the same plastic] used to make some false teeth and mouth guards for hockey players, he said.

He stained the [new beak] yellow, to make it look realistic. The bird took to it immediately.

"He's tearing at his prey. When we first put it on, he gave us this nice, great big yawn and squawk, and we were quite thrilled that it stayed together," Andrews said. ...

"I'm fond of wildlife. I'm a carver and I make duck <u>decoys</u> as a hobby. I figured: I can carve a wooden beak, maybe I can make a plastic one for this guy," he said.

From: "Canadian dentist gives eagle new beak, waives bill," *Planet Ark*, August 19, 2002.

dental technician: someone who makes devices for dentists
replica: copy

decoys: wooden animals carved to look like the real thing

notes:

> How did missing most of its beak cause problems for the eagle?

It could only eat small morsels of food because it didn't have its full beak.

(155)

UNIT 5 CHAPTER 23 (155)

Write to Learn

Write a Story Have students write a short story in which a child finds an injured animal and how technology is used to repair the injury. Stories can be read aloud to the class or posted on a bulletin board.

Differentiating Instruction

Verbal/Linguistic Encourage interested students to do research on how technology is used to clean up oil spills and/or save the lives of animals that have been contaminated with oil.

Students should use notes to develop and present an oral report of their findings. Students should be told that they can use visual aids as part of their presentation.

After students underline the passage of the reading that explains what Dr. Andrews based his beak design on, ask: *How do you suppose each of these things helped Dr. Andrews come up with a good model?* (The photograph showed what a beak looks like on a live eagle, and the dried specimen gave him a physical model to work with.)

Science Background
Dr. Andrews and Fred Leak used orthodontic acrylic to make the prosthetic beak. This is the same material used to make dentures and fake fingernails. When heated, it can be poured into a mold of any shape. When cooled, it is very hard and durable.

Check Understanding
Skill: Communicate
Why did the people who rescued the injured eagle turn to a team of dentists to help the eagle? (Dentists make prosthetic teeth and a beak is similar to teeth in form and function.)

Connections

Physical Education Invite a physician or medical technician who works with prosthetic devices to visit the class and discuss his or her work with students. Suggest that your guest bring along several prosthetic devices and give a presentation showing how each one works.

Have students ask some of the following questions during the presentation:

1. What body part is this device meant to replace?
2. Why is the function of this body part important.
3. Why would it be important for a person's health to get a prosthesis for this body part?
4. How is the device operated?
5. What things can it do that the original body part did?
6. What things can't it do that the original body part could do?

Look Back

Answer the following questions based on what you learned in the reading about the prosthesis that the injured eagle wore.

> **What body part did the prosthesis replace?**

the beak

> **What material did they use to make it?**

plastic

> **How was it attached to the eagle?**

It was pinned to the bit of real beak that was still left after the gunshot.

> **What did the eagle use the prosthesis for?**

for tearing up its food

Explore

USING PROTOTYPES

A **prototype** is an early model of a design. Engineers—people who design technology—usually build many different designs before they get one that works well.

Fred Leak made four prototypes of the prosthetic beak before he got the one that worked best. The eagle ripped the first beak right off. The second beak trapped water between what was left of the real beak and the prosthetic beak. This caused the real beak to soften. The third beak was too big. The fourth beak was the one that worked.

> **How did prototypes help Fred Leak get a design that worked well?**

Each prototype told Fred Leak something new—what was working and what wasn't. He was able to learn from each trial and improve each version.

Look Back

You may want to explain to students that the material the team used to make the prosthesis is a special kind of plastic called "acrylic." Explain that acrylic is transparent, very hard, and weather resistant. Also, it can be easily molded into any shape. ***Why was acrylic a good choice for the prosthetic beak?*** (The beak needed to be beaked-shaped, strong, and able to withstand weather.)

Explore

Using Prototypes Explain that engineers usually brainstorm many possible ideas before building and testing a prototype. After they make a list of ideas, they analyze the expected benefits, costs, and drawbacks of each. Then they choose the best one.

What was different about each prototype Fred Leak made? Was each one made of a different material? (No, they were all made of plastic. What changed was the size and shape of the beak.)

Suppose you were in charge of building the prosthetic beak. In testing the first prototype, you found that the beak snapped in half when the eagle tried to tear at food. How might you modify your design? (Students may suggest that they would use a different material as the material was not strong enough. Accept all reasonable responses.)

Explore

DESIGNING TECHNOLOGY

The diagram on the left shows the steps engineers follow when designing a new technology.

> **Study the diagram on the left. Then complete the diagram on the right to show the steps the dentists followed when they designed the prosthetic beak.**

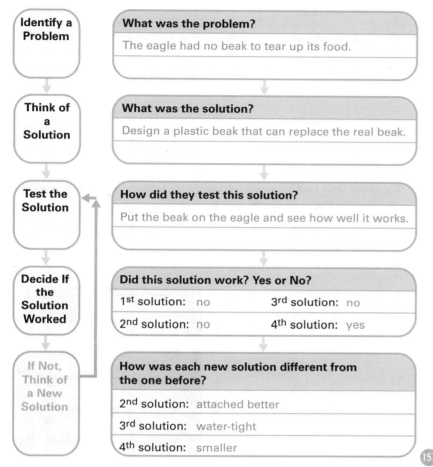

Identify a Problem

What was the problem?

The eagle had no beak to tear up its food.

Think of a Solution

What was the solution?

Design a plastic beak that can replace the real beak.

Test the Solution

How did they test this solution?

Put the beak on the eagle and see how well it works.

Decide If the Solution Worked

Did this solution work? Yes or No?

1st solution: no   3rd solution: no

2nd solution: no   4th solution: yes

If Not, Think of a New Solution

How was each new solution different from the one before?

2nd solution: attached better

3rd solution: water-tight

4th solution: smaller

157

Explore

Designing Technology You may choose to recreate this flow chart on the board and have students complete it as a class exercise.

Point out that each new solution, or prototype, needed to be tested again to see whether it worked. Explain that sometimes it takes hundreds of prototypes before a design is successful.

Once students have completed the flow chart, have them fill in a second flow chart using the information from their egg-drop challenge experience. (See **Enrichment**, in the side column above.)

Once the flow charts are complete, ask: **What did you learn from each design that failed?** (Answers will vary. Students may report that they found that foam peanuts shifted around too much in the box, allowing the egg to jostle about. Or that the stocking used to suspend the egg in the center of the box was too elastic and allowed the egg to

strike the bottom of the box when it hit the ground. Accept all ideas.)

How would you modify your own egg drop contraption based on all the group's results? (Answers will vary. Students should report that each new design should correct a problem that existed in the previous design.)

Assessment

Skill: Sequence

Use the following question to assess each student's progress.

What are the basic steps in technology design? (1. Identify a problem, 2. think of a solution, 3. test the solution, 4. decide if the solution worked, and if not, 5. design and test a new solution.)

Review "Find Out" Question

Review the question for Chapter 23 in the Unit Opener on page 146: ***Why don't bald eagles mind going to the dentist?*** Have students use what they learned in the chapter to suggest an answer to the question. (Because injured eagles can be helped by dentists and the technology they design.) Use their responses as the basis for a class discussion.

⌐Explore

USING SKILLS TO DESIGN TECHNOLOGY

Sometimes people lose teeth that have rotted or died. A dentist, such as Dr. Andrews, can replace these teeth with false teeth. A dental technician, such as Fred Leak, makes the false teeth out of plastic or another material. They both make sure that the new teeth are the right size and shape so that they work as well as the original teeth. Sometimes they have to keep adjusting the false teeth until they fit and work just right.

> **What skills from his profession—or work—allowed Fred Leak to help the bald eagle?**

He could make plastic parts that could replace parts of the mouth that were lost or damaged. He also knew how to adjust the parts until they worked right.

> **What skills from his personal interests—or hobbies—allowed Dr. Andrews to help the bald eagle? (Hint: Look back at the reading.)**

He carved duck decoys as a hobby, so he knew something about how to shape a bill.

This case displays several of the different prosthetic beaks that Fred Leak designed for the eagle.

⌐Explore

Using Skills to Design Technology

Have students discuss the skills and knowledge that are required of someone who designs prosthetic teeth. Be sure to discuss the function of different kinds of teeth and how this might affect the design of different kinds of teeth.

What is the function of teeth? (To bite, chew, and grind food until it is small enough to be efficiently digested and easily swallowed.) ***What properties should false teeth have?*** (Some should be sharp enough to cut food. Some should be hard enough to grind food. And all should be strong enough to withstand chewing food.) Point out that for cosmetic purposes false teeth should also look like real teeth.

Have students think back to the properties of acrylic. (transparent, hard, resistant to weather, moldable into any shape) ***Why is acrylic a good choice for false teeth?*** (It can be molded into tooth shapes, including sharp teeth, and it is strong enough to withstand chewing, and it won't break down in a wet environment.) Explain that acrylic can be colored white to look like a real tooth.

After students answer the questions on the page, hold a class discussion on the role of professional training and personal interests in problem solving. Help students see that professional skills can be applied to solve new problems, as was the case with the dentist and the eagle.

Animated Movies

Chapter 24

He's green, he's mean, but is he real?

The Incredible Hulk is a comic book character that was first created in 1962 by writer Stan Lee. The Hulk was an ordinary man who turned into a giant, green monster when he got very angry. In 2003, the movie *The Hulk* came out. The movie had real actors, but it also had a character made using computer technology—the big, green Hulk himself.

In this chapter, you will learn how technology was used to create the Hulk. You'll also see how a team of people with different skills worked together on the project.

Before You Read

How is a picture of an object different from the object itself?

> **Draw a picture of a pencil in the space below.**

> **Compare your drawing to the pencil. What information about the pencil can you get by looking at the actual pencil but not by looking at the picture?**

The picture doesn't show all sides of the

pencil. You can't see the back of the pencil.

You can't see how "deep" it is, only how

long and wide.

www.scilinks.org
Keyword:
Computer
Technology
Code: GS5D125

159

Key Idea

Creating an animated movie character requires many types of technology and the participation of a team of people with different skills.

Focus

* Position and motion of objects
* Understandings about science and technology
* Science as a human endeavor
* Science and technology in society

Skills and Strategies

* Sequence
* Concept map
* Interpret scientific illustrations
* Apply knowledge
* *Communicate (TG)*

Vocabulary*

Before beginning the chapter, make sure students understand these terms.

* computer
* laser
* technology
* three-dimensional (3-D)

* Definitions are found in the Glossary on pages 166-172.

Introducing the Chapter

This chapter looks at how the animated movie character the Hulk was created. To generate interest and familiarize students with animation in movies, ask students to identify and describe an animated movie they have seen.

After the discussion, ask students the following questions: *How is a movie character physically different from a comic book character?* (A movie character is three-dimensional while a comic book character is two-dimensional)

How do you think movie makers made the Hulk move around like a human character on film? (Answers will vary.)

Before You Read

Lead students to conclude that real objects have three dimensions, but drawings only show objects in two dimensions.

What device do you suppose the creators of The Hulk *might have used to turn this 2-D comic book character into a 3-D movie star?* (Accept all answers for now. Students may guess that computers were involved.)

More Resources

The following resources are also available from Great Source and NSTA.

Reader's Handbook

Writers Express

www.scilinks.org
Keyword: Computer
Technology
Code: GS5D125

Connections

Language Arts Early animation developed as flip books. Flip books hold a sequence of slightly different pictures. When the pages are flipped, the pictures seem to be in motion, i.e., animated. After you have explained the mechanics and contents of a flip book, ask: **How is a flip book like a book you read?** (Both tell a story. The flip book uses pictures. The book I read uses words and pictures.)

⌐Read

Read about how a special team of people used technology to create the Hulk on the big screen.

"The Hulk Comes Alive!"

notes:

> What tool did the technicians use to scan the sculpture and make a 3-D picture of it on the computer?

laser light

In the new movie *The Hulk* the monstrous green superhero stands 15 feet tall and weighs two tons. Scary! But the huge star didn't start out so impressive. He <u>evolved</u> from pencil sketches on paper and a ten-inch-tall clay model. How'd he become the monster he is today? It took artists, sculptors, animators, and a ton of cool technology.

1 <u>Laser</u> Scan A clay sculpture is created from sketches of the Hulk. Technicians place the sculpture onto a <u>turntable</u>. "As it <u>rotates</u>, we <u>scan</u> the model with a laser light," explains Paul Giacoppo, Creature Supervisor (yep, that's a real job title!). "The laser makes a 3-D picture on a computer of the mini-Hulk that can then be <u>altered</u>."

evolved: was developed
laser: concentrated light beam
turntable: disk that turns around, like a merry-go-round
rotates: turns around
scan: move across
altered: changed

160

⌐Read

Paired Reading As students read, invite them to take notes regarding people's roles (artists, sculptors, animators, technicians, Creature Supervisor, computer animators, digital artists, creature developers) and words related to technology (laser, scan, computer, computer mouse clicks, digital) mentioned in the reading.

Have students continue to focus on the people and technology mentioned in the reading. Have them note how many different types of people and technology went into creating the Hulk.

Help students as needed to understand how the clay figure is scanned into the computer using a laser light and converted to computer images. You may choose to do the simulation of the laser scan suggested in ***Differentiating Instruction*** (side column, page 161).

After students have completed the simulation, ask: **Why did Paul Giacoppo place the clay sculpture of** **the Hulk on a turntable while he scanned it with the laser?** (Students should infer that he needed to scan all sides of the figure, and rotating it while shining a beam on it allowed him to scan all sides.)

Help students see that either the scanner needed to move around the figure, or the figure needed to rotate in the laser light. The rotating figure was the easier solution. Point out that part of using technology effectively is figuring out the best and simplest way to do a task.

2 Inside The Computer The 3-D computer model is "the real starting point for what our <u>digital</u> character will look like," says Giacoppo. With clicks of a computer mouse, Giacoppo and his team add more muscles to the Hulk's body, alter his face to look meaner, and make the Hulk appear as powerful and impressive as possible.

3 <u>Animating</u> The Muscled Monster Now the computer animators take over. They're the people who draw (in the computer) everything the Hulk does in the movie. The movie director shot the movie with someone moving a stick with a picture of Hulk's face on it to <u>represent</u> the Hulk's movements. That's what the human actors reacted to. Later the stick is replaced with the animated drawings made of the Hulk playing his part as a digital character.

4 The Hulk Comes Alive! The team that includes 42 animators, 7 <u>digital artists</u>, and 10 creature developers works for about three months to finish the Hulk. When he finally jumps onto the screen, the superhero is capable of running 150 miles an hour and leaping two miles. It takes *a lot* to create a giant green <u>humanoid</u>!

From: "The Hulk Comes Alive!"
National Geographic Kids, July/August 2003.

digital: made on the computer
animating: bringing to "life" on the computer

represent: stand for
digital artists: people who draw using computers

humanoid: human-like creature

notes:

> What do the animators do to the Hulk's image?
They draw in the computer everything the Hulk does in the movie.

Differentiating Instruction

Materials turntable or rotating cake plate, laser pointer or narrow-beam flashlight, 3-D action figure

Naturalist Recreate the set-up described in the reading for converting the sculpture into a 3-D computer image.

Safety Note: If you choose to use the laser pointer, maintain control of it at all times. Tell students that the laser should never be pointed at anyone's eyes.

1. Place the action figure in the center of the turntable or rotating cake plate. Turn down the lights.
2. Shine the laser light or narrow flashlight beam at the figure from one side. Do not move the light.
3. Turn on the turntable or begin rotating the cake plate.
4. Have students note where the beam falls as the disk turns around. Explain that information about every part of the figure touched by the laser light is transmitted to a camera. The information is then transmitted to a computer.
5. Now raise the laser pointer to the top of the figure. Then lower it slowly to the bottom as the table or plate turns. Have students note that every part of the figure was touched by the beam, so every part of it can be recreated in the computer.

Help students understand that the movie director shot the movie on film like any other movie, using real actors and movie sets. Later, the images of the Hulk created by the computer animators were "cut and pasted" into the film. So although it looks like the human actors are interacting with the Hulk on film, the actors never actually saw the monster.

Check Understanding

Skill: Communicate

What were the first and last tools used to create the Hulk? (The first tool was a pencil. The last tool was a computer.)

Enrichment

Making an "Animated Movie"

Materials unlined pads or packages of stiff paper, which can be obtained at a stationary store; pencils or pens

Give students the following instructions for making their own "animated movie" using a flip book.

1. Think of a simple story to tell in the "movie." (dog running and leaping in the air, horse jumping over a fence, car zooming down the street) The story should be made up of at least 15 frames.

2. Place the pad on your desk so that the binding is on the left.

3. Draw your first image on the second sheet of the notepad, near the edge.

4. Draw the next image on the next sheet. Each image should be only slightly different from the one before. Here's an extra challenge. You can draw the image from different angles, so it looks like it is rotating when you flip the pages.

5. Continue until you have completed the story. Make a cover for your book on the first sheet of the pad.

6. Holding the binding in your left hand, flip the pages of the pad quickly so that you see the object or character in your story move.

Look Back

The reading describes a process with many steps for creating an animated character.

> **Put the following steps in order to show how the animated Hulk was created.**
> • Change the appearance of the 3-D image.
> • Create clay model of the Hulk.
> • Create pencil sketches of the Hulk.
> • Make the Hulk move around in the movie.
> • Create a 3-D image of the Hulk on the computer.

Step 1
Create pencil sketches of the Hulk.

Step 2
Create clay model of the Hulk.

Step 3
Create a 3-D image of the Hulk on the computer.

Step 4
Change the appearance of the 3-D image.

Step 5
Make the Hulk move around in the movie.

162

Look Back

Materials index cards

As an added challenge, you may complete this page as a class exercise:

1. Break the class up into small groups.
2. Cover up the steps listed on page 162.
3. Have half the groups identify the procedures for creating an animated character described in the reading.
4. Tell the groups to verify their final lists against the list provided on page 162.
5. Then have groups write each step on a separate index card and mix the cards.
6. Challenge the other half of the groups to put the index cards in the *correct order*.

(2-D sketch
to 3-D sculpture
to 3-D computer image
to enhanced 3-D computer image
to moving 3-D computer image)

Then help students identify the technologies used at each step, even the simple technologies. (pencil, sculpting tools, laser light/scan, computer, computer)

Explore

It took lots of different people working together to create the animated Hulk, including artists, sculptors, technicians, and animators.

> Fill in the concept map below to show how each group of people contributed to the project. In your descriptions, focus on how each group's task depended on the work done by the group before it. Use the information from the reading and in the chart on the previous page to help you.

Artists
The artists drew pencil sketches of the Hulk.

↓

Sculptors
The sculptors created a clay model of the Hulk based on the pencil sketches.

↓

Technicians
The technicians used the clay model to create a 3-D image of the Hulk on a computer screen.

↓

Animators
Animators then changed that image and made the Hulk move and do things on the screen.

163

Writing an Explanation Explain how animation "fools" your eyes. Each picture in an animated movie is a still picture. As a matter of fact, each frame in any movie shows only a still picture. Do research to find out how your brain turns these still pictures into what seems to be motion. Write an explanation that your classmates will understand.

NSTA Activity

Seeing in 3-D

See page 145A for an NSTA activity on seeing 2-D drawings in 3-D.

After students finish looking at the paired images with their tubes, explain why they saw the image in 3-D: We see the world in three dimensions because each of our eyes gets a slightly different view of what we are looking at. By using the tubes to separate the view received by each eye, we set the brain's three-dimensional processing into high gear. It analyzes the two different views and uses the information to "paint" depth onto the view.

Explore

Team Effort After students have completed the concept map, get them to focus on the skills each professional brings to his or her job. *What training and skills do you suppose artists have?* (Students may guess that artists are good at representing real-life objects on paper. They probably were good at drawing when they were young and later went to art school to learn different kinds of drawing and painting.)

Continue in this fashion through the other three professions listed on page 163. You may choose to point out that artists, sculptors, technicians, and animators may not all attend the same sort of school. Some may go to a liberal arts college while others attend a technical or vocational college. Take this opportunity to talk about careers. You might want to bring in a career counselor from a local high school to discuss career options further.

Finally, draw out students' own experience with working on a team of people with diverse skills. *In a science or technology project you have worked on in a team, how did the different skills and knowledge of each member of the team contribute to the success of the project?* (Answers may include the following: Students good at math did the calculations. Students good at building things constructed models. Students good at drawing made the displays. Accept all responses that reveal how students with different skills contribute to a team effort.)

Assessment

Skill: Apply Knowledge

Use the following question to assess each student's progress.

How is a flip book like an animated movie? (Both use a series of slightly different images to give the impression of movement.)

Review "Find Out" Question

Review the question for Chapter 24 in the Unit Opener on page 146. Ask: *How many people did it take to create The Hulk?* Have students use what they learned in the chapter to suggest an answer to the question. (A team of 59 artists, sculptors, technicians, and animators.) Use their responses as the basis for a class discussion.

Explore

MAKING A 3-D IMAGE

A pencil sketch shows an object in two dimensions (2-D). A clay sculpture shows an object in three dimensions (3-D). You can turn a sculpture around and see all sides of it. You can't see all sides of an object in a sketch.

Laser scanning is a technology that lets us make a computer image of a 3-D object. In laser scanning, a laser beam is pointed at an object. The laser light bounces off the object and gives information to a camera about how far away every part of the object is. A computer attached to the camera gets information about the ups and downs, ins and outs, and everything about the object's shape. This information is used by the computer to map the object and create an image of it on a screen. To make a complete image, the laser must scan all sides of the object.

> You need a clay sculpture of the Hulk in order to create the 3-D image on the computer. What would happen if you laser-scanned the artists' pencil sketches instead?

The pencil sketches are a 2-D model. Every part of the sketch would be the same distance away from the laser, so it wouldn't give the computer useful information about the shape of the image.

Explore

Making a 3-D Image Help students as needed to understand what is going on in the illustration. (The laser/camera is pointed at the sculpture of an elephant on a turntable. The laser/camera is attached to the computer. As the laser scans the sculpture, images of it from all sides will be reproduced on the computer screen. The technician (see hands) is deciding between laser scanning the 2-D sketch or the 3-D sculpture of the elephant.)

To help students further visualize the set-up, you may choose to do the simulation of the laser scan suggested in *Differentiating Instruction* (side column, page 161).

Help students to conclude that a 3-D sculpture must be placed on the turntable in order for a 3-D image to be created on the computer screen.

UNIT 5: Science, Technology, and Society

What Did We Learn?

CHAPTER 22 What did wasps know about making paper long before people did?
Paper can be made out of chewed up wood pulp and something sticky.

CHAPTER 23 How can technology improve the life of a wild animal that is injured?
Engineers can design technology that replaces injured body parts in both people and wild animals.

CHAPTER 24 What kinds of people are needed to create an animated movie character?
Creating an animated character requires the work of artists, sculptors, technicians, and animators.

165

What Did We Learn?

The questions on this page complement the questions in the Unit Opener on page 146. Discuss the questions as a class. Invite students to share their ideas about the chapters they have completed. What new questions do they have after completing these chapters?

Write an essay Have students write an essay describing what it takes to be a successful engineer—a person who designs new technology.

Have them look for qualities exhibited by each of the engineers or other creative people described in the chapters of this unit. (observant, curious, resourceful, creative, able to apply skills to new problems, passionate, artistic, perseverant, technically adept, imaginative, and so on)

Once they have brainstormed a list of adjectives and descriptions, have them come up with a structure for their essays. Encourage them to create an outline, complete with paragraph ideas and topic sentences, before starting their essays.

Post student essays around the classroom and invite students to read one another's work.

Glossary of Science Terms

A

adaptation: a structure or behavior that helps an organism meet its basic needs (36)

amphibian: an animal that lives in water when it is young and on land when it is an adult (135)

artificial: made by people (154)

astronomy: the study of planet Earth and objects in space (82)

B

biodiversity: the variety of different species in an area (144)

brain: the organ in the nervous system that is the control center of the body (20)

C

canyon: steep-sided river valley (65)

carnivore: an organism that eats animals (26)

cavern: a large cave (58)

chemical change: a change that produces a new substance when two or more chemicals are combined to produce new chemicals (98)

chemical compound: a substance made up of two or more elements (89)

chemical property: the ability of a substance to react with other substances and to change into a new substance with different properties (93)

chemistry: the science of elements and chemical compounds (90)

classification system: a system that groups organisms based on similarities and differences of their traits (16)

computer: an electronic machine that stores and processes information (161)

D

deformity: a body part that is not "normal" (133, 134)

dental technician: someone who makes devices for dentists (155)

deposition: the process in which rock eroded by water, wind, or ice is dropped in a new place (62)

digest: break food down into nutrients that the body can use (29)

digital: made on the computer (161)

dinosaur: an extinct reptile that lived long ago (69, 70)

dung: poop (128)

E

earthquake: movements of Earth's crust that produce waves that pass through Earth (51)

earth science: the study of planet Earth and objects in space (50)

eclipse: one object in space casting its shadow on another object in space (81)

ecosystem: all the living and nonliving things that are found in an area (43)

electrical energy: a form of energy that is produced when negative electric charges move from one place to another place; also called electricity (105)

electricity: a form of energy that is produced when negative electric charges move from one place to another place; also called electrical energy (101)

element: the most basic kind of matter; a pure substance made of only one kind of atom (89)

embryo: the body of an unhatched animal (72)

energy: the ability to cause motion or change (107)

energy of motion: the energy of a moving object due to its motion; also called kinetic energy (105, 111)

engineer: someone who designs technology to solve problems (150)

environment: the surroundings that an organism lives in (126)

erosion: the movement of weathered rock by water, wind, or ice (62, 66)

evaporate: to change from a liquid to a gas (115, 116)

evidence: proof; facts that support an idea

experiment: a scientific investigation that tests a hypothesis

extinction: the dying out of a species (134)

F

fertilizer: chemical used to help grass grow (135)

force: a push or pull (112)

fossil: the remains or traces of an organism that lived long ago (69)

friction: a force that makes it hard for two surfaces to slide past one another; friction works against motion (112)

fuel: a material that is burned to produce heat energy (127)

G

generator: a device that uses magnets to change the energy of motion to electrical energy (105)

gravity: the force that pulls objects toward each other

H

heat energy: the energy of moving particles in a substance; also called thermal energy

herbal supplement: a product made from a type of leafy plant called an herb (141)

I

image: what you see at the place where an object would be if light rays reflecting off the object did not change direction slightly (124)

indicator species: a kind of plant or animal that reacts quickly to changes in the environment (136)

inference: an idea that explains an observation or answers a question (71)

inherit: receive characteristics that are passed from parents to their offspring (40)

insect: a small animal, such as a ladybug, that usually has six legs, two wings, and a hard shell (16)

introduced species: species of plants and animals that have been brought to a new area (43)

invention: a new device usually designed from scientific knowledge or study (147)

L

landform: a natural structure or feature on Earth's surface **(63)**

laser: concentrated light beam **(160)**

life science: the study of plants, animals, and all other living things; also called biology **(12)**

light: a form of energy that travels in waves and can move through empty space where there is no air **(119)**

M

machine: a tool that makes work easier, usually by letting you use less force **(107)**

malaria: a serious tropical disease that gives people a high fever, which is caused by a germ that is carried by mosquitoes **(142)**

mammal: an animal that has a backbone and hair or fur, breathes with lungs, gives birth to live young, and feeds milk to its young **(16)**

mate: to make more organisms of the same kind

mesa: flat-topped land with cliffs at the edges **(64)**

mineral: a solid natural material that has a crystal form and its own set of properties **(58)**

motor: a device that uses electricity to produce motion

mutation: a change in traits that happens when the traits are being passed from parent to offspring **(41)**

N

native species: species of plants and animals that have lived in an area for a very long time **(43)**

natural resources: materials in the environment that are useful to people **(126)**

nerve cell: a cell in the nervous system that carries messages to and from the spinal cord and brain **(20)**

nutrients: substances that an organism needs in order to survive and grow **(27)**

O

observation: something that you note using your senses **(71)**

offspring: young organisms that come from parent organisms **(37)**

organism: a living thing

P

perpetual motion machine: an imaginary machine that runs forever without any outside energy **(108)**

pesticide: a chemical used to kill insects and other small animals **(134)**

phase (of the moon): one stage in the regular changes in the way the moon looks from Earth **(82)**

photosynthesis: the process of using the energy in sunlight to make food from water and carbon dioxide **(28)**

physical science: the study of matter, forces, motion, and energy **(88)**

plant fibers: tough strands of material found in all plants **(150)**

plate: a huge piece of Earth's crust that moves very slowly **(56)**

polluted: harmed or damaged by waste material that is not part of the natural environment **(133)**

predator: an animal that catches and eats another animal **(47)**

prey: an animal that is hunted, caught, and eaten by another animal for food **(47, 91)**

prosthesis: an artificial body part used to replace a natural part that is damaged or missing **(153)**

prototype: an early model of a design **(154, 156)**

Q

quinine: a drug used to treat patients with malaria **(143)**

R

reagent: a chemical that causes another chemical to change **(96)**

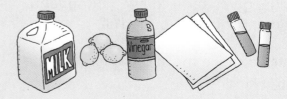

recycle: turn in waste items so the materials they are made of can be used to make new items **(151)**

reflect: bounce back (121)

reflection: the bouncing back of light rays from a surface (121)

refract: change direction slightly (light rays) (124)

refraction: the bending of light rays as they move from one material into another material (124)

relief map: a map that shows features of the land by showing the shadows that they cast (67)

reproduce: to make more organisms of the same kind (37)

S

scientist: someone who studies the natural world

seismograph: a science tool that measures the strength of earthquakes (54)

society: a group of people who all live under the same set of rules (146)

solution: a mixture with one substance spread out so evenly in another substance that you cannot tell the two substances apart; liquid mixture (96)

species: one kind of living thing; a group of organisms of the same kind that can mate and produce offspring like themselves (17, 134)

stalactite: cave formation that extends down from the ceiling of a cavern (58)

stalagmite: cave formation that rises from the floor of a cavern (58)

stored energy: energy that is stored in an object due to its position; also called potential energy (111)

synthetic: made by people in the laboratory (142)

T

technology: any tool or product that helps people in some way and that was created using scientific knowledge (118, 150, 153)

telescope: a tool for observing distant objects (84)

temperature: the average speed of the particles in a substance

thermometer: a tool that measures temperature

three-dimensional (3-D): an object, such as a sculpture, that has height, width, and depth **(160)**

tool: a device used to make a job easier **(33)**

tornado: a funnel-shaped storm cloud caused by rotating, high-speed winds **(75)**

toxin: poison **(90)**

trait: a characteristic or feature of an organism **(16)**

tundra: regions where it is very cold and there are almost no trees **(128)**

V

vortex: a swirling, twirling, moving shape in water or air **(78)**

W

wave: a repeating up-and-down or back-and-forth movement of matter

weathering: the breaking down, dissolving, and wearing away of rock **(62, 66)**

Assessment Rubric

Name _____ Assignment _____ Date _____

	Gold 4	Silver 3	Bronze 2	Copper 1
Comprehension _____ %	Specific facts and relationships are identified and well-defined.	Most facts and relationships are defined.	Some facts are identified but relationships are missing.	No facts or relationships are stated.
Application and Analysis _____ %	A strong plan is developed and executed correctly.	A plan is developed and implemented with some scientific errors.	Some organized ideas toward a weak plan.	Random statements with little relation to the question. No plan present.
Science Content _____ %	Appropriate, complete, and correct scientific facts, ideas, and representations.	Appropriate and correct but incomplete scientific facts, ideas, and representations.	Some inappropriate, incomplete, and/or incorrect ideas, leading to further errors.	Lacking understanding of scientific facts or ideas.
Communication _____ %	Strong and succinct communication of results.	Strong communication of results. Justification for outcome may be weak.	Communication of results is present, but lacks any justification.	No results are communicated. No justification is to be found. A correct answer may have appeared.
Aesthetics _____ %	Exceptional. Attractive. Encourages attention. All requirements exceeded.	Neat and orderly. Requirements met.	Messy and disorganized. Some requirements missing.	Illegible and random information. Most or all requirements missing.

Black Line Masters

Name _____ Assignment _____ Date _____

Major Classes of Arthropods Key

1a. Typically with three pairs of legs, with or without wings, and three distinct body regions	**insects (INSECTA)**
1b. More than three pairs of legs and wings never present	Go to 2
2a. With four pairs of legs, no antennae, and head and thorax fused into one segment	**arachnids (ARACHNIDA)**
2b. More than four pairs of legs present	Go to 3
3a. Body broadly oval with stout spine-like tail	**horseshoe crabs (XIPHOSURA)**
3b. Body not as above	Go to 4
4a. Usually with 5 to 7 pairs of legs and two pairs of antennae	**crustaceans (CRUSTACEA)**
4b. With more than ten pairs of legs and only one pair of antennae; body long and wormlike	Go to 5
5a. Body cylindrical; two pairs of legs on each segment; antennae short	**millipedes (DIPLOPODA)**
5b. Body more-or-less flattened; one pair of legs per segment; antennae long	**centipedes (CHILOPODA)**

Name _____ Assignment _____ Date _____

Relief Map

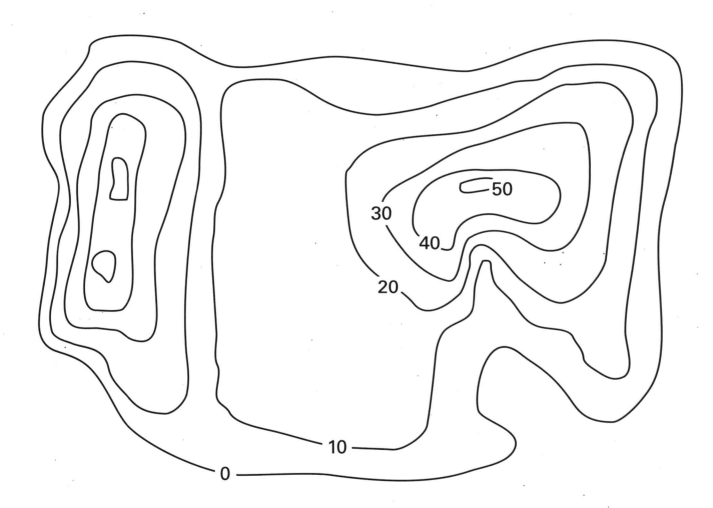

Name _____ Assignment _____ Date _____

World Outline Map

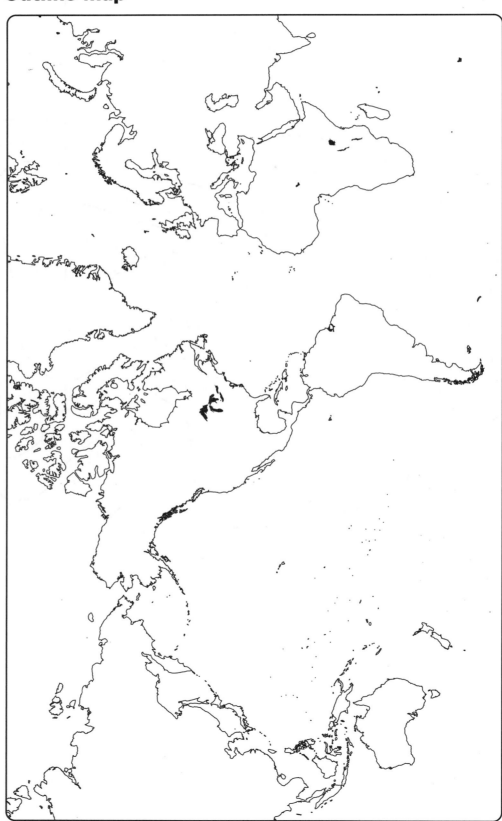

Name _____ Assignment _____ Date _____

Fishing for Clean Water Script Cards

Card #1

Close your eyes. Imagine a clean river as it meanders through a protected wilderness area. In your imagination, listen to the sound of clean water bubbling and splashing over the rocks of a small waterfall. Take a closer look in the river; look at all the different forms of life. Especially notice one particular fish. Open your eyes. (put the sponge fish into the jar of water.) The fish has lived in this stretch of river since it hatched from its egg. Now that it is older, the fish explores the area downstream. It will encounter many dangers, but the fish will still swim.

Card #3

The fish continues to swim. It enters an area with lush green lawns and flower beds that have been fertilized and watered frequently. The people who live in this area have watered their lawns and gardens so much that some of the **fertilizer** has washed into the river. (Dump cup#3, "fertilizer," into the jar.) Even more of the fertilizer washes into the river when it rains. The increase in nutrients in the river caused the aquatic plants to grow very fast and thick. These plants grow so fast that eventually the river can not furnish them with all the nutrients they need. The plants die and decay, using up much of the oxygen in the river. **How does this affect the fish?**

Card #2

The fish swims into an area where there are farms on both sides of the river. The farms have just been plowed in preparation for planting. As the fish swims, rain begins to fall. The rain washes **soil** from the freshly plowed fields into the river. (Dump cup #2, soil into the jar.) Imagine how this looks to the fish. **How does this affect the fish?**

Card #4

The fish quickly swims away from this polluted area. As the fish swims, it passes under a busy highway bridge. Some of the cars traveling over the bridge are leaking **oil and gasoline**. These pollutants have been washed into the river by the rain. (Dump cup #4, oil, into the jar.) **How does this affect the fish?**

(continued on page 178)

(continued from page 177)

Name _____ Assignment _____ Date _____

Card #5

The weather begins to turn cold. Rainwater left on the bridge and road freezes during the night. To avoid accidents, the highway department sends out trucks to spread salt on the roads and bridges. The next day, the temperature increases enough so the ice begins to melt. As it melts, the water and **salt** are washed into the river by the rain. (Dump cup #5, rock salt, into the jar.) **How does this affect the fish?**

Card #8

Also on this part of the river is the city's wastewater treatment plant. A section of the plant has broken down and **raw sewage** is being dumped into the river. (Dump cup #8, "sewage," into the jar.) **How does this affect the fish?**

Card #6

The fish continues on its journey, it swims past a city park. Some people did not put their trash in bins. Now the wind is blowing **trash** into the river. (dump cup #6, paper dots, into the jar.) **How does this affect the fish?**

Card #9

The fish continues to swim downstream. It passes a hazardous waste dump located on the b anks of the river. The rain is washing even more of the **toxic chemical** into the river. (Dump cup #9, three drops of red "toxic waste,", into the jar.) **How does this affect the fish?**

Card #7

Down river from the city are several factories. The city regulates the amount of pollution the factories can dump into the river. However, the factories do not always follow the regulations. Many **pollutants** are being dumped into the river today. (Dump cup#7, liquid dish detergent, into the jar.) **How does this affect the fish?**

Name _____ Assignment _____ Date _____

Images for Tube-Viewing

What You Need:

• 2 sheets of 8" x 11" plain paper

• transparent tape

What To Do:

1. Roll each piece of paper into a tube 11" long.

2. Use tape to hold the edges in place.

3. Hold the tubes so that your thumb and index finger form a soft cup at the top.

4. Holding the tubes like a pair of binoculars, position the tubes directly above one of the image pairs below.

5. Allow the images to drift together and fuse. Be patient! This might take some practice. What do you see?

Index